The Language Dynamic

The Language Dynamic

Gerard O'Grady and Tom Bartlett

SHEFFIELD UK   BRISTOL CT

Published by Equinox Publishing Ltd.

UK: Office 415, The Workstation, 15 Paternoster Row, Sheffield, South Yorkshire S1 2BX

USA: ISD, 70 Enterprise Drive, Bristol, CT 06010

www.equinoxpub.com

First published 2023

British Library Cataloguing-in-Publication Data
A catalogue record for this book is available from the British Library.

ISBN-13   978 1 80050 333 5   (hardback)
          978 1 80050 334 2   (paperback)
          978 1 80050 335 9   (ePDF)
          978 1 80050 409 7   (ePub)

Library of Congress Cataloging-in-Publication Data

Names: O'Grady, Gerard, author. | Bartlett, Tom, 1962- author.
Title: The language dynamic / Gerard O'Grady and Tom Bartlett.
Description: Sheffield, South Yorkshire ; Bristol, CT : Equinox Publishing
  Ltd, 2023. | Includes bibliographical references and index. | Summary:
  "The Language Dynamic identifies a number of mechanisms that enable the
  meaning potential of language from the phoneme through grammar and
  discourse and onto ideological systems. This book, which underpins
  functional theories of language with concepts from biological and
  cultural evolution, social semiotics and systems theory, is relevant to
  all who are interested in how and why we can mean and what it means for
  us as humans to be semiotic agents"-- Provided by publisher.
Identifiers: LCCN 2023016390 (print) | LCCN 2023016391 (ebook) | ISBN
  9781800503335 (hardback) | ISBN 9781800503342 (paperback) | ISBN
  9781800503359 (ePDF) | ISBN 9781800504097 (ePub)
Subjects: LCSH: Linguistics. | Semiotics. | Meaning (Philosophy)
Classification: LCC P121 .L38545 2023 (print) | LCC P121 (ebook) | DDC
  410--dc23/eng/20230717
LC record available at https://lccn.loc.gov/2023016390
LC ebook record available at https://lccn.loc.gov/2023016391

Typeset by Sparks Publishing Services Ltd – www.sparkspublishing.com

Like all books this one has benefited from the input of numerous colleagues and students who we have interacted with over the years. We would like to thank John Bateman and Bob Hodge for their incisive reading of an earlier and messier draft of this work. Naturally, though, any remaining errors or bloopers are ours and ours alone. We would not have been able to complete this work without being awarded a Cardiff University Research Leave and thanks are due to colleagues for covering the daily necessities of university life. Thanks also to Miriam Taverniers for hosting both of us in Ghent. Finally we are grateful for the support and professionalism of Janet Joyce, Val Hall and Sarah Lee at Equinox and John Duggan at Sparks.

We dedicate this book to the dynamic legacy of Ruqaiya Hasan and Michael Halliday.

Στη Γεωργία, που ήταν μαζί μου.
Gerard

Para María Veranos, mi compañera eterna.
Tom

Contents

Chapter 1

The language dynamic: Recursive processes from morpheme to ideology

1.1 INTRODUCTION: INTRA- AND INTERDISCIPLINARITY IN LINGUISTICS

The aim of this book is to identify a small set of processes and attendant properties that recur repeatedly within and across different orders of linguistic organisation and which demonstrate, in the words of Ruqaiya Hasan (1984:57), 'a continuity from the living of life on the one hand right down to the morpheme on the other'.

The processes we discuss are *distinction, articulation and prospection*, and the attendant properties of these processes are *systematicity, redundancy, stratality, metaredundancy, criteriality and serviceable noise*[1].

While we claim that these features are essential to the dynamics of language and that they recur at various spatiotemporal scales, we do not suggest that they comprise absolute rules or linguistic universals, nor that the list is comprehensive. Quite the contrary. The processes and properties we describe are essentially fluid and indeterminate and hence, by their very nature, they predict the absence of *linguistic universals* of the kind suggested within innatist models of language. Moreover, they interact in complex ways with other properties of language, both substantial and accidental, and their role in the reproduction, adaptation, diversification and complexification of language can only be properly comprehended when language is seen as one system within an irreducible triad, alongside the embodied mind of the individual speaker and the network of relations between individuals that we call society.

---

1   With thanks to Wray (2014:29), who refers to a connected concept as *serviceable language*. We have previously employed the relatively unserviceable term *functionable noise*.

The book has been a decade and a half in the making, a period in which the two authors have worked extensively together[2] on a number of projects in which it has been necessary to interconnect concepts from critical, applied, descriptive and theoretical linguists. Consequently, while each of us has expertise in a specific field of linguistics, we see ourselves as generalists as much as specialists. Gerard has, for example, published within his own research specialisms of phonology, intonation, information structure and linear grammar (2013a, 2016, 2017, 2020a, 2020b), and has applied this work in the analysis of register (2020a) and political discourse (2013b, 2022). Tom sees himself primarily as a critical discourse analyst, with a focus on context (Bartlett 2008, 2013, 2015, 2017, 2018a, 2018b, 2019) and the sociolinguistic concept of *voice* (Bartlett 2005, 2012, 2020; Bartlett and Erling 2007), but his first linguistic heartthrob was grammar, and he has publications on the mood system and unmarked atopicality in Scottish Gaelic (Bartlett 2021a, forthcoming). As a team, Gerard and Tom have cowritten articles (Bartlett and O'Grady 2017, 2019; O'Grady and Bartlett 2017, 2019) and coedited books (Bartlett and O'Grady 2017; Fontaine, Bartlett and O'Grady 2013; O'Grady, Bartlett and Fontaine 2013) and edit a book series (*Key Concepts in Systemic Functional Linguistics*, with Rebekah Wegener). Within these individual and joint endeavours, we have had the recurrent experience of coming across concepts in one area of study that correspond, to varying degrees, with concepts from other fields, often at several disciplinary removes. At times these concepts go by the same name in fields and genres as diverse as, say, neurobiology and French Discourse Analysis, but are used to explain phenomena which, superficially at least, are not only distinct, but often at different orders of abstraction; or conversely, at other times, different words are used, yet the explanatory power of the concepts seems to be roughly equivalent; while, at other times again, the concepts in one field seem well designed to test assumptions, generate insights and propose equivalences in others.

These different degrees of overlap and separation can be explained by the comparative 'siloisation' of linguistics as a discipline and the resultant isolation and insulation of the various sub-disciplines that comprise it. The lesson linguists can take from linguistics here is that long-term insulation transforms dialects into mutually unintelligible languages. Within theoretical linguistics, for example, formalist models of language tend to treat language as an autonomous or quasi-autonomous system and, in the extreme case, consider the investigation of language in use to be outwith the domain of 'linguistics proper'. Functionalist theories, in contrast, take it as axiomatic that language is a tool for social interaction, yet tend to engage primarily with the grammar *qua* grammar, to the relative exclusion of 'the cognitive structures and operations involved in language processing, as well as the sociocultural

---

2   And not forgetting long-term collaboration with colleagues such as Lise Fontaine, Kristin Davidse, Alison Moore, Rebekah Wegener, Ed McDonald, Jorge Arús and colleagues in Cardiff and Leuven.

structures and practices in which language is embedded' (Butler 2009b:2). Conversely, within more critical and socially-oriented disciplines, such as interactional sociolinguistics and linguistic anthropology/linguistic ethnography, language is viewed as a resource for speakers to draw on and linguistic data and linguistic categories are used to investigate the situated construction of cultural, social and (inter)personal relations, yet there is little in the way of an underlying and coherent model of language as a system in its own right. There is, moreover, a general wariness within critical circles of such a totalising concept and the structuralist or cognitive tendencies in linguistic theories generally, which are seen as fundamentally counter to concepts such as embodiment, intersubjectivity, fluidity, transgression and emergence that are the object of enquiry in interactional sociolinguistics (e.g. Blommaert 2018a; Silverstein 2003).

Commenting on this situation, and looking outwards from the perspective of functional grammar, Wray (2014:20) follows Butler (2009a, 2009b) in proposing 'that it should be possible to reconcile cognitive, sociocultural, discoursal, acquisitional, typological and diachronic explanations of language, besides accommodating observational evidence from corpora, experiments and intuition'. While it is obviously beyond our ambition to reconcile these approaches in a single volume, we hope that the framework we outline here, which embraces a broad scope of linguistic enquiry while moving away from a 'finely tuned set of rules' (Wray 2014:33), will be compatible with, and have something to offer to each of the broad gamut of interests that share the crowded disciplinary space of linguistics and language studies.

In the following two sections we set out our position with respect to three enduring points of contention in linguistic theory: embodiment, autonomy and the primacy of form or function. This discussion provides an essential backdrop to our theorising of language dynamics and the place within this of the core processes and properties introduced above. We finish the chapter with a preview of the remaining chapters of the book, in which we develop the ideas introduced in this overview and draw on examples from specific languages to illustrate these features at work. The book will therefore be characterised by a continual to-and-fro between abstract theorising and model-making on the one hand and, on the other, detailed illustrations of language phenomena as they emerge, survive (if fit) and adapt (if not).

We hope that this book will contribute to a materialist theory of language (*cf.* Halliday 2015) that rejects both the dualism of mind and body (Maturana and Varela 1980; Barbieri 1985, 2015, 2019; Pennisi and Falzone 2016; Eagleman 2015) and the dualism of the individual and their lived environment (Abram 1996; Maturana et al. 2016). In doing so, our focus will be on language as the *mediational means* (Wertsch 1998) for human existence, a system of relations that is external to both the individual embodied mind and the collective social body, but through which each constitutes itself in relation to the other without recourse to gods, black boxes or homunculi.

1.2   LANGUAGE, PERSON AND SOCIETY: AN IRREDUCIBLE TRIAD

Ferdinand de Saussure provides the following metaphor for the relationship between language and its social and material context (Holquist 2014:13; see also de Saussure 2006:202):

> A sign system must be part of a community. Indeed, any semiological system is not a ship in dry dock, but a ship in the open sea. Which is the real ship: one in the covered yard surrounded by engineers, or a ship at sea? Quite clearly only a ship at sea may yield information about the nature of a ship. A community environment changes everything. A sign system is destined for a community just as a ship is destined for the sea.

This quote is initially surprising, as Saussurean structuralism is generally considered as a markedly asocial approach in which language is formulated as a self-contained system of *pure values*, of abstract and immaterial contrasts. It seems clear from this quote, however, that this is a reductionist view of Saussure's intention, and that his abstraction of the language system from its social and material context was merely a temporary necessity that allowed the ship of language to be described *qua* ship, while postponing the inevitability that the full test of any ship is its functioning at sea. A similar approach is taken by Hjelmslev (1961 [1943]:127), who talks of 'the temporary restriction of the field of vision [as] the price that had to be paid to elicit from language itself its secret'. And, in like manner, Bergman (2009:3) defends Peirce from the charge that his 'interpretative process disconnects the sign relation from social practice', arguing that 'the generality of the abstracted sign relation does not imply the autonomy of semiosis; signs function as signs in purposive and pragmatic contexts'. It would appear, then, that for each of these foundational thinkers, the system of language needs to be considered not only in terms of its own internal organisation, but also – if belatedly – in terms of how that system operates when put to use. With specific reference to Saussure, but in terms that can be adapted to fit the cases of Hjelmslev and Peirce, Thibault (1997:60*ff*) discusses how the concept of *pure values* is only one aspect of Saussure's theory, a necessary reaction to the essentialist view dominant in Saussure's time that linguistic terms served merely to label a preexisting reality. As Thibault (1997:46; *cf.* Corballis 2017:33; Taylor 2016: Chapter 1; Torfing 1999:95) explains, therefore, Saussure's concept of a system of pure values:

> ...does not mean that language does not, in part, function to classify objects, events, happenings and so on in the material world. It does; but it is wrong to think that it does so on the basis of a direct and unmediated

link between word and object. Saussure's argument is that the value producing resources which are internal to a given language system cross-couple with the 'concrete real'. Further, the ways in which it does so are specific to particular cultures. It is these culturally specific cross-couplings which produce the consciousness, awareness and experience which agents have of phenomena in the 'concrete real'.

In these terms, Saussure's well-known bipartite division of a sign into a signified and a signifier would imply the additional presence of a culturally situated agent by means of whose perceptual and cognitive faculties the signs 'make sense'. This brings Saussure's conception of the sign closer to – but not identical[3] to – Peirce's tripartite division of the sign relation into 'a sign (or representamen[4]) that represents an object for an interpretant or, alternatively, that mediates between object and interpretant' (Bergman 2009:67; see also Atkin 2010). Saussure's aim, therefore, is not to suggest that pure values in the semiotic realm are independent of the concrete real, as if the sign system served purely to communicate itself, nor to suggest that there is no real outside of language; rather Saussure makes the point that the semiotic and the material are distinct yet integrally linked through the very process of cross-coupling by which the ultimately unknowable nature of concrete reality is transformed, via semiosis, into a knowable and culturally contingent system of values[5]. Such transformations are not, of course, carried out *ab initio* by individual agents, but through their gradual socialisation into the existing system of relations established by their contemporaries and forebears as they continue to make sense of their material environment. In other words, while the *formal* relationship between a signifier and signified might be said to be arbitrary and the relationship between signs that of pure value, *the partitioning of material reality through the conjunction of a signifier and a signified within a given system of relations is a functionally significant act that relates to the material and social conditions of existence of the interpreting agent in accordance with their perceptual and cognitive capacities* (see also Bartlett and Montesano Montessori 2021). Or, in the words of Hodge (2017:11), 'value does not oppose signification…it inflects it.'

---

3   It would be foolhardy ever to claim that an idea, even one of Peirce's own, corresponds precisely to Peirce's thinking. Peirce's works comprise a continuous trajectory of thought and the number of different interpretations of his ideas appears to be the same as the number of interpreters. Bergman (2009) provides a helpful and non-dogmatic commentary on the development of Peirce's views and the different interpretations of these.

4   Peirce later dispensed with the term *representamen* as he began to question whether signs truly 'represented' their object.

5   A similar point is made by Peirce (1998 [1907]:204) when he talks of the role of collateral knowledge, gained from experience, in the use of signs.

In these terms, the language system is at once a product and an enabler of social organisation in material contexts – it is an 'enhanced/enhancing intelligence' (Dennett 2017:135) – and having access to such external tools makes us 'Gregorian creatures' (Dennett 2017:98), freed from the shackles of unreflective bodily impulses. This does not, mean, however, that we can ignore the constraints and affordances that our biologies impose on us as interpreting agents (e.g. Gibson 1979) and the conduits through which language passes into society and society into language (*cf.* Bowcher and Yameng Liang 2015). At a bare minimum, biological constraints on interpretation demand that, while signs may be defined entirely in opposition to each other, the differences in both signifier/representamen and signified/object must themselves be *sensible* to the speaking subject in order for the differences to be understandable and reproducible (*cf.* Tomasello 2003:75). This requirement, however, does not preclude abstract thinking. Once language learning is under way and, along with this, socialisation into an existing network of meanings embedded as signs and relations in the language system, then the *representations* of the social and material world that the language system enables become sensible and distinguishable input in their own right and allow for the meta-representations we call reflection (Maturana and Varela 1980:39; Peirce 1909:26, discussed in Bergman 2009:106). Furthermore, a comparison between the perceptions of the moment with the stored representations of previous experiences allows us to evaluate our ongoing activities and to assess possible futures (Eagleman 2015:53, 56–57; Lamb 1999; Feldman Barrett 2017:27), with the hippocampus in particular playing 'a key role in assembling an imagined future by recombining information from our past' (Eagleman 2015:28).

Pennisi and Falzone colourfully refer to meta-representational processes as the *cognitive catastrophe* of a new linguistic mind[6] (2016:178) by which 'our individual and social cognition is doomed to achieve the fulfilment of its purposes' in accordance with the constraints and affordances of the language system (Ibid:98). We refer to this post-linguistic instinct, paraphrasing Nietzsche, as *the will to semiosis*, an embodied tendency to interpret our environment and the activities of others as they come into contact within us as meaningful elements and activities within a wider system of meanings. This is apparent in Scollon's (2001) analysis of parent–child interaction in which parents interpret the pre-linguistic reflexes of their children from the perspective of the parents' own social semiotic system – as, for example, when the biologically-programmed instinct of 'reaching' is resemioticised

---

6   Here Pennisi and Falzone are using the term 'catastrophe' not to propose a saltationist account of biological evolution, but to dismiss such a view. Their view is that the emergence of language was the result of multiple and gradual evolutionary adaptations and that the rapid leap forward implied by 'catastrophe' was a cognitive consequence of the language system once this had emerged, and not vice versa (*cf* Reboul 2017).

as the social and communicative act of 'handing'. Such one-sided meaning-creating practices can be seen as examples of the Saussurean/Peircean framework discussed above, but also as preludes to the internalisation of meanings and the gradual socialisation of the developing child through joint interaction, as described by Vygotsky (1978).

Meta-representations, reflection and the will to semiosis allow individuals to form impressions of themselves as coherent identities across space and time within the social systems into which they have been socialised as members and within which they interact with other members. Thus, when interacting with others, individuals respond cognitively and emotionally to the ongoing situation as this is evaluated in relation to their stored representations of previous encounters – what Scollon and Scollon (2004:19) refer to as 'the historical body'. On the basis of this emotional and cognitive response, individuals use (amongst other things) the shared conventions of the (distributed) language system in order to take up positions that serve to maintain or recalibrate their self-perception as coherent identities in relation to the activity at hand, as this is situated within and overdetermined by multiple activities across different spatiotemporal frames (Harré and van Langenhove 1999; Bartlett 2012:119; Wray 2017:571–573). Co-participants in the ongoing activity do likewise and the social system (imperfectly) reproduces itself through the linguistic (and other) actions of individuals in response to the pressures of that same social system and by means of the shared conventions of language as these are made accessible and reproducible to them through their biocognitive capacities.

By means of this rather dense formulation, we can make the provisional statement that language, society and the person are three separate but interrelated systems. More precisely, and predicting ideas to be developed throughout the book, we can refer to *mutually-triggering autopoetic systems*. Following Maturana and Varela (1980:78–79, *their emphasis*), an autopoietic system (or machine) is one which is:

> *...organized (defined as a unity) as a network of processes of production (transformation and destruction) of components that produces the components which: (i) through their interactions and transformations continuously regenerate and realize the network of processes (relations) that produce them; and (ii) constitute it (the machine) as a concrete unity in the space in which they (the components) exist by specifying the topological domain of its realization as a network.* It follows that an autopoietic machine continuously generates and specifies its own organization through its operation as a system of production of its own components under conditions of continuous perturbations and compensation of perturbations.

Briefly, and more simply, this means that autopoietic machines are self-sustaining systems which maintain their internal coherence, or unity, by reproducing the components that both organise them and enable them to reproduce. Further, they are able to maintain this cycle, in the face of external shocks, by reorganising themselves in such a way as to maintain their essential unity, if not their earlier form. This reorganisation is achieved by means of the same internal interactions by which they function and reproduce themselves under normal conditions.

The concept of autopoiesis was developed in the field of theoretical biology by Maturana and Varela, whose 1980 work seeks to provide a unified, materialist account of biological and cognitive processes. While the two authors disagreed at the time of writing on whether social systems were autopoietic (Maturana and Varela 1980:118), their book is prefaced with a commentary by Stafford Beer, professor and consultant at Manchester Business School, who concludes (Beer 1980:70) that:

> ...any cohesive social system is an autopoietic system – because it survives, because its method of survival answers the autopoietic criteria, and because it may well change its entire appearance and its apparent purpose in the process. As examples, I list: firms and industries, schools and universities, clinics and hospitals, professional bodies, departments of state, and whole countries.

Many authors subsequently have used Maturana and Varela's framework to analyse social systems operating across different spatiotemporal scales (see https://en.wikipedia.org/wiki/Autopoiesis). These developments notwithstanding, and in view of our distinction above – between individual languages and language as a system – we are unsure whether such institutions are autopoietic systems in their own right or simply the ripples of a more general system of 'society', imagined as unities from a specific spatiotemporal vantage point by interpreting agents with an irrepressible will to semiosis.

We can bring this section to an end by stating our position that language is external to and distinct from both the biocognitive individual, or person, and the social collective, though it is internalised by individuals and distributed in different forms and in different measures across collectives of different scales. As a consequence, while persons, societies and languages are all systems in their own right, it is simply impossible to conceive of the workings of one of them without consideration of each of the others (*cf.* Lemke 1992, 1993, 2000). Bodies emerge as persons through socialisation via language; language emerges through the continuous social interaction of persons; and societies emerge as persons interact through language. In what follows, therefore, we will be discussing language not solely on its own terms, nor as either simply a *social semiotic* (Halliday 1978) or a biological facility (Chomsky 1965; Chomsky and Berwick 2016), but as one element of an

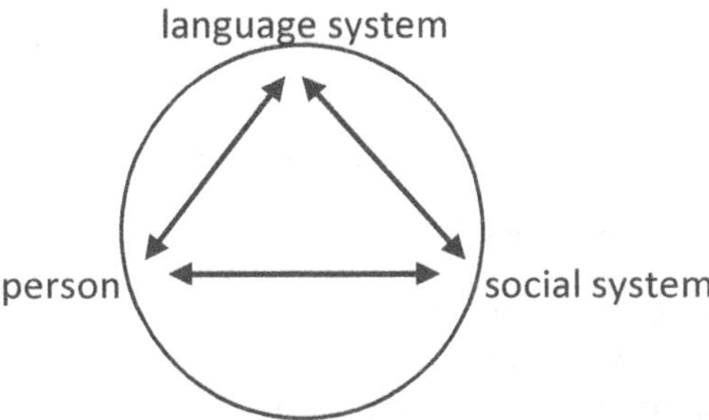

Figure 1.1 The irreducible socio-bio-linguistic triad

irreducible socio-bio-linguistic triad in which language, the person and society are interacting systems that must be accounted for both *within their own terms* and *in relation to each other*. In other words, while our primary goal in this book is to explore this triad from the perspective of the language system, we need to consider the ship, the ocean it sails in, and the sailors that navigate it.

The above discussion has brought in by the back door, so to speak, another dichotomy in the field of linguistics: the division into generally hostile camps of self-proclaimed formalists and functionalists. While both of us would describe ourselves as functionalists, in that we find it impossible to explain the dynamics of language in terms of their structural properties alone, this book is precisely about recurring structural characteristics of language. We should therefore take a little time to explain precisely how we see the relationship between form and function.

1.3 NEITHER STRUCTURE NOR FUNCTION FIRST

The entrenchment of formalists and functionalists into opposite camps is illustrated by Thomas (2021:107, 110) in terms of the stark contrast between the webpages of the departments of linguistics at the Massachusetts Institute of Technology (MIT) and the University of California Santa Barbara (UCSB), often considered the homes of formalist and functionalist approaches to language respectively, in the US context at least. Information on the MIT page is prefaced with the proclamation that:

> Our research aims to discover the rules and representations underlying the structure of particular languages and what they reveal about the general principles that determine the form and development of language in the individual and the species.

> https://linguistics.mit.edu/ accessed 21/3/22

On the top left of the UCSB page, in contrast, there is a banner heading proclaiming that

FORM FOLLOWS FUNCTION

https://www.linguistics.ucsb.edu/home (accessed 21/3/22)

The different stances adopted here represent the two poles in what can appear at times like an irreconcilable conflict. Formalists, in the most extreme cases, reduce language to an innate algorithm for generating syntactic strings devoid of meaning, with communication reduced to a by-product. Such a position is anathema to functionalists, who take the view that 'only a functionalist approach from the beginning to the end can lead to a proper description and explanation' (Foolen 2002:99, cited in Thomas 2021:98). Within the authors' own home discipline of Systemic Functional Linguistics, the guiding principle is, as the name would suggest, close to the UCSB statement. This is evident in Halliday's (1978:4) oft-repeated aphorism that 'language is as it is because of the functions it has evolved to serve in people's lives'. We would, however, add to Halliday's statement the corollary that *social life has evolved the way it has because of the functions that language has made possible.* While this may seem, on first reading, like an affirmation of the primacy of functionalism in the UCSB motto, what we are in fact saying is that – in the general case – neither form nor function follows the other[7].

To suggest that function precedes form is to adopt a teleological position that is at odds with the materialist position advocated in the present book. The teleological position, that structures evolve to meet preexisting metaphysical goals, is well exemplified by Reboul's (2017) arguments against language having evolved primarily for communication. Reboul (2017:15) asks 'Why did humans (and only humans) need a communication system that allowed them to produce an infinity of different sentences, with different contents?' And her conclusion (2017:6) is that language must have evolved *for* something that needed such structural possibilities and that the relevant structures were only later exapted for communication. This is not the only possibility, however, and one alternative explanation is that 'discrete infinity' (Chomsky 2005) is an accidental property of language as it developed alongside communication, just as mirrors can reflect to infinity, though there is no need for them to do so. The teleological position is rejected by cognitive biologists such as Maturana and Varela (1980) and Darwinian biolinguists such as Pennisi and Falzone (2016:34). And, as noted by Barbieri (1985:147), Darwin himself preferred the term 'adaptation' to 'evolution' precisely because he saw the latter term as implying progress rather than a continuous process of ad hoc accommodation to external perturbations.

---

7   See Butler 2003 for an overview of the relationship between form and function in three prominent theories identifying as functionalist.

Conversely, to suggest that language systems develop on the basis of structures alone is to deny the cross-coupling between language and context described above and to remove from language both the motivation to adapt and the means of its own reproduction. This is not to say that we deny the central place of structure; in particular, we recognise the recursive force of existing structural patterns in constraining the possibilities for future structures as languages adapt and expand their meaning potential (Halliday 1978:19) in ways that maintain their essential unity – or what Mathesius (1964 [1928]; see also Halliday 2014) would call their *characterology*. We do not, however, see any need to assume that such structures are innately located in the brain, in some universal form, as opposed to being distributed norms of shared behaviour that are internalised through processes of association and imitation and the gradual strengthening of neural connections within the individual brain (Edelman 2004:538; Lamb 1999; Garcia, Sullivan and Tsiang 2017; Corballis 2017:20)[8].

While we generally want to avoid absolutes and contentious dichotomies in this book, our own position can be summed up, briefly, in the idea that – in the general case – form and function emerge simultaneously when *mutations in structure fulfil a function in a previously non-existent niche*. There is no primacy of either form or function[9]. Or, in the words of Maturana and Varela (1980:56):

> Living systems in general, and their nervous systems in particular, are not made to handle a medium, although it has been through the evolution of their handling of their medium that they have become what they are, such that we can say what we can say about them.

In other words, in their interaction with their environmental niche, living systems – including language – may produce structural novelties (or mutations) and, if these mutations enhance the system's operations within their environmental niche (which may be altered in the process), then such adaptations are likely to

---

8   Following Peirce (as discussed in Bergman 2009:81), we would agree that formalism is a useful tool for the elimination of a priori and 'one-side opinions' (Peirce 1907:36) but that 'formal logic must not be too purely formal' or it may degenerate into 'a mathematical recreation' (Peirce 1883:421). As Bergman (2009:81) summarises, a mathematical and formalist approach to the nature of signs 'inevitably falls short when faced with the experiential grounding of semiotic concepts' and 'ought to be followed by an *a posteriori* phase in which the inquirer checks whether there really is something in experience that would match the forms.'

9   This is the case for a single idealised and non-reflective system. In the case of language, reflection allows speakers to devise structures to fill what they see as a missing niche. This process could be taken as a case of form following function and attributed to *techne* as opposed to organic emergence. However, if reflection is a recursive material process, as argued here, then techne is a recursive organic operation.

be reproduced so as to become defining features of the systems themselves. This is the standard theory of natural selection. Following Barbieri (1985:169–170) and Maturana and Varela (1980:93–94), however, we would add that natural selection is only possible if the novel form (or mutation) finds a place within the existing system of relations that define the organism in question. Such a situation is described by Pennisi and Falzone (2016:191) when they state that 'unexpected cases "oblige" the central structure by reincorporating them within our knowledge...creating new algorithms' and the possibility of 'innovative types of behaviour'. Completing the Gothic tryptic begun with their metaphors of *doom* and *catastrophe*, Pennisi and Falzone (2016:182) describe the role of the brain in restoring at least temporary equilibrium to the continually bombarded senses as 'supporting the organism to free it from the anguish of uncertainty, from the horror vacuity of the inapplicability'.

In sum, then, we can say that the structure of any operational system determines the properties of its components, while the properties of these components maintain the structure of that system. The function of an element is its place within the structure of the system in which it functions and the existence of a function 'predicts' a niche in the structure. If, for any reason, a novel structure or mutation is introduced into the system, this novelty will be maintained over the long term if and only if: (i) the novel structure fulfils a function that can be accommodated into the previously existing relations by which the system maintained itself; and (ii) the system so reorganised is better able to operate within its environmental niche, which it may modify in the process. As Barbieri (1985:170) puts it:

> Competition is real, but adaptation to natural cycles is fundamental. First and foremost the forms of life had to create natural cycles by co-operating and complementing one another. Only after that was there some space for competition and minor readjustments. Natural selection is the mechanism of these readjustments and necessarily takes second place.

In linguistic terms, this means we should not focus on individual form–function relations within a given language, but on the interconnectedness of such relations and their combined contribution to that language as a (relatively) coherent system. This takes us back to Mathesius's (1964 [1928]:59) concept of *linguistic characterology*, foreshadowed by Sapir (1921:129), who wrote that:

> ...it must be obvious to any one who has thought about the question at all or who has felt something of the spirit of a foreign language that there is such a thing as a basic plan, a certain cut, to each language. This type or plan or structural 'genius' of the language is something much more fundamental, much more pervasive, than any single feature of it

that we can mention, nor can we gain an adequate idea of its nature by a mere recital of the sundry facts that make up the grammar of the language.

While this is a picture that appears to be incompatible with Chomsky's account of an innate universal grammar, it would predict the type of universals identified by Greenberg (1963), which can be seen as individual languages chasing their own tails as they continuously attempt to make sense of themselves as functional systems. Both Greenberg's perspective on universals and Mathesius's concept of characterology are concerned with form–function relations within the lexicogrammar of individual languages. The present book, in contrast, aims to demonstrate that the form–function relations and the adaptational processes outlined in this section have enabled language – and hence languages – to operate at ever-higher levels of sophistication as they develop in an irreducibly triadic relationship with human society and human persons' understandings of themselves. This theory is built up piece by piece in the following chapters and is summarised in concise terms at the end of the book.

1.4   OUTLINE OF THE BOOK

In Chapter 2, *Embodiment* we have two main aims. The first of these is to set out our view of embodiment and to distinguish it from the cognitive linguistic view that language, like other cognitive resources, is grounded in bodily perception, the sensorimotor system and emotions. While we are largely in agreement with this point, we further argue that as language is a distributed system, that exists at different scales and times, only some aspects of it can be said to be embodied within an individual at any one time. We argue that through reiterated contextualised interactions language is enacted in the sense that it becomes internally represented within individuals. This leads us to our second major point, which is that as the linguistic system is itself metastable and extravagant, what is embodied has the potential for change and will obey the logic of A-curves, where roughly 20% of the tokens do 80% of the work, this is also known as the Pareto Principle. The long tail of roughly 80% of the tokens comprises items which are declining and also ones which have the potential for growth.

In order to illustrate our points the chapter is divided into a number of sections. The first of which details the cognitive and emotional skills a language-ready-made brain would require – before moving on, in the second section, to consider what capacities have evolved within humans and what functions have coevolved in language. In this section redundancy will be introduced to illustrate the stark differences between animal communication systems and human language while at the same time showing how animal communication systems may have evolved into human language. Redundancy refers to the predictability between two occurring things. To illustrate a response is 100% redundant if the presence of one form entails the other. In language there is no 100% redundancy between form and function; though, as we will see, form and function are mutually predictive. In the fourth section we will illustrate the evolution of a linguistic feature: vowels, in order to show not only how the primary function of distinctiveness appeared but also how vowels developed a 2nd order contingent indexical meaning (a point developed in Chapter 3). Finally we end the chapter by examining the relationship between syllable onsets and vowels in English. We do this to illustrate the complexity of the metastable system that has evolved and to show that it follows the logic of the A curve.

In Chapter 3, *A systemic and stratal account of language and society*, our discussion moves from phylogenetic accounts of the emergence of language in the species to consider the ontogenesis of the capacity for language within the individual speaker. Drawing on the work of Tomasello (2003), we highlight the importance of children's capacity to distinguish structures and their uses as they attend to the contextualised talk of socialised speakers. Turning to the language system, we then illustrate how such distinctions function within networks of interrelated meanings and emphasise that the distinctions captured in linguistic forms are not universal but language specific, reflecting alternative ways of carving up the concrete real into functional elements. We then introduce the twin concepts of articulation and stratality to explain how combinations of meanings at one order of abstraction create new higher-order meanings in a recursive and open-ended cycle. This entails a discussion of *metaredundancy* and the regular but not absolute correlation between meanings at one level of abstraction and their realisation by features from the next stratum down. We then expand on the indeterminacy inherent in the concept of metaredundancy to discuss different registers as subcategories within an overall language system that are distinguishable in terms of both their semantic content and the characteristic ways by which the lexicogrammar is used to realise the semantics. In this way we see that systems are not only language specific, but also context specific. Once again, these relations are relative rather than absolute, an idea we explore in terms of cultural evolution and an embodied human tendency to balance copying and risk-taking as an effective strategy in adapting to new contexts.

In Chapter 4, *Stratification, Redundancy and the Mechanisms of Change* we revisit the conception of stratification in order to illustrate that an open, dynamic and cyclical system must be stratal and that the relationship between strata must be realisational. We specifically examine the relationship between the higher semantic stratum and the lower lexicogrammatical stratum and suggest a modification to the content expression boundary. Our arguments are grounded in a close textual and prosodic analysis of a short political statement. We show that slippage between strata leads to creativity and illustrate how the use of explicit objective interpersonal meanings rearticulates meanings. This is a topic we will examine further in a follow up companion volume, where we will argue that such rearticulations are a major driver in ideological formations such as populist discourse.

The opening part reintroduces metafunctional meaning (discussed in Chapters 2 and 3) in order to illustrate how a text is simultaneously the aggregate of particulate, prosodic and wave-like meaning-bearing elements. We conduct a close textual analysis and examine the choices made in field, tenor and mode. Our analysis includes both lexicogrammar and prosody. We note that recombinations of lexicogrammar and prosody have the effect of shifting experiential-like meanings into prosodic interpersonal meanings. We further note that while many of the prosodic choices were predicted by the lexicogrammar – and hence redundant – others were not. The recombination of prosody and lexicogrammar in order to realise a thought illustrates how both Halliday's and Hjelmslev's notions of stratification require some minor modification. The chapter will propose a slightly amended model of stratification with a more central role for prosody.

While earlier chapters have looked at how linguistic systems emerged through contextualised interactions, Chapter 5, *Prospection: The Emergence of Target States and Common Ground in Text*, by contrast, examines how in a metastable linguistic system the deployment of lexicogrammar and prosody allows for meanings to emerge within and across a text. While this chapter focuses on the instantiation of syntagms, reference is made to the fact that the syntagm itself results from paradigmatic choices. We introduce the key notion of prospection which states that the production of an element requires the production of a further element and that this continues until certain grammatical criteria have been satisfied. In the chapter we examine a short English source text and two translations (Japanese and Greek). We do this to illustrate how the linguistic structure of each language creates expectancies which result in the realisation of semantic meaning at two scales. The first is a local level and realises a proposition which then acts as the ground for the following proposition until the overall communicative intention, the second scale, is achieved. We then examine a reading of each of the three texts in order to examine the contribution prosody makes to prospecting further elements in tandem with the lexicogrammatical choices. The chapter demonstrates that the overall principle of prospection is valid for the three languages though the actual operation of what is prospected depends on the characterology of the language. Our take-home point is that the emergence of meaning in the three metastable linguistic systems results in perturbation in the overall system and once again affords the opportunity for change.

In Chapter 6, *Emergent Creativity*, we compare the processes of reception discussed in Chapter 3 with processes of production in context. We explore how these both respond to the expectations set up by previous productions and recalibrate these in real time as speakers respond to both the centripetal forces of conventionalised structures and the centrifugal forces generated by an overdetermined and multilayered context. We analyse in detail three texts from nursing handover meetings to illustrate the core principles we have been developing throughout the book as these operate across extended interactions and, on the basis of this analysis, to demonstrate how the nursing team involved has drawn on the serviceable noise of the conventional format to recalibrate the system of meanings open to them as they respond to contextual pressures. In this way we illustrate the emergence of distinctive language systems operating across specific spatiotemporal scales.

Chapter 7, *Outline of a Socio-Biosemiotc Theory of Language Dynamics*, does exactly what it says on the tin, presenting the essential elements of our socio-biosemiotic approach to language dynamics in concise and stepwise form.

Chapter 2
Embodiment

2.1 INTRODUCTION

In this chapter we will develop our materialist theory of language as a complex dynamic system by focusing on the relation between language and the body. As noted in Chapter 1 we argue that language is a distributed system but one that as languaging animals we produce and perceive through our bodies. Thus we argue that the systemic possibilities and the somatic resources which humans use to produce language have co-evolved. To illustrate, speech sounds must be both perceptible by the ear and interpretable by the auditory cortex, and utterances must not be too complex for the memory systems in the brain to process. This simple truism allows us to predict that the speech signal will pattern in a manner that enables humans to utilise language in order to interact with their eco-social environment, and to satisfy their communicative needs. So, despite the fact that each language will have evolved to serve the (social) needs of its speakers (Halliday 1978), we can predict that at a more abstract level the same sort of patternings will emerge cross linguistically e.g., the division of the signal into given and new, the marking of speech function, metaredundancy, etc. In this chapter we examine how language has evolved into a metastable system. We illustrate this by detailing how the emergence of syllable onset systems in English entrains patterns which conform to the logic of the A-curve and which results in the formation of a metastable complex and learnable system. First though we will explain more clearly what we mean by our use of the term 'language' as an evolving metastable system.

Language, as Sydney Lamb (1999:284) reminds us, is a term which creates the illusion of unity when in fact the term describes a myriad of different objects. It is in many ways best depicted as a hyperobject, to borrow the term from the ecological philosopher Timothy Morton. We take Morton's term as referring to an object which cannot be seen in its entirety, only its local effects can be measured. A hyperobject, which we claim language is, is huge and distributed temporally and spatially (Morton 2018:22). Our claim is that the obsession with the unitary nature of language has obfuscated its real nature. As it presently stands the umbrella of language includes shared cultural conventions, spoken and written texts, the grammatical analysis of clauses and phrases, multilingualism, dialectology, prosody, acquisition and how it is represented within the brain. It is somehow simultaneously a cultural object and a biological system as demonstrated in Chapter 1. It is both a system and a process which is mediated by – and which in turn mediates – culture and the biological person. As such it represents a daunting edifice which is seemingly remote from anything else. But so presumably, to adopt an analogy from Pinker (1994), from the elephant's point of view must its trunk seem special. Anatomically an elephant's proboscis is simply the fusion of an extended nose with the upper lip. Yet it is a wonder in that its functions include breathing, olfaction, touching, grasping, sound production and comforting. In short it is far more than an extended nose. We are left wondering though if it would seem quite so wondrous if today's Asian and African elephants, and the perhaps soon to be reborn woolly mammoth, were not the sole surviving members of the order *proboscidea*. We are also left wondering whether language would seem quite so mysteriously wondrous if we were not the sole extant human species, and we could trace its continuity within our mammalian heritage.

However, as we are the sole surviving human species remaining on the planet, language, like the elephant's proboscis, is in some sense an isolate; and evidence of how much language, if any, other humans may have possessed is unclear. We can, however, be certain that for a language capacity to have evolved it must have been selected for. We are genetically endowed to be languaging animals; indeed ones who are doomed to semiosis (Pennisi and Falzone, 2016) or, as we phrase it more positively, have 'a will to semiosis'. Simply put, humans have the ability to learn the native language of the community they grow up in regardless of their ancestral origin.

Despite this ability to learn any language there is some potential evidence indicating a link between the genome and the ability to acquire a specific language Dediu & Ladd (2007) propose that two genes involved in brain development, ASPM and MCHP1, may influence sensitivity towards an individual's preference to use lexical tone to encode meaning. But as a non-Chinese child adopted by Mandarin speaking parents in Shanghai would learn Mandarin as a native language, such biases if they exist must be weak and violable. Dediu and Ladd's findings may be explainable in terms of Arbib's (2005:131) concept of vocality, which argues that language evolved as it has because of the physical and semiotic affordances of the vocal tract producing articulatory gestures that in turn led to the brain developing plastically.[1] And so before going on to develop our view of language as a dynamic cultural system embodied in the individual and distributed across the society, we will first briefly sketch out the evidence for what is unique about language and set out the cognitive tools required for language capacity to develop in the brain.

---

1   This in turn seems to be no more than a specific manifestation of the 'Baldwin effect' which describes the effect of learned behaviour on natural selection and is a mechanism by which culturally acquired traits are inscribed in the genome in order to boost reproductive success (Dennett 2003; Burman 2013; Eagleman 2020).

2.2 TOWARDS LANGUAGE

It is clear that language is not simply an extended animal communication system. In a justly famous paper Hockett (1960) proposed 15 features for oral language[2] of which the following 9 features seem unique to language: *arbitrariness, discreteness, displacement, productivity, cultural transmission, duality of patterning, prevarication, reflexiveness and learnability.* While these have been highly influential in allowing us to distinguish human language from animal communication systems, they are not fully in accord with more current views of language evolution (e.g. Christiansen & Kirby 2003). Hockett's focus on the language code rather than the underlying cognitive abilities creates some rather puzzling evolutionary continuities between bees signalling the location of honey and humans telling stories, while at the same time failing to capture more interesting examples of displacement grounded in episodic memory, such as corvids stashing food (Wacewicz & Zywicynski 2015). This is not to say that that Hockett's features are not useful for distinguishing the emerged metastable human language system from animal communication systems.

For language to emerge, speakers as users and transmitters of the system need to demonstrate a number of abilities: chiefly cooperation and intentionality. Intentionality relies on the communicator recognising that their interactant, like the communicator, has goals and perceptions which can merge into jointly shared goals (Tomasello 2008, 2019). Communicators can engage in recursive mind reading. They can reason that the signal they sent will be interpreted by a mind like theirs who, in turn, will know that the communicator intended the communication and recognise that the hearer will interpret the message in a manner similar to the communicator's intention, and so on. Shared intentionality is itself grounded in cooperation. Extended cooperation allows for the development of mutual assumptions where communicators can recognise that they share an overlapping world view which further boosts the development of joint reasoning which itself further strengthens the common ground existing between the communicators. Socially this has the evolutionary advantage of strengthening community/group bonds which in turn increases the individual survival and reproductive opportunities.

Yet, while language is exclusive to humans, communication in its broadest sense pervades the natural world. Damasio (2018:234–39) proposes that all life from bacterial existence to the management of human emotions is subject to *the homeostatic*

---

2   There is much debate in the literature as to the modality in which language initially evolved. Scholars such as Tomasello (2008 and 2014) and Corballis (2017) argue for a gestural origin while others e.g. Everett (2017) argue for a vocal origin. Yet, as it is a fact that, outside groups of deaf signing communities, there is not a single community which uses gestures as its primary mode of communication, we, while not taking sides, focus on oral language in this book.

principle. He defines homeostasis as ensuring that 'life is regulated within a range that is not just compatible with survival but also conducive to flourishing, to a projection of life into the future of an organism or a species' (ibid:25).[3] For a mindless organism, such as a bacterium, homeostasis entails the ability to interact and communicate with the external world. Survival dictates that it sense and respond to the presence of other single celled organisms, food and heat sources, etc. For humankind, it entails amongst other things our ability to respond to our own and others' feelings which are frequently expressed by linguistic means.

Language is a world apart from the chemical coded signals which allow bacteria to interact with their environment. Yet, while language in one sense is unbounded – permeating and populating both the physical and virtual worlds – in another real sense it is constrained by physiology: it is the way it is because we are the way we are.[4] Morphology constrains how living organisms interact and communicate with the affordances which are perceivable and relevant to the living organisms, (Gibson 1979). Laland (2017:77–99) reports on two types of genetically related fish: the threespine stickleback and the ninespine stickleback. Both types of fishes eat similar food, shoal together and apparently exhibit similar cognitive abilities, but yet only ninespines appear capable of using the behaviour of conspecifics as cues to where rich food sources exist. In a series of careful experiments, Laland and his colleagues demonstrated the robustness of this odd and unexpected result. After all, the stimuli both fishes had received were the same but the affordances so generated differed. Laland concluded that the differences in behaviour between the fish were due to their morphology. Threespines are better armoured than ninespines and, as a result, relatively less at risk from predation. This allows them more freedom to explore their environment themselves and so they have less of a need to rely on cues from their conspecifics as to the location of rich food sources. Ninespines by contrast spend more of their time hiding and hence have less opportunity to directly sample their environment for food – so they have evolved the ability to extract foraging information from their environment while hiding.

Threespines would appear to be, in Daniel Dennett's terminology, Skinnerian Creatures: who in addition to hardwired behaviour have the ability to respond and adjust their behaviour in reaction to reinforcement (2017:92). They sample the world through trial and error. Ninespines, though, would appear to be Popperian creatures who extract information from the external world and use it to generate

---

3   In a similar manner the physicist, Paul Davies, argues that life is matter plus information and that it is the regulation of information which keeps entropy at bay, (Davies: 2019). Without homeostatic regulation cells would be unable to reproduce and organise themselves into complex multi-cellular organisms such as humans.

4   Though clearly language has also reshaped the human brain and afforded us the opportunity to be both socio-cultural and biological creatures.

hypothetical behaviours (ibid:98): in this case depending on the signal whether or not to leave the safety of the reeds. We are Gregorian creatures who have access to an environment well stocked with thinking tools: chief of which is of course language (ibid:98). In other words our umwelt allows us to deploy symbolic and abstract reasoning to construe the material and social worlds we exist in.

Language is constrained by our physiology. The type of speech sounds we can produce and hear are dependent on: the amount of air in our lungs, the thickness of our vocal folds, the shape of our mouths, the flexibility of our tongues, the air pressure in the cochlea, the number of hair cells in the inner ear, the auditory nerve, the speech centres in the neo-cortex and working memory. But yet, like the threespines and ninespines, our ability to communicate and make meaning arises from our interaction with the world. Language is therefore simultaneously a physical and cultural system. We are, in other words, in complete agreement with Chomsky (2005) and his proposal for three factors necessary for language design, namely (i) genetics, (ii) experience and (iii) mental operations not specific to language such as auditory perception and memory. However, unlike Chomsky, we argue that the primary motivating function of language was communication and hence, for us, language is a distributed system and not located within an organism. It is the capacity for language which is within the organism. Language is as it is because we are constrained by our physiology and the system that has coevolved with our mental operations and vocal apparatus is constrained by our limitations. We further believe that the accumulation of contextualised linguistic interactions which we interpret as the phylogenetic development of a language variety is key to explaining the existence of different languages all suited to their communicative niches and within the varieties the emergence of registers. So rather than espouse a biolinguistic framework our work could be labelled *socio-biosemiotics*.

For a communicative signal to be linguistic, Sperber and Wilson (1995) note that the signal must be ostensive and intentional. It must be ostensive in that it is recognisable to the intended hearer in the manner that a dog's growl signals a warning, and intentional in the sense that it cannot be simply a response to an external stimulus irrespective of the presence of a recipient. Hence the ninespine capacity for the sharing of relevant environmental information is a long way removed from language; it is neither intentional nor ostensive. Ninespines convey the same signals regardless of whether or not a conspecific is present.

It is estimated that the last common ancestor between sticklebacks and humankind lived approximately 440,000,000 years ago (Dawkins 2004:274). The oft cited work of Cheney and Seyfarth (1980) details an example of seemingly intentional communication from a species more closely related to humankind, vervet monkeys: our common lineage split approximately 25,000,000 years ago (Dawkins 2004:118). It is widely known that vervet monkeys have three distinct alarm calls which signal the presence of predatory eagles, leopards and snakes. Upon hearing a particular alarm call the hearing monkey takes the most appropriate evasive action. Yet, despite these signals being ostensive and apparently intentional (Cheney and Seyfarth 1996:62)[5], these calls remain far removed from language. Language is not a code with fixed meanings; rather it is a signal which the hearer interprets within the context in which it is produced. Neither is language a system with static and fixed meanings, rather it is a complex and adaptive system. While, at best, vervet alarm calls might be the equivalent of proto-words, they are evidence that primate minds can produce and interpret ostensive and perhaps intentional signals as communicative messages.[6]

The closest related living primates to humankind are chimpanzees and bonobos with the last common ancestor estimated to have lived between 5 and 7 million years ago (Dawkins 2004:88). Tomasello (2014) reports that while ape's vocal repertoires are largely genetically fixed, they have the ability to produce novel and flexible gestural signs in response to communicative pressures when interacting with conspecifics and human keepers. This, he notes, is evidence that they have the ability to recognise that individuals have goals which they pursue and that others may perceive things in a manner different from theirs. Benson & Greaves (2005) detail an extended 'non-verbal negotiation' between the primatologist Sue Savage-Rumbaugh and the bonobo Kanzi which demonstrates that Kanzi was, at the very least, aware that his and Savage-Rumbaugh's communicative moves were ostensive and intentional – though it is debatable whether Kanzi was attending to anything other than his own needs. Furthermore, apes in the wild engage in a number of foraging and hunting activities which require joint intentionality and planning. Bonobos have even been witnessed saving tools for future use, which indicates that they have some ability to make inferences about hypothetical and displaced states based upon their previous experiences (Mulcahy and Call 2006).

Apes engage in forms of social learning such as learning from conspecifics, the use of novel tools, or how to wash food items. However, Tomasello (2008:loc 90) is quite clear that humans, and humans alone, cooperate communicatively. He argues that were a distressed chimpanzee baby to be searching for its mother, a neighbouring chimpanzee adult with sufficient knowledge would not produce a gesture pointing the child in its mother's direction. This is despite the adult being perfectly capable of gesturing if it so desired. Yet, while apes do not engage in activities such

---

5   Though without empirical evidence of whether vervet monkeys produce alarm calls in the presence of predators but in the absence of conspecifics it is not entirely clear whether their calls are intentional rather than instinctual.

6   Though as vervet monkeys have spent the previous 25 million or so years evolving to fit their own biological niche we cannot automatically assume that their cognitive abilities equate with that of our last common ancestor.

as phatic communication, Dunbar (2014:37) is clearly correct in his claim that primates are intensely social. They form stable relationships which allow them to live in enduring groups where they form long-term relationships. De Waal (2016:61–62) reports altruistic behaviour in chimpanzees living in the wild. On one occasion a frail elderly chimpanzee who was no longer able to climb a fruit tree waited patiently at the bottom of the tree for her daughter to collect fruit for both of them to eat. On another occasion De Waal reports younger females carrying water in their mouths to bring to an infirm elderly chimpanzee. On yet another occasion, he reports that in order to stop their offspring fighting a mother chimpanzee poked at a more senior ape and gestured towards the fight in order to successfully enlist her help in ending the fight. De Waal (2016:61) illustrates the extent of ape cooperation by recounting the story of a group of 25 chimpanzees who cooperated together to lift a heavy tree trunk in order to prop it against a wall and facilitate their escape from a zoo compound. Thus, it seems that Tomasello's claim that humans alone communicate cooperatively may be too strong. Apes may engage in communicative behaviour when it is in their own or their kin's self-interest to do so. Yet, as we will argue below, it is possible that reactive aggression, at least in the wild, constrains apes' ability to cooperate and hence hinders their ability to develop a richer communicative repertoire.

Evidence for ego-centeredness in apes comes from the work of ape communication researchers. Some such as Savage-Rumbaugh et al (1986) have taught apes to communicate using keyboards. These captive apes have shown the ability to produce instrumental language such as responding to commands, or asking for food. But the apes have not produced messages indicating their concern or interest in the mental or emotional states of their human interlocutors. Nor have they produced speech acts such as offers and promises. Though, as they show the ability to respond to their human interlocutors, they have the ability to understand a much richer set of speech acts than they themselves employ. But it is noticeable that, unlike humans, apes rarely initiate conversation unless they are begging for food or attempting to fulfil a need such as asking for a toy or to be allowed into another room.[7] So in short we can see that apes and presumably our last common ancestor (though see caveat in fn6) have developed a communicative and interacting brain that is almost ready to host language.

---

7   While dogs have much more limited abilities to communicate their own desires to their human companions, they are much more tuned into human desires and needs. For instance, dogs have been known to lead rescuers to their injured companions. Thus, it seems that dogs may have developed some of what is missing from ape communication – presumably from a rewiring of their brains caused by thousands of years of close interactions and cohabitation with humans.

We do not know why humans alone developed language and why evolutionary pressures have not yet led to apes developing their communication skills into full-fledged language. Hood (2014) and Wrangham (2019) argue that humans have self-domesticated as a species with a more pro-social behaviour necessary for communal living. Self-domestication has resulted in morphological and psychological changes leading to more juvenile features and less sexual dimorphism. In the fossil record it is argued that the more gracile *Homo sapiens* represents a self-domesticated archaic human. For instance it has been noted that the 600,000-year-old fossil of a young male shares many modern facial features absent in the accompanying archaic adult fossils (Bermúdez de Castro et al. 1997:1392). Wrangham's specific proposal is that the driver for self-domestication is the diminution of reactive aggression. Supporting evidence for his view comes from the Siberian silver fox breeding experiments where, over generations, silver foxes have been bred for friendliness to humans. This has resulted in the creation of two morphologically and behaviourally distinct but genetically identical cohorts. The foxes bred over generations for friendliness are, as to be expected, far less wary than the other foxes who have retained the aggressive and wary behaviour of the ancestral population. But, surprisingly, the selected friendly foxes have changed morphologically over the generations, preserving juvenile features such as floppy ears, splotchy coats, curly tails, smaller teeth and more gracile skulls, (Hare 2013).

Apes, with the possible exception of the bonobo, have not self-domesticated and hence remain wary and fearful of conspecifics, with the consequence that they are seemingly unable to cooperate with each other in a manner akin to that of children. Their failure to do so may be the result of the fact that their innate reactive aggression constrains them from adopting a perspective based on common ground rather than a selfish position based on their own instrumental desires. In theory, at least, it might be possible to breed apes in a manner akin to the silver foxes in order to reduce reactiveness and perhaps increase their ability to cooperate. Some evidence that apes may have more latent communicative and cooperative ability than manifested in the wild is the fact that apes who have been hand raised by humans display a higher degree of social learning, cooperation and the ability to imitate compared to their wild conspecifics (Tomasello 2019:138). They are also better communicators! Yet even the human raised apes reproduce gestures for instrumental reasons (ibid:143) and, as noted above, their communications are egocentric and instrumental. If this reasoning is correct we can predict that bonobos would prove to be the most effective at communicating with humans which may well be the case (see Savage-Rumbaugh & Lewin 1994).[8]

---

8   Of the apes that have communicated using keyboards, bonobos such as Kanzi have been the top performers. If the neurologist David Eagleman is correct in his argument that extended meaningful interaction leads to a rewiring of the brain, we could also predict that

Now that we have looked at why a fully human language capacity has not evolved in apes, the remainder of this section will narrow its focus and survey some of the reasons posited for language evolution in humans. Numerous theories have been advanced in the literature purporting to explain the evolution of human language. For instance, Chomsky and Berwick (2016) state that language capacity is a spandrel[9] which automatically results from the emergence of a large brain. However, this seems to simply raise a new issue: what evolutionary pressures led to the emergence of large brains in humans; and, to flip the question around, what evolutionary pressures have constrained the growth of larger brains in apes?[10] It also provides an all-or-nothing explanation with more or less fully formed language arising in a flash. While we share the atelic view that language arose by chance mutations that proved functional, we can only see this as being accounted for through the gradual emergence of embodied behaviours which facilitated social cohesion and hence survival, and which then modified other behaviours which in turn provided altered functional niches in which language continued to evolve in tandem with other sociocognitive tools and faculties.

Dunbar (1996) proposes that language emerged as a form of vocal grooming required to replace primate grooming once primate colonies grew past the size where physical grooming was no longer possible. Yet words, unlike physical grooming, take little physical effort and hence do not necessarily represent an honest signal. An interesting and plausible suggestion in how speakers and hearers overcame the lack of honesty in the signal is Ladd (2014:101), who proposes that the speech signal is simultaneously decomposable into meaningful lexicogrammatical content and analysable as a sequence of meaningless prosodies in order to ameliorate the problem of cheaters employing empty words. The prosodies provide cues to allow hearers to infer indexical information in the signal and to enable hearers to more accurately

---

the longer the cross species interaction continues the more the language capacity of bonobos will increase, (Eagleman 2020). So perhaps in 10 or so generations bonobos may be able to interact in a manner more in tune with human communication.

9   A spandrel is not a direct product of natural selection but rather a trait which arises as a by-product of the evolution of another trait but may be co-opted for a further use. For instance, the lungs were selected as part of the respiratory system but subsequently co-opted as the power source for speech. See Gould & Lewontin (1979).

10   Though see Dunbar (2009) whose article shows that primates brains are unusually large when compared with their body size. Interestingly, Neanderthal brains were at least as large as those of modern humans. Though it may well be that their neo-cortex was smaller but it is supposed that they had at least some language ability (Papagianni & Morse 2015). Chomsky himself ascribes a much more recent birth to language (2005: 3) of sometime in the last 100,000 years. But by language he means the development of syntax and especially merge, see also (Berwick et al. 2013; and Bolhuis et al. 2014).

evaluate the source of the proposition. Regardless of whether Ladd is correct or not, his argument illustrates the importance of not viewing language in narrow terms as a mere conveyor of propositional meaning. In short, as the song almost said, it is not what you say but the way that you say it.

Returning to the discussion of how language may have emerged, authors such as Tomasello (2008, 2014, 2019) and Corballis (2003, 2017) have argued that as (i) apes have very limited ability to vocalise, (ii) people on the phone still gesticulate when talking and (iii) deaf people develop the ability to communicate using sign, then language must be grounded in gesture. However, the counter-argument is that this view does not explain how and why the voice became the dominant modality: see Pennisi and Falzone (2016) who argue that vocal gestures led to a restructuring of the mind which made it a more suitable host for language. Barbieri (2015:135) suggests that the growth in human language capacity is the result of key aspects of brain formation occurring postnatally. The infant's maturing brain is stimulated by the extra-somatic environment and this results in human language capacity[11]. Bickerton (2002), while emphasising the role of social intelligence, argues that language emerged from the evolutionary pressures of a changed lifestyle, bipedalism, foraging and life on a dusty and dry savannah surrounded by dangerous predators. Conversely, the aquatic ape hypothesis equally plausibly claims that our hominin ancestors lived on the shoreline and spent a lot of time immersed in water (Morgan 2011). Blackmore (1999) has argued that lexical items invaded the brain as parasitic memes which eventually proved to be able to promote human fitness after re-shaping our minds to ensure their and not our survival. Language in her thinking is akin to a virus which epiphenomenally turned out to be beneficial. Corballis (2017) speculates that fire was the spark for language by lengthening the day and allowing us to develop the pleasure of storytelling and coincidentally fostering stronger in-group ties. While we would see this only as a potential factor in an already fairly advanced linguistic system developing further, we are in complete agreement of the importance of language as a means of fostering group identity. This is a point we will return to in Chapter 6.

Others have argued that the development of tool use was the spur that turned humans into talking apes by creating the communicative pressure and need for linkage between vocal/gestural sign and a physical referent (Hurford 2012:loc2260). Yet, we are not the only tool users[12], though human tool making is quantitatively different from that of other animals. Tomasello (2008) notes that we alone learn

---

11   Eagleman (2015:7) reports that over two million synapses are formed every second in the developing infant's brain.

12   It is possible that our last common ancestor with chimpanzees may have had far greater tool making abilities than present day chimpanzees, and that modern chimpanzees may have evolved in an environment where tool use and with it language have been suppressed.

by imitation, whereas chimpanzees copy through 'ontogenetic ritualization'[13] and thus filter out redundant movement. Apes focus on the producer rather than the mechanism of the gesture. This naturally entails some limited variability in primate actions and is not necessarily optimal for the emergence of a shared and flexible social practice such as language where slavish adherence to a gesture is vital for distinguishing between meaningful choices.

Arbib (2012) like Tomasello is a proponent of the view that language has a gestural origin. He bases his argument on the fact that Positron Emission Tomography scans of human brains have found evidence of a mirror neuron system analogous to that found in Macaque monkeys, in the frontal cortex in or near Broca's area (page 28).[14] He argues (ibid:173–180) that the neural processes and networks which support language evolved 'on top' of a mirror system for hand movement. This, he argues, provides the evolutionary basis for why an utterance means roughly the same for both speaker and hearer. Mirror neurons in or near Broca's area fire inside a hearer when he/she perceives a speaker's auditory gesture. Briefly, the hypothesis argues that the ancestor of all extant primates had a mirror neuron system which enabled them to match executed actions with observed actions. This, coupled with the ability to copy the specific actions of conspecifics, afforded the evolution of a more complex imitation system in hominins. Through repeated use and practice the link between action and observation as complex imitation entailed attention to what was being imitated and understanding of what was being imitated.[15] Communicatively this is akin to communication via pantomime.[16] Repeated use led to conventionalisation and the emergence of proto-sign where more of the shared intended meaning was encoded in the signal. Finally, proto-speech emerged from the expansion

---

Thus the last common ancestor may have exhibited greater linguistic abilities then modern primates.

13   Arbib's mirror system hypothesis similarly separates what he calls pre-hominid imitation from humans' complex imitation system (2012: 174).

14   Rizzolatti et al. (1996) discovered that some neurons in brain region F5 in Macaque monkeys fire not only when the monkey grasps an object but also fire when the monkey observes a conspecific or human make a similar grasping gesture. An alternative view is found in Hickok (2014) who denies the importance of mirror neurons in linguistic processing but accepts the importance of imitation.

15   Eagleman (2015:156) reports that people with Botox can't read emotions as well as other people owing to the fact that their facial muscles have been weakened resulting in a lowered ability to mirror others' gestures.

16   This was perhaps something like a parlour game of charades which itself is a paradigmatic example of Gricean communication. The mirror system hypothesis also shows how conventionalised language emerged and hence avoids the criticism of Gricean approaches found in the scenario presented in Azzouni 2013:348) where two speakers with different languages struggle to communicate using gestures.

of the mirror system to adjacent neural regions which control mouth muscles and proto-sign was superseded but not fully replaced by proto-speech. The McGurk effect, where hearers, if presented with an aural stimulus which does not match the seen articulatory gesture, misperceive the spoken stimulus is evidence in favour of the multimodal perception of spoken language (see McGurk and McDonald 1976).

It is clear that all of the above address what the philosopher Daniel Dennett describes as the how come question: how come language evolved? But perhaps a more interesting question is the what for question: what did language achieve that boosted our survival as individuals and hence fostered the further development of our species? All of the above scenarios are plausible and, indeed, by no means mutually exclusive. But, regardless, the one thing that is certain is that language did evolve, though what this actually means is itself not entirely clear.

2.3   WHAT EVOLVED?

The Chomskyan revolution (e.g. Chomsky 1957, 1965, 1981, 1994) created a view of language based on Universal Grammar (UG) and the autonomy of syntax. The study of discourse phenomena or, indeed, how language functioned and was put together in texts was cast outside the pale. Instances of language use were designated performance and marginalised. No attempt was made to link language with society, or indeed to explore how language is processed and neurally encoded in the brain. Instead, the internal system of language was idealised and abstracted, and it was studied as if it were a physical organ; rather as if biologists studied the heart without recourse to the circulatory system. Language was equated with syntax and ultimately with merge[17] (Hauser, Chomsky and Fitch 2002 and Fitch, Hauser and Chomsky 2005). While the earlier versions of UG, such as Chomsky 1965, proposed a rich innate encoding of linguistic features within the genome, the more recent minimalist programme does not. The traditional Chomskyan view of language is fundamentally anti-Darwinian (Pennisi & Falzone (2016:18), as it allows for no adaptive path between animal communication systems and human language. Rather, it argues for a saltationist adaption, which propelled a fortunate hominin towards sudden linguistic competence. But the more recent version (e.g. Chomsky 2005) does appear to allow some potential room for communicative pressures to emerge as an evolutionary pressure through the 2nd factor of experience. Thus, it

---

17   Merge is the basic operation in minimalism where two syntactic objects are combined to form a new one (Chomsky 1995:226). While it clearly bears some similarities to what we call articulation, the latter concept refers to the creation not just of more complex meanings, but of meanings at different levels of abstraction (see Chapter 3).

would appear to be potentially compatible with Darwinian approaches (though see Chomsky and Berwick 2016).

A view of language and how it evolved that ignores communicative pressures is in some senses odd. Comparative ethologists studying the evolution of the wing do not consider their description complete until they have described the function of the wing; namely flight. Wings, like language, represent perceived challenges to evolutionary adaption. After all, what is the function of half a wing, or indeed how can one posit a non-teleological account of language development? Coyne (2009:42) states that, in reality, it is entirely possible to imagine intermediate stages between flight and non-flight. Gliding, he notes, is an obvious first step, and today flying squirrels use flaps of skin which extend along their sides to glide from tree to tree. More impressively, flying lemurs, who have more extensive membranes surrounding their bodies, have been witnessed to glide for over 135 metres. It is clearly not difficult to imagine a later stage where the flapping of the membranes adds to the flight efficiency or an earlier one where gliding itself emerged out of the use of jumping behaviour. The coupling of a wing with feathers led to streamlined flight though feathers themselves are an exaptation as they appear to have evolved on the basis of their functionality in insulation and/or for sexual display. Similarly, the use of the vocal organs for speech is an exaptation from the basic biological needs of breathing and eating.

In the following paragraphs we consider the issues of (i) what role has the evolution of language played in completing the overall system of human life, (ii) how does this make the human cultural system a better fit for its niche, and (iii) what might this mean for how the capacity for language is represented in our brains. Kahneman (2012:19) segments thought into system 1 and system 2. The former operates automatically, while the latter allocates attention to effortful mental activities, frequently involves complex calculation, and is associated with the subjective feelings of logical effort. It is hard to see how language could aid system 1 thinking, which is far too rapid for conscious reflection; our hominin ancestors would not have survived long if they had stopped to weigh up the pros and cons of various escape options when faced with a hungry predator. Conversely, it is obvious how language could bootstrap system 2 thinking when employed in planning a hunt or in tool making. This then raises the issue of the extremely controversial relationship between language and thought. Various views have been posited ranging from the strawman argument (discussed below), where language determines thought, to the view that language is simply a vehicle for conveying the universal grammar of thought 'mentalese' (Fodor: 1975). Our view, which we hope will emerge over the next few pages in particular, is that neither of the above views is sustainable and that the relation between language and thought is both richer and more nuanced.

It is clear that language and thought can be disaggregated, and that the language we speak does not determine our conceptual abilities and that no serious scholar currently holds this position. Despite the popular association of a position – that language determines thought – with the anthropological linguist, Benjamin Lee Whorf, Whorf himself was not an advocate of linguistic determinism. He wrote (1956:239):

> The tremendous importance of language cannot, in my opinion, be taken to mean necessarily that nothing is back of it of the nature of what has traditionally been called 'mind'. My own studies suggest, to me, that language for all its kingly role, is in some sense a superficial embroidery upon deeper processes of communication, which are necessary before any communication, signalling, or symbolism whatsoever can occur.

To prefigure and introduce the discussion in Chapters 3 and 4, Halliday and Matthiessen (2014) argue that the relationship between language and thought is best considered to be stratal. In Chapter 1 we mentioned that a proposition and utterance are linked in a redundancy relationship. We will briefly preview this view here, but will extensively discuss the concept of stratification in Chapters 3, 4 and 5. The context which includes the interaction between individual organisms and their environment (both intra and intersomatic) is realised as meaning on the semantic layer which itself is realised as wording on the lexicogrammatical layer. However, that does not mean that there is no relationship between context and language: they exist in what in Chapter 4 will be defined as a meta-redundancy relationship. Realise is a two way relation. In other words the fact that the context is realised in the semantics entails that the semantics realises the context. The strata exist in a redundancy relationship. Furthermore, as the context realises semantics which realises lexico-grammar we can say that context and lexico-grammar are in a meta-redundancy relationship. In other words, thoughts are articulated not as wordings but as patterns of wordings and are shaped by the context while also shaping what is permissible in the context.

Language is a cultural tool, an enabler of cultural evolution and the external output of cultural evolution. It influences how we conceptualise external stimuli. Were this not to be the case it is highly unlikely that industries such as advertising and public relations could profitably exist. Furthermore, significant evidence exists that speakers of different languages do perceive the world in differing ways. For instance, Thierry et al. (2009) using brain potentials established that (i) 20 Greek speakers were faster than 20 English speakers in distinguishing between dark and light shades of blue but (ii) performed at the same speed as their native English speaking counterparts in distinguishing light and dark shades of green. Greek employs the basic colour terms γαλάζιο (galazio) and μπλε (ble) to distinguish light from dark blue but, like English, only employs one basic colour term πράσινος (prasinos) for all hues of green. Thierry et al. (2009) measured brain activity prior to the mind being consciously aware of what was being presented and therefore there could be no question that conscious reflection influenced task performance (ibid:4568). A further study using the same methodology has shown that the presence and absence of grammatical gender influences categorisation:

> The current study shows that humans may automatically utilise grammatical categories such as gender when asked to make judgements about semantic relationships unrelated to the grammatical categories in question. The fact that we have found such effects in the domain of grammatical gender is particularly important, since previous empirical attempts to address the Whorfian question in this domain used methods and task instructions, mostly based on behavioural measures, that might promote strategic use of grammatical gender categories.

> (Boutonnet et al. (2012:76)

Other work has demonstrated similar effects for the categorisation of space and time (Levinson 2003 and Boroditsky 2001); though as both of these studies have not measured brain activity, critics of linguistic relativity could argue that they have simply shown an interesting correlation between a language and categorisation. Linguistic relativity illustrates sensitivity between speakers and their cultural milieu; we shape our environment but it simultaneously shapes us.

Language opens up new ways for humans to directly manipulate the physical and social environment. It affords humans unique opportunities to regulate our environment: through strengthening group identity and by streamlining the transmission of cultural and technological innovation. Language, by enabling humans to share and reflect on our feelings and thoughts, functions as a homeostatic regulatory device (Damasio 2018). It is social action and it has evolved to have perlocutionary effects (Austin 1961, Searle 1969).

Were we to attempt to reverse engineer a communicative tool which functions to regulate our environment, we would predict that the tool would be flexible and dynamic, learnable but embellished with local flavour (there will be a discussion of redundancy and learnability in Chapters 4 and 5). And language, as we will see, is flexible, dynamic, learnable but contains local embellishments which not only capture intragroup cultural specifics but further serve to create group identity by creating barriers between speakers and outsiders. We would further expect that the social and physical environment in which the speakers operate would feed back into the language system. This, in turn, would result in the language system adapting to the particular environment in which it is spoken, by foregrounding semiotic and physical affordances found in the environment; and this, as was seen above in the discussion of linguistic relativity, appears to be the case. Language is both biological and cultural: it is simultaneously housed in human brains and is a part of the material social setting. Our view in other words is very different from Chomskyan I and E language. We do not draw a distinction between knowledge and use of language but argue that while the language system is mediated through individual brains no speaker has or can have access to the full system. But speakers do have the ability to utilise those parts of the system that they have internalised, when and as appropriate, though their sociolinguistic competence may need explicit instruction (Bernstein 1971).

2.4   A LANGUAGE-READY BRAIN

In order to have access to the affordances generated by language, humans uniquely have evolved a brain capable of utilising language. Our brains consist of a brain stem, cerebellum, diencephalon and the cerebrum. The brain stem is the most primitive part of the brain and is in charge of ensuring that automatic cardiac and respiratory functions are maintained. The cerebellum is involved in regulating motor control including articulatory gestures and in the regulation of pain. The diencephalon consists of the thalamus and the hypothalamus and morphologically may be considered part of the brain stem. However, functionally it is a relay station between the cerebral hemispheres and the lower part of the brain. It links the nervous and endocrine systems and hence is centrally involved in the regulation of feeling and hence subjectivity. The cerebrum represents the largest and superior part of the brain and is divided into two hemispheres. Both hemispheres are covered by an outer layer of grey matter and connected by the corpus callosum – a thick bundle of nerve fibres.

Language capacity is lateralised in the brain and, for most people, it is housed in the left hemisphere[18], though in the case of young children who have to have their left hemisphere surgically removed language can occupy their right hemisphere.[19] In addition, pitch – at least in tonal languages – is located in the right hemisphere for most people (Patel 2007: 76). The hemisphere itself is divided into four lobes:

---

18   Because of the difficulty of testing which hemisphere is linguistically dominant it is by no means certain how many right dominant language people exist. Mazoyer et al. (2014) in a relatively small survey found little evidence of correlation between handedness and linguistic processing. In other words, left handed people were as likely to have left hemisphere dominance for language processing as right handed people. They estimated that fewer than 1% of people have right hemisphere dominance for language (ibid:13).

19   Recent evidence suggests that while the left hemisphere is dominant some linguistic processing such as the recognition of phonemes and graphemes occurs in the right hemisphere (Taylor and Regard 2003). So it is not strictly true to assume that language processing occurs by default in the left hemisphere.

the frontal lobe, the parietal lobe, the temporal lobe and the occipital lobe. While all four lobes are to some extent involved in processing language the occipital lobe is mainly concerned with the processing of visual input. The frontal lobe houses the motor centres of the cortex which control the execution and planning of gestures. It contains Broca's area which has been traditionally associated with activities which involve joining and segmenting syntactic and phonological information. Pennisi and Falzone (2016) have proposed that Broca's area is also involved in the integrating of contextual information. It is also, as mentioned on page 27, the site of (or exists close to the site of) the mirror neuron systems; hence, work such as Friederici (2002) and Caplan (2006) has proposed that Broca's area plays a role in comprehension as well as production. The other traditional site for language namely Wernicke's area is found in the temporal lobe and damage to Wernicke's area results in comprehension difficulties. The parietal lobe is responsible for processing and integrating somatic and extra somatic sensory information including language.

The brain is both highly plastic and individual, so it is important to note that no morphology of any two brains is identical (Friederici 2002). The brain is sculpted by experience as it continuously rehearses and activates responses to situations in a timely manner. In a series of publications, Eagleman (2011, 2015, 2020) notes that the brains of experts engaging in activities use less energy than do those of novices. Through practice the routines used by experts are embodied in the neo cortex and automatised. Such divergences can be identified via brain imaging. Similarly, there is some evidence for sexual dimorphism with more grey matter in female brains in Broca's area (Kurth et al. 2017). This may explain why females tend to perform better in verbal comprehension tasks, though whether this advantage is genetic or the result of lived experiences is unclear. However, as all brains are unique we need to remember that models of neurolinguistic processing are idealisations of a brain which is not necessarily any one brain in particular.

Within the cortex, grey matter is made up of nerve cell bodies, and it is where processing occurs. Nerve cells or neurons typically form into neural networks and are connected together by firing together. A typical neuron[20] consists of a cell body with an input and output. Inputs are received through dendrites and pass directly to the cell body. A neuron may contain numerous dendrites and so may receive simultaneous inputs from different sources. Outputs are sent along the axons. Each

---

20   In reality there are different types of neurons. It is by no means clear how scientists should classify the form and function of the neurons found within the brain. Thus, it may be that morphologically different neurons may have different functions. In 1909, the German neurologist Korbinian Brodmann mapped the cortex into 52 regions based on the different types of neurons, but the functional differences, if any, between such regions have not yet been fully worked out; see Ziles (2018) for a recent review. Hence current modules of processing which assume that all nodes function in the same manner may need revising.

neuron contains only a single axon which, however, typically branches into numerous fibres, thus allowing a single output to be received by more than one neuron. Axons are typically myelinated and are the white matter which lies beneath the cortex. They link the various regions of the cortex and also connect the cortex with various subcortical structures such as the amygdala which is known to play a role in the processing of emotions, memory and decision making. Myelination allows for the faster transmission of electrical activity across long distances in the brain. Neuronal signals may be excitatory or inhibitory. Edelman (2004:loc538) proposes a theory of neuronal group selection which argues that developmental selection leads to the brain containing numerous potential networks. Interaction with the environment results in the favouring of some networks which outcompete their peers. This results in the strengthening of some networks and the atrophy of others. This is a recurrent and dynamic process which continues over a lifetime. Crudely put, this can be rephrased as 'use it or lose it' – and if you use it you have more of it. Learning, in this view, is the result of the strengthening and weakening of neural pathways.

Lamb (1999) and Garcia, Sullivan and Tsiang (2017) illustrate a neurolinguistic theory which is broadly compatible with the above neurological description. They propose networks of a functional unit called nections which, they argue, are neurologically encoded as cortical columns (groupings of a 100 or so neurons). The networks are distributed, bi-directional and consist of *and* and *or* nodes. Localisation is achieved through the proximity hypothesis which states that nections that are physically close to one another will tend to have similar functions. Different but overlapping networks are proposed for production and reception as well as for different linguistic subsystems. In this view of language, there is no need for mental modules to read and write symbols. Instead, language becomes embodied directly in the hardware of the brain as processing information, and each time the system is used or experienced it changes and reorganises itself. The system of language which emerges is hierarchical with the conceptual network determining the lexical network which, in turn, determines the phonological network (Garcia Sullivan and Tsiang 2017:199).

While such a model can, we claim, account for the systematisation of language distinctions at all strata, in the next section we will consider what a phonological system would look like. The first thing to note is that in a relational network there is no need for rules and categorisations. Each and every token is recorded, and each and every token restructures the system (Lamb 1999, Bybee 1999). Thus, the representation of the phonological form clusters around the most common representation of the phone or series of phones and, as we will see, the presence of a phone skews the presence of a neighbouring one. The second thing to note is that, akin to Edelman's neural networks, phonological networks exist only through use – and possibilities that are not exploited wither away. Finally, and most significantly, the phonological systems which emerge conform to the homeostatic principle. They not only allow speakers to operate with a shared, regulated and metastable system but with one which is not just compatible with communicative efficiency but is itself maximally efficient. From chaos order emerges in the form of regular and predictable phonological patterns. In the next section we will consider how order emerges from chaos by looking at the evolution of vowel systems. This will allow us to see how the interaction of physiological constraints, cultural interaction and communicative pressure results in the emergence of a metastable but sub-optimal system.

2.5   THE EVOLUTION OF VOWEL SYSTEMS

Vowels are the centre of syllables and their articulation is constrained by the physiology of the tongue and the length and shape of the vocal tract. Vowels are traditionally classed in terms of where they are produced in the mouth: front vs back, whether they are produced towards the roof of the mouth or not; high/close vs low/open and whether or not the lips are rounded or spread. Yet, despite this, there remains both enormous diversity between vowels produced cross linguistically and also enormous symmetry within and between vowel systems. Vowel systems are metastable with vowels historically engaging in chain shifts, splits and mergers. De Boer (2001) discussing the similarities between vowel systems argues that similarities in vowel systems found across languages are based on a combination of properties of the human brain, historical processes and the functions of language. Sound systems represent a trade-off between articulatory and auditory needs (Stevens 1972, 1989).

Carré's *distinctive regions model* considers the speech signal as representing an optimal solution to the physiological difficulties inherent in producing distinctive and meaningful sounds. It models deformations in the acoustic space which correspond to the vowel space and tongue gestures. This allows the model to predict which vowel spaces and physical properties will produce optimally distinctive sounds but does not say which choices any given language will utilise (Carré & Chennoukh 1995). De Boer (2001:13) notes that a weakness of both Carré's and Stevens' work is that speech sounds are considered in isolation and not in relation to other extant sounds within the language system. In other words, sounds must be considered as optimal not in universal terms, but in terms of the individual language and the phonological patterns which emerge within the language. This implies that as vowel sounds are not distinct in absolute but in relative terms they will tend to spread out and occupy the vowel space in a manner analogous to repelling magnets.

Languages have vowel systems which are by no means identical. Ladefoged and Maddieson (1996:281) caution that, in practice, it is not easy to draw a sharp distinction either phonetically or phonologically between vowels and consonants.[21] But, as noted above, they recognise that the basic parameters of most vowel systems are high/low, front/back and rounded/unrounded (ibid: 282). In the discussion that follows we will restrict our discussion to these three qualities and ignore phonation, nasalization, tenseness, length, diphthongisation and pharyngealization so that we can examine the cross-linguistic category of vowels presented in the *World Atlas of Linguistic Structures* which samples the vowel systems of 564 languages (Maddieson 2013)[22]. The smallest vowel inventory found is 2 and the sole distinction is vowel height. More common are 3 vowel inventory languages such as Inuit – where vowels of the form /i, u, a/ which are distinguished by vowel height and front/back are found.

The most common number of vowels found in a language is 5 which occurs in 188 languages including Japanese, Greek and Spanish. These languages typically have vowel inventories of the following kind /i, e, a, o, u/. In these languages, and the other 100 which contained 6 vowels, the distinguishing features are high/low and front/back. For languages with more vowel qualities other options are required to distinguish vowels. For instance, French has 11 vowels and distinguishes 6 front vowels /i, e, ɛ, y, ø, œ/ as being unrounded or rounded. The first three vowels are unrounded and the last three are rounded. So /i and y/ are both front and high vowels and are distinguished only be the fact that the former is unrounded and the later rounded. By contrast British English, which has a vowel quality inventory of 13 vowels. does not use the unrounded and round distinction. Instead British English vowel qualities can be grouped into the following three groups which are themselves distinguished in terms of vowel height: front /i, ɪ, e, ɛ, æ/; centre /ʌ, ɜ, ə/; and back /u, ʊ, ɔ, ɒ, ɑ/. British English obeys the general universal tendency that front vowels are unrounded and non-open back vowels are rounded. Rounding in other words appears to be distinctive only in some larger vowel inventory systems. However, such tendencies are overridden within certain languages – for instance, Japanese, which has a 5 vowel inventory[23] that includes /ɯ/ an unrounded high back vowel.

---

21   For instance there is no simple way of deciding whether the /l/ in the second syllable of little [lɪtɬ] is (i) phonetically a vowel or a consonant or (ii) functioning as a vowel or a consonant.

22   Some caution is required in generalising findings from 564 languages as it is estimated that there are 7079 extant languages (Eberhard et al. 2020) and that there may have been 100,000 languages spoken until now.

23   And indeed 5 vowel phonemes.

De Boer (2001) in his extensive investigation of the origin of vowel systems argues that vowel systems have evolved to be self-organizing and complex systems. Thus, while the initial spur must have resulted in a selectional gain, presumably through more optimal communication, the evolution of vowel systems towards a steady but metastable state is driven by cultural factors. Order emerges on a large scale in the system as a result of numerous local contextually appropriate interactions. Perhaps the best example of a complex adaptive and self-organised system in nature is a termites' castle which emerges unplanned from the interactions of thousands of insects and produces a castle like edifice. For self-organisation to emerge there exists a need for boundedness which, in the case of vowels, is provided by biological constraints on the actuality and possibility of certain articulatory gestures. Within the bounded system positive feedback loops lead to the emergence of attractors or central members of a prototype. In the emergence of vowel systems, the interactions are the communicative acts of individual speakers. The interactions (the tokens) result in the formation of the system or types.

The sole evidence that speakers can draw on in building their internal representations of the vowel system is the language they hear around them. Thus *parole* underpins *langue* (Steels 1997, Bybee 2002). This view implies that the system which will emerge will be learnable, but not fully optimal, as not all possible distinctions will be heard. The input will contain redundancies with no one fit between form and function. Pierrehumbert (2001) argues that language learning is stochastic; the proportion in which a pattern has previously been experienced predicts its future emergence. While we accept this point, we argue that a stochastic approach on its own is unable to account for dynamism and change. The wider communicative and social contexts also play a role. For instance, language is an important means of maintaining homeostasis within a community, and thus communities which have denser social networks and are less open to outside pressures maintain sub-optimal linguistic systems including phonological features (Dunbar 2003, Trudgill 2009). The maintenance of sub-optimal features such as the unnecessarily extensive British English vowel system hampers learning while at the same time strengthening affiliative links between speakers.[24]

De Boer's (2001) computer modelling of the evolution of vowel systems assumes as a starting point that the ability to reproduce and perceive vowels has evolved through Darwinian mechanisms. Vowels are learned and spread through repeated interactions between imitators. In order to make the model more realistic the spoken vowel is masked by noise and the population of imitators refreshed through simulated death, birth and migration. De Boer found that every

---

24   As dialect forms of English such as Singapore Standard English are spoken with fewer vowel phonemes than Standard Southern English, some of the SSE vowels are necessarily redundant and not needed to maintain functional distinctions.

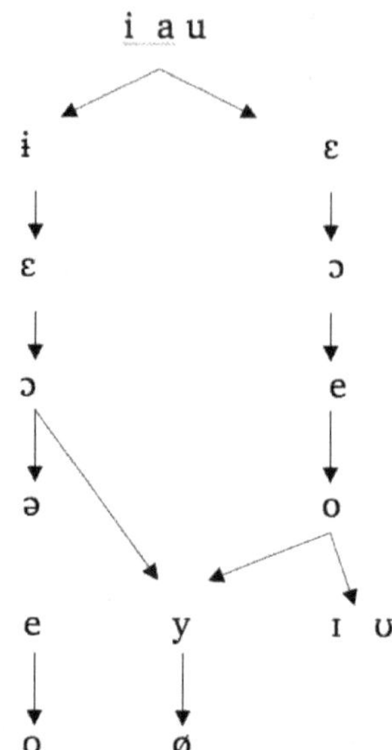

Figure 2.1 Vowel system hierarchy based on Crothers 1978

simulation resulted in realistic looking vowel systems of varying sizes with a reasonable similarity to the attested vowel systems of human languages. The simulation games generated vowel systems with vowel qualities of between 3 and 9 vowels with the most frequently occurring vowel system containing 4 vowels. This is unlike human language where 5 vowel quality systems are as noted above the most frequent. Yet, the systems that emerged were largely in agreement with Crothers (1978), whose observations on possible vowel systems, and in which order vowel qualities emerge, remains the theoretical gold standard. Figure 2.1 illustrates the order in which vowel qualities are predicted to emerge typically.

It can be seen that for a language such as Southern Standard British English, which has more than 6 vowel qualities, the predicted optimal order does not fully emerge, with neither /e/ or /i/ emerging. Thus, we should not be surprised that the vowel quality systems produced by De Boer's simulations were also in a sense suboptimal: in the sense that they did not maintain the articulatory distance between vowels required for optimal functional distinction.

Table 2.1[25] details the vowel systems generated by De Boer's computer simulations. Grey shading indicates vowel systems that have not been attested in human languages.

---

25   The symbol /a/ represents both an open-front unrounded vowel and an open-centralised unrounded vowel. In order to distinguish between the two forms, I have underlined the 4 instances where it represents a centralised vowel.

Table 2.1 Vowel quality systems that emerged in De Boer (2001)

3 Vowel system	/i, a, u/ (78%)	/a, ə, ɨ/[26] (22%)	
4 Vowel system	/i, a, ə, u/ (55%)	/i, e, a, u/ (45%)	
5 Vowel system	/i, e, a, o, u/ (88%)	/i, e, a̲, ə, u/ (8%)	/i, ə, a̲, o, u/ (4%)
6 Vowel system	/i, e, a, ə, o, u/ (55%)	/i, e, ɛ, a, o, u/ (18%)	/i, e, a, ɑ, o, u/ (13%)
	/i, e, a, ɔ, o, u/ (6%)	/i, e, a, ɨ, ɔ, u/ (6%)	/i, a, ɨ, ə, o, u/ (2%)
7 Vowel system	/i, e, ɛ, a, ɔ, o, u/ (24%)	/i, ɛ, a, ɨ, ɑ, ɔ, u/ (20%)	/i, e, a, ə, ɑ, o, u/ (20%)
		/i, ɛ, a, ɨ, ə, ɔ, u/ (20%)	/i, e, ɛ, a, ɨ, ɔ, u/ (16%)
8 Vowel system	/i, e, ɛ, a, ɨ, ɔ, o, u/ (49%)	/i, e, ɛ, a, ɑ, ɔ, o, u/ (16%)	
	/i, e, ɛ, a, ɨ, ə, o, u/ (14%)	/i, ɛ, a, ɨ, ə, ɔ, o, u/ (9%)	
	/i, e, ɛ, a, ɨ, ɑ, ɔ, u/ (5%)	/i, e, a, ɨ, ə, ɑ, o, u/ (5%)	
9 Vowel system	/i, e, ɛ, ɨ, ə, a̲, ɔ, o, u/ (33%)	/i, e, ɛ, a, ɨ, ɑ, ɔ, o, u/ (33%)	
	/i, e, ɛ, a, ɨ, ə, ɔ, o, u/ (22%)	/i, e, ɛ, ɨ, ɤ, ɔ, o, u/ (6%)	
	/i, e, ɛ, æ, ɨ, ə, a̲, ɔ, u/ (6%)		

While Table 2.1 does not by any means illustrate all the possibilities found in human languages with 3 to 9 vowel quality systems, it does show that De Boer's simulations were more than capable of illustrating how such systems evolve. Different interactions defined by the noise filter and the variations in the imitators' knowledge of the vowels lead to different systems. In each case the metastable system which emerges is not dependent on a particular cognitive or biological ability. Instead, once the ability to produce and perceive vowels exists, and assuming a need and drive to produce sounds which are distinct, interactions between users of the sounds results in a self-organised and dynamic system.

Since the pioneering work of Roman Jakobson – see Jakobson & Waugh (1987:chp2) and Waugh & Monville-Bateson (1990:259–260) – phonological theory employs distinctive feature analysis to describe speech sounds and to explicate relationships between sounds. Distinctive features enable the study of how rules and constraints interact with natural classes. Jakobson's pioneering work defined features in terms of 12 acoustic binary features, 10 of which it was claimed were sufficient to account for the English phonemic system. The relevant features for English vowels are presented in Table 2.2. The star indicates that the '–' feature option is not available in English.

---

26   It is worth emphasising that the fact that the systems that have been shaded in grey have not been recorded does not necessarily entail their impossibility. They may exist in languages that have not yet been studied or have existed in languages which have gone extinct. Nor is the reader to understand that these are the sole types of vowel systems that have been recorded.

Table 2.2 Vowel binary features based on Jakobson

Feature	Acoustic description	Articulatory description
+/− vocalic	Clearly defined formant structure	No obstruction in vocal tract
+/− tense	Higher energy with greater spread across the spectrum	More strain or duration or a stronger airflow
+/− voice*	Periodic low frequency excitation	Vocal fold vibration
+/− continuant*	Interrupted sound	Rapid opening and closing of the oral tract
+/− grave	Energy concentrated in lower frequencies	Articulated at peripheries of the mouth
+/− flat	Weakening of upper frequencies	Lip-rounding or other forms of aperture narrowing

Since Chomsky & Halle (1968), features have been mostly defined in terms of sets of articulatory gestures with the current view being that it is more realistic and economic to describe the phonemic system of a language using a mixture of unary and binary features e.g. Nathan (2008). The roof of the mouth or the place of articulation consists of 4 primary regions: LABIAL, CORONAL, DORSAL and GUTTURAL which can be described in terms of a unary feature, i.e. an option that is available or not. A unary feature governs sets of binary features. This view reflects the understanding that phonological processes typically affect some related combination of features rather than others (O'Grady 2013a:42). As can be seen in Table 2.3 the feature LABIAL only applies to 4 monophthongs /uː, ʊ, ɔː, ɒ/. Unlike older models the other vowels are not classed as [− Rounded]. The feature simply does not apply. The advantage is that it more easily identifies phonologically active classes and provides both a more elegant and simpler explanation. Distinctive features are not simply lists but rather represent hierarchical configurations of features (Clements and Hume 1995).[27] In relation to English vowels Halle (1995) proposes the description set out in Table 2.3.

---

27   While there is a growing recognition (which can perhaps be classed as a consensus) that rule-based phonology rooted in the Chomsky and Halle (1968) tradition needs to be supplemented with a constraint based approach (Iosad 2018:17), this does not affect the discussion of distinctive features as a way of systematising phonemes. For an alternate view see Berent (2013).

Table 2.3 The monophthongs of Standard British English based on Halle (1995)

Feature	iː	ɪ	uː	ʊ	ɛ	æ	ʌ	ɔː	ɒ	ɜː	ɑː	ə
Labial			√	√				√	√			
Rounded			+	+				+	+			
Dorsal	√	√	√	√	√	√	√	√	√	√	√	√
High	+	+	+	+	−	−	−	−	−	−	−	−
Low	−	−	−	−	−	+	−	−	+	−	+	−
Back	−	−	+	+	−	−	+	+	+	−	+	−
Radical	√		√					√		√	√	
Tense	+		+					+		+	+	

Jakobson in his early writing argued that each language needed to be described in its own terms. In other words, only emic descriptions of systems made sense (1942:241). Yet in later work such as Jakobson and Halle (1956) he argued that the description of the phonemic pattern of a language needed to take account of universal tendencies. We, as the following paragraphs make clear, are aligned with Jakobson's earlier views.[28]

While the feature descriptions in Chomsky and Halle (1968) have been amended, the underlying assumptions posited by Chomsky and Halle that features are innate and part of universal grammar has remained largely unchallenged (Mielke 2008:27). Mielke, though, argues (ibid:9) that features are abstract categories based on generalisations which emerge from the perception of phonological patterns. We saw earlier that there is debate as to whether language is best described as a biolinguistic system or in terms of a system grounded in biology and culture.[29] The evolution of vowel systems would seem to shed light on this debate. Innate views of features ground them directly in phonetics, and thus ultimately in the shared human biological ability to articulate distinct speech sounds. Emergent

---

28   Within the tradition of Systemic Functional Linguistics works that has inspired us, there have been a number of phonological studies which have demonstrated the importance of describing each language in its own terms, e.g. Halliday (2005/1992), Matthiessen (2021), Mc Gregor (1992), Tench (2017) and O'Grady (forthcoming). Broadly speaking these studies take seriously J R Firth's admonition, that every language must be described in its own terms as it is a specific cultural product, and attempt to map out the systems of an individual language before producing cross-linguistic descriptions.

29   This is reminiscent of the 19th century debate between those who saw languages as biological systems akin to species and those who argued that languages were cultural products. Saussure (1957) provides cogent arguments, which we agree with, against an exclusively biological view.

views conversely predict that, as features merely reflect phonetic detail as perceived by speakers' recategorisation into phonological patterns, each language (or perhaps closely related groupings of languages) should have different sets of features, though of course language contact may also play a role in the spreading of features. A major testable difference between the innate and emergent views is therefore that, for the former but not the latter, features should pattern in a similar manner cross linguistically in the identification of natural or productive classes.

Mielke (ibid:13) defines a natural class of sounds as follows:

> A group of sounds in an inventory which do at least one of the following to the exclusion of all other sounds in the inventory: (i) undergo a phonological process; such as nasal stops in English which all assimilate to the place of articulation of a following consonant, (ii) trigger a phonological process; such as the voiceless stops in English which in initial position trigger aspiration, or (iii) exemplify a static distributional restriction; such as the semi vowels /j/ and /w/ in English are restricted to syllable onsets.

In order to test whether the evidence best supported innate or emergent views of features Mielke surveyed 549 languages from a wide range of language families and found that innatist theories[30] of features were unable to account for around 30% of the data. In other words, 30% of the identified phonologically active classes were not predicted on the basis of the phonetic similarity of the features. Furthermore, the 70% of the surveyed cross-linguistic patterns that are accounted for by innatist views are similarly accounted for by emergent views of features (ibid:197), and many of the unpredicted or unusual patterns can be explained as emerging from phonetically driven sound change. It is hard to disagree with his conclusion that as innatist views of language do not lead to any increased explanatory clarity, it seems unnecessary to posit them.

Steels (1997), an opponent of innatist views, has argued that for a language system to evolve three factors are required: (i) imitation, (ii) imperfect imitation leading to creative change and (iii) efficiency and effectiveness which result in the language system itself co-evolving to become more learnable. The maximisation of efficiency entails the minimisation of the amount of effort required to produce a lexical item: higher frequency words tend to be shorter and words tend to shorten by use. Deutscher (2005:98) has likened this process to the erosion of rocks by waves; linguistic items are worn down through use. An illustration from English is

---

30   Mielke tested using three feature theories, Jakobson's original model, Chomsky and Halle (1968) and unified feature theory e.g. Clements and Hume (1995).

the pronunciation of the English counties (and London square and road) Leicester and Gloucester as ˈlɛstə/ not /ˈlaɪsɛstə/ and /ˈglɒstə/ not /ˈglɒsɛstə/. The maximisation of effectiveness recognises that hearers' perceptual abilities are a bottleneck in the reproduction of linguistic meaning: some potential distinctions are not perceptible. Language has adapted to ameliorate perceptual difficulties by allowing redundancy, case marking and word order. In the next section we will illustrate, by using phonological examples, how linguistic features emerge as a result of interaction and show that they form into metastable systems which follow the logic of the A-curve with a minority of items doing most of the functional work.

2.6   THE EMERGENCE OF SYLLABLE ONSETS

In this section we will examine syllable onsets in English in order to further explore how systems evolve and become learnable while maintaining functional distinctions. We do this to demonstrate that most of the work is done by a minority of the available resources as we would expect in a dynamic and metastable system. Prior to so doing we will take a brief excursion to introduce the term *prospection* which we mentioned in Chapter 1 and will discuss in detail in Chapter 5. The term itself, as far as we know, originates in the corpus linguistic literature. Sinclair and Coulthard (1975) and Tadros (1985) employed the term to refer to something occurring in the discourse which creates the expectation that something else will occur; or, to put it another way, that the production of an element anticipates a following element. Our argument is that prospection occurs at all scales from the phonemic up to the discursive (see Chapter 6) and its occurrence is entirely in accord with Steels' evolutionary arguments in relation to efficiency and effectiveness. In this section we will illustrate its occurrence in syllable onset+vowel sequences.

In speech, vowels are normally not produced in isolation and lexical items are formed out of one or more syllables. Each syllable typically contains a vowel.[31] Languages can be divided into those which allow only open syllables where consonants are restricted to prevocalic position and those which allow closed syllables where consonants are not restricted to prevocalic position. The presence of closed syllables in a language such as English entails that the language also contains open syllables. Table 2.4 presents some example English syllables

---

31   Even in English speech it is not strictly true to say that syllables always contain vowels; e.g., listen and bottle may be realised as [ˈlɪsn̩] and [ˈbɒtl̩] with the vowel in the final syllable elided. See Pike (1943) for distinction between vowel and vocoid.

Table 2.4 Some open and closed syllables in British English

Open Syllables	Closed Syllables
/eɪ/(ay)	/æt/ (at)
/peɪ/ (pay)	/hæts/ (hats)
/pɹeɪ/ (pray)	/bɛndz/ (bends)
/spɹeɪ/ (spray)	/sɪksθs/ (sixths)

Within the innatist literature two violable principles are usually evoked in order to determine the division of words into syllables: (i) the maximal onset principle which states that all phonotactically legal consonants clusters in the language should be placed into the onset e.g. the syllabification of *petrol* is /ˈpɛ.tɹəl/ and not /ˈpɛt.ɹəl/ (Roca and Johnson 1999). The second principle is the sonority scale which states that consonants on both margins of syllables successively decrease in loudness the further they are away from the vowel or syllable nucleus (MacNeilage 2008:80). Sonority is therefore predicted to increase throughout the onset, reach a peak in the nucleus and decrease again through the coda. Obstruents are the least sonorant sounds with voiceless sounds less so. O'Grady (2013a:130) illustrates sonority in English consonants.

Sonority restrictions are almost certainly grounded, to an extent, in the opening and closing of the mouth (MacNeilage 2008:57); but, as Berent (2013:175) argues, the sonority profiles of syllables in real languages cannot be solely explained by articulatory pressures. She argues that actual sonority profiles are to some extent arbitrary as illustrated by the fact that sonority restrictions in Ancient Greek were sensitive to voicing while this is not the case in English.[32]

In English onset clusters, voice is determined by the presence or absence of voicing in the initial phone.[33] This entails that activation of a voiceless stop in initial onset position prospects the preservation of devoicing until the articulation of the vowel. The frequent English onset clusters /sp, spj, spl, spɹ/ are examples of non-phonetically motivated breaches of the sonority hierarchy. By comparison the /ps/

---

32   Berent's main point is that a cross linguistic comparison of phonological systems is supportive of a weak view of the innatist position which argues for the presence of a specific phonological module, but one that develops according to the timing and amount of input. For a fuller and accessible description of Evo-Devo see Carroll (2011). Berent's views though are equally compatible with an emergent view of phonology and the issue is simply whether or not there are specifically innate language networks or not.

33   The determination of voice in coda clusters is slightly different in that voice is determined by its presence or absence in the first obstruent (oral stop, fricative or affricate) as long as the cluster is monomorphemic. This chapter will present networks of onset consonant clusters only, but the basic point holds.

Table 2.5 Sonority in English Consonants

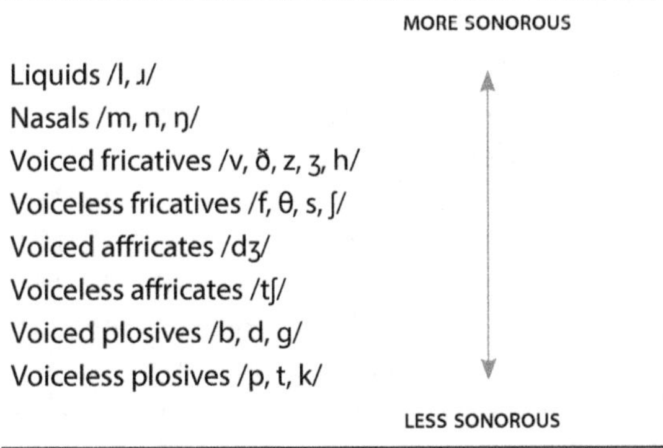

onset cluster which obeys the sonority hierarchy is phonotactically illegal in English in onset position but not for instance in Greek e.g /psoˈmi/ (bread) /ˈpsari/ (fish).[34] Conversely, /ps/ despite contravening the sonority hierarchy in coda position can along with /sp/ appear in coda position in English eg. /mæps/ and /klæsps/.

This discussion illustrates that syllabification, while grounded in the articulatory process of opening and closing the mouth, is not so determined. Languages have – as would be expected from the discussion of vowel systems above – evolved differing and metastable syllable templates. Yet, it would also seem reasonable to suggest that the evolved templates would respect Steel's view of maximum effectiveness – the presence of a consonant or consonant phoneme predicts the following vowel phoneme in English. In order to test our hypothesis, we examined all instances of consonant clusters found in stressed syllables in lexical items as recorded in the *Longman Pronunciation Dictionary of English* (Wells 2000). We examined onset and not coda consonant clusters because of the tight connection between vowels (syllable nuclei) and consonants in codas (MacNeilage 2008:81). In order to ensure that we gleaned a representative but manageable sample of the lexical items found in the standard English we included all words except:

1   Those clearly indicating a recent foreign borrowing, i.e. words which may not yet have been assimilated into the English sound system, e.g. words such as *babiroussa* but not *babushka* were excluded.

2   Those with variant spellings such as *labour/labor* and *jail/gaol* were counted only once.

---

34   One of the authors can, despite the phonetic naturalness of the cluster, attest to the extreme difficulty for a native English speaker in attempting to pronounce the /ps/ onset cluster, and the resulting general merriment when he attempts to do so.

3   Entries commencing with capital letters such as personal names, place names or brand names were excluded[35].

We found 90 English consonant onset clusters in the data set comprising 1, 2 and 3 consonants. Rather than consider onsets such as /sp/, /pl/ and /stɹ/ as sequences of phonemes, we chose to treat them as single clusters or prosodies (Firth 1948)[36]. This was for a number of reasons: (i) the issue of archiphonemes (Trubetzkoy 1969): we cannot confidently class the second consonant in /sp/ as /p/or /b/; (ii) different phonetic realisations e.g. /l/ in the sequence /bl/ is voiced but in the sequence /pl/ it is not; and (iii) work on sound symbolism has demonstrated that such sequences have the potential to connote meaning, e.g /gl/ signals the presence or the absence of light (Willett 2015, Monaghan et al. 2012, Ohala et al. 1994 and Kanero et al 2014).

We located 35,694 consonant onsets ranging from the most frequent /s/ which occurred 2,595 times to the sequences /bw/, /vr/, /mw/, /hw/, / ʃp/, / smj/, /tm/ and /sθ/ which were only found once. Table 2.6 lists the 16 most frequent onset clusters, which amount to 73% of the data set, and shows their distribution by vowel.

In order to investigate whether or not the onsets associated with the vowels were in a non-linear distribution, we ran a series of chi squares in order to see if the distribution of onsets and following vowels were drawn from the same population. As Table 2.7 illustrates we found that there was a significant difference in the distribution of all onsets; in all cases a p value of <0.001. The difference in patterning between /t/ and /st/ and between /d/ and /st/ supports our view that onset clusters were better treated as unitary gestures rather than sequences of discrete phonemes. The second element of /st/ creates differing expectations than do /d/ and /t/.

Kretzschmar (2009 and 2015) has extended Zipf's work by showing that numerous features of spoken language, such as lexical and phonetic variation, have a non-linear distribution. He has dubbed this the A-curve (asympiotic hyperbolic curve) which can be calculated by the formula that roughly 20% of the features make up roughly 80% of the instances and that the most frequent value is roughly twice as frequent as the following one and so on. We will discuss this in more detail in Chapters 3 and 4. We examined the distribution of onsets with vowels and found a non-linear distribution for each vowel. Figure 2.2 illustrates for the six most frequent vowels, /ɪ, ɛ, æ, ɒ, eɪ and ʌ /.

---

35   This was solely done to ensure that the data set was of a manageable size.

36   Lamb (1999:164) quotes early 20th century work by Noreen to argue for the presence of *complex phonemes* such as /kɹ/ based upon the fact that in the sequence /ɹ/ will, because of the presence of the aspirated voiceless stop, be devoiced and realised as [ɹ̥] (see also Firth 1948). The argument is that the word 'crow' comprises only one consonant element (decomposable into two phonemes) and a vowel.

Table 2.6   The most frequent onsets + vowels found in Wells (2000)

	iː	ɪ	ɛ	æ	ɑː	ʌ	ɔ	ɒ	ɜː	ʊ	uː	ɪə	ɛə	ʊə	eɪ	aɪ	əʊ	aʊ	ɔɪ	All
/s/	233	455	489	196	43	226	102	146	148	3	79	19	5	4	115	207	86	31	8	2595
/m/	93	331	326	367	95	149	90	186	60	2	40	8	8	5	171	109	73	102	7	2222
/k/	55	78	43	318	112	296	158	463	62	25	55	1	14	0	237	32	121	79	15	2164
/l/	134	367	246	245	69	81	49	213	17	13	134	10	9	8	239	184	111	25	10	2164
/p/	106	228	252	299	119	132	114	225	130	54	27	25	27	1	138	61	120	28	25	2111
/t/	133	257	306	205	28	75	98	155	130	12	63	29	31	7	247	142	96	22	10	2046
/ɹ/	198	203	315	232	62	116	27	122	2	4	94	27	12	2	275	99	147	37	15	1989
/f/	86	219	167	151	44	61	222	108	94	55	23	10	18	0	108	127	74	22	5	1594
/b/	108	308	97	175	80	149	79	95	74	66	52	3	19	4	75	61	46	27	16	1534
/d/	103	234	272	106	38	165	61	113	18	0	36	21	9	5	120	88	46	53	3	1491
/n/	103	149	136	142	30	69	38	189	27	3	18	20	34	0	212	118	118	71	14	1491
/h/	54	80	205	184	113	64	50	89	5	4	11	20	29	1	56	108	83	53	7	1216
/w/	74	206	82	20	4	26	87	143	113	67	9	5	20	0	68	95	12	2	0	1033
/v/	43	131	131	95	18	19	29	34	133	0	1	8	23	0	75	98	32	11	22	903
/st/	46	122	85	63	52	8	51	55	24	4	13	21	9	0	121	27	45	5	0	751
/g/	7	53	56	130	45	82	30	79	9	18	30	2	2	3	90	12	73	7	3	731
All	1576	3412	3208	2928	952	1718	1285	2415	1046	330	685	229	269	40	2347	1568	1283	575	160	26035

Table 2.7 The Summary of chi square tests for onset distribution

	s	m	k	l	p	t	r	f	b	d	n	h	w	v	st	g
s		314***	1248***	370***	426***	235***	423***	367***	338***	136***	495***	481***	521***	263***	340***	490***
m	314***		677***	252***	228***	258**	318**	340***	283***	141***	908***	217***	605***	372***	215***	247***
k	1248***	677***		871***	523***	872***	898***	745***	628***	786***	551***	668***	927***	945***	537***	183***
l	370***	252***	871***		392***	210***	171***	399***	352***	231***	220***	345***	586***	426***	191***	248***
p	426***	228***	523***	392***		232***	416***	204***	193***	310***	296***	247***	408***	288***	168***	172***
t	235***	258**	872***	210***	232***		256***	202***	340***	214***	198***	354***	366***	158***	134***	317***
r	423***	318**	898***	171***	416***	256***		540***	490***	214***	214***	293***	849***	471***	239***	257***
f	367***	340***	745***	399***	204***	202***	540***		217***	321***	338***	346***	221***	227***	171***	319***
b	338***	283***	628***	352***	193***	340***	490***	217***		284***	414***	410***	344***	329***	249***	245***
d	136***	141***	786***	231***	310***	214***	214***	321***	284***		236***	264***	497***	344***	205***	310***
n	495***	908***	5551***	220***	296***	198***	214***	338***	414***	236***		244***	490***	302***	177***	259***
h	481***	217***	668***	345***	247***	354***	293***	346***	410***	264***	244***		646***	359***	255***	242***
w	521***	605***	927***	586***	408***	366***	849***	221***	344***	497***	490***	646***		297***	313***	555***
v	263***	372***	945***	426***	288***	158***	471***	227***	329***	344***	302***	359***	297***		217***	452***
st	340***	215***	537***	191***	168***	134***	239***	171***	249***	205***	177***	255***	313***	217***		217***
g	490***	247***	183***	248***	172***	317***	257***	319***	245***	310***	259***	242***	555***	452***	217***	

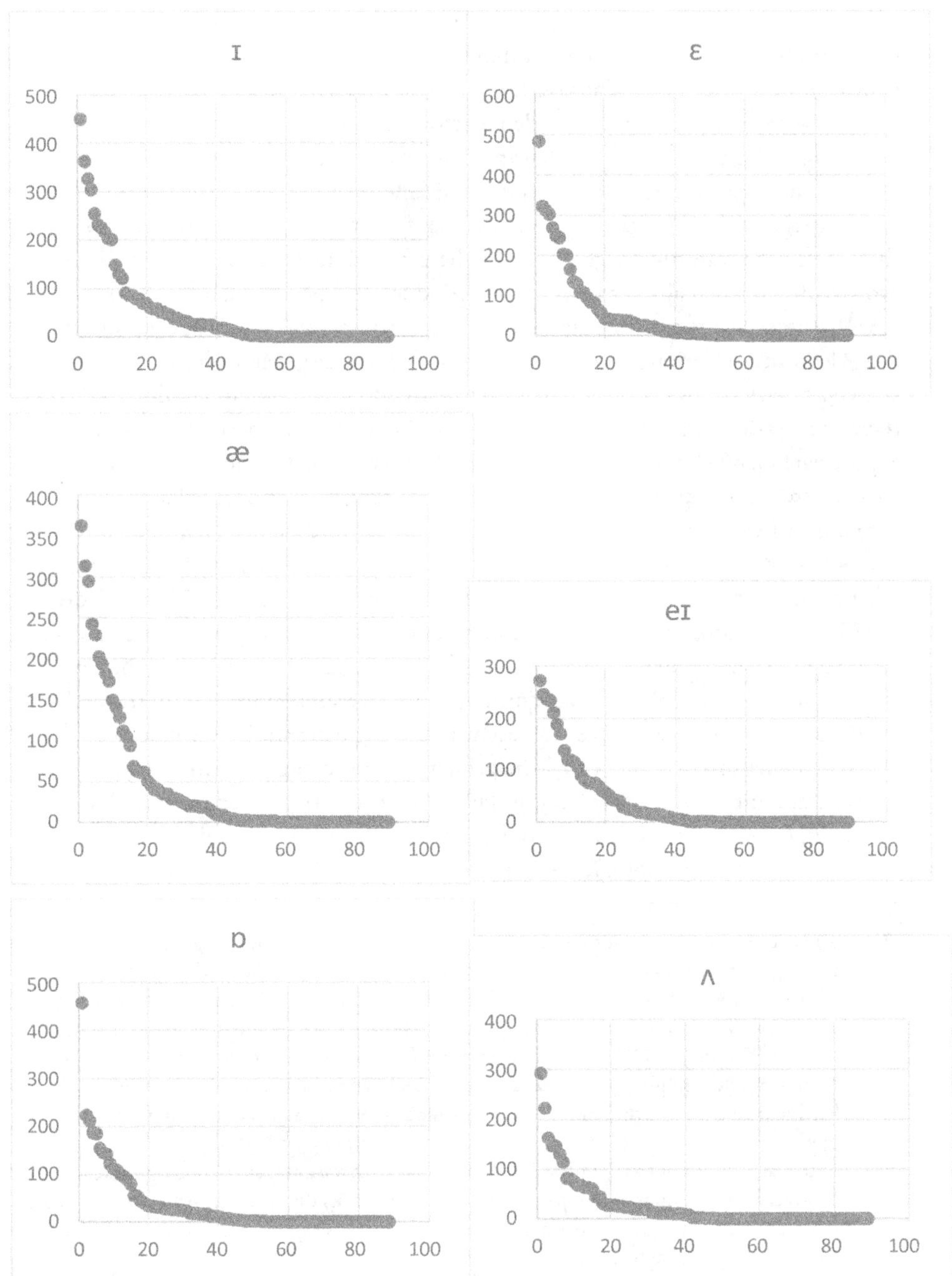

Figure 2.2 The distribution of onsets with 6 most frequent vowels

This suggests that in the continuing evolution of a language, in this case English, the occurrence of vowels and onsets follows the principle of effectiveness and is evidence against innate views. The non-linear distribution facilitates perception by ensuring that the sequence onset + nucleus narrows the probability of likely sequences occurring and hence aids lexical identification. We see that the results are compatible with the logic of the A-curve and thus the emergent systems are learnable.

Language as a self-organising and complex system has evolved, but humans as the agents who transmit language across the generations have simultaneously co-evolved the mental capacity to efficiently produce and perceive language.[37] Lamb (1999) argues that the recognition system is the primary system because (i) in language learning reception precedes production, (ii) people generally have larger passive vocabularies, (iii) people monitor their articulatory production in fine-tuning their vocalisations and more generally in ensuring that their speech unfolds in an appropriate manner to achieve its intended effects (what, in Chapter 5, we will label 'target state'). Some psycholinguistic and neurolinguistic support for Lamb's work is found in Levelt (1993, 1999). Speakers, in other words, constantly and actively monitor the speech signal. Thus, we would expect the presence within the brain of a neural mechanism to facilitate input. Studies such as Warren (1970) and Cole (1973) have demonstrated that phoneme recognition is biased by preceding lexical context and shared knowledge[38] but less is known about how the actual phonetic cues in the speech signal assist recognition, and hence subsequently form the basis for the speaker's own utterances. A recent neurolinguistic study (Gwilliams et al. 2018) provides some evidence that the primary audio cortex is sensitive to phonological ambiguity as regards voicing and place of articulation when presented with /p, b, t, d, k, g/ onsets and makes rapid auditory judgements as to phonemic identity. However, the phonological evidence is retained within the auditory cortex

---

37   The issue of whether or not multilingual speakers have discrete, overlapping or even single language networks remains an unresolved issue, e.g. Paradis (2001), Lein et al. (2016) who argue for separate and discrete systems. When one system is activated the other is turned off. By contrast Amengual (2019) argues for interlocking and interacting systems, and MacWhinney (2005) argues for a single unifed system. The difference between an interlocking and a single system appears to us to be a matter of a perspective: it is, after all, hard to define how many connections are needed before two separate systems merge into one.

    It is also worth noting Lamb's (1999:130–131) observation that language production and reception are housed in separate though by no means discrete networks. Hence the representations presented above are necessarily idealised simplifications of the real complexity of language in use.

38   To illustrate, suppose a hearer knows that the speaker has a brother named John and believes that John is the speaker's only sibling. And the speaker says *My little brother Don is coming to visit next week,* we would expect the hearer to perceive the initial onset phoneme as /dʒ/ and not /d/.

allowing for the signal to be reinterpreted in the light of subsequent phonological and contextual information. In other words, as the authors claim, the future sheds light on the past.

If we interpret our findings above in light of Gwilliams et al. (2018), we can see that their work provides a potential Hebbian mechanism linking onsets with the remainder of the word. And in more frequently perceived tokens[39] greater binding will take place between neurons representing the onset and those that follow. While it is clear that the language that humans produce is subject to morphological and physiological constraints, it is also clear that such constraints empower our languaging abilities by enabling us to creatively exploit the demarked space set aside for language. And, within that space, languages have had to adopt to pressures of transmission imposed by "the arena of use" (Kirby 1999:132).

Our argument here is that, once an organism has developed a brain capable of receiving and producing language, biological mechanisms are superseded by cultural ones.[40] Steels (2015) similarly notes that once the neural mechanisms are in place to allow for language to emerge, further development may not necessarily be coded within the genes but reside solely within the space created by cultural development. He (ibid:336) proposes four factors which determine whether the output produced is likely to be evolutionarily successful by being a variant which reproduces and spreads through the population. The factors are:

(i)   expressive adequacy – is the variant produced able to achieve the communicative state or as we shall describe it 'achieve target state';

(ii) cognitive effort – is the amount of effort involved in producing or perceiving a message adequate[41];

(iii) learnability – the language must evolve in ways that new variants accommodate both the speakers and the hearers ability to perceive and produce language; and

(iv) social conformity where hearers and speakers optimise their language perception and production by aligning their language systems.

---

39   Our reported findings of relations between onsets and nuclei report on types and we have no way of predicting whether the same relationships would hold for co-occurrence between onset and nucleus had we investigated tokens. Though we rather suspect that the relationship would hold.

40   Here one thinks of the claim made by the American evolutionary biologist Stephen Jay Gould that because of the morphological constraints imposed by bones, tendons and muscles, wheels could not have emerged through natural selection – though of course they are the highly successful output of cultural evolution (Gould 1983)

41   Though as noted earlier what is efficient for a speaker may most definitely not be so for a hearer and vice-versa.

This is clearly in accord with the idea in the previous chapter, following Barbieri (1985:169–170) and Maturana & Varela (1980:93–94) that, within a system, the introduction of new element (i) must serve a function; (ii) must be able to be adopted into the existing system of relations (with consequent perturbation of the existing arrangement; and (iii) the whole new system must function better. We would add that the same logic applies to the subtraction of an existing element.

Bartlett (2012) explores the concept of voice in order to illustrate how innovative discourses require cultural capital to enable them to be reproduced. In other words, it is not just what you say, nor even the way that you say it that matters; it is how the saying relates to who you are that matters. But for the moment we will park voice to one side and argue that the A-curves we have presented above evidence how the English phonological system has itself evolved to be learnable. To this description, couched in terms of efficiency, we will argue in the following chapters that we need to include the twin insights that language did not solely develop to foster communication but that it also indexes identity and enacts social relations, and consider the role of redundancy in achieving and balancing the demands of hearers and speakers.

We are conscious that the view of embodiment we have presented in this chapter is not entirely in line with the way the term is understood in the cognitive linguistic literature (see, for instance, Gibbs 2005, Lakoff 1987, Lakoff and Johnson 1999, Lakoff and Turner 1989, Turner 2014). But we expect that readers will have recognised that our work does not oppose such views. Cognitive linguists argue that language is grounded in bodily perception, the sensorimotor system and emotion. We are largely in agreement, but argue that as language is a distributed system and as it exists at different scales and times only some of it can be said to be embodied within an individual at any one time and in any one place. We have argued above that through reiterated contextualised interactions, language is enacted in the sense that part of the distributed language system becomes internally represented within individual people. The internalised language system is embodied in neurological networks with potentially shifting connection weights which strengthen or weaken in response to external and internal stimuli. The external stimuli comprise interactions with the language system in different manifestations, such as interaction with other language users or with textual artefacts of various kinds. The internal stimuli comprise neurological networks which interact with the language system, such as those situated in the amygdala, which regulates emotion, and the memory systems which encode experience and generate expectancies based on past occurrences.

2.7   CONCLUSION

In this chapter we have covered a wide range of topics in order to illustrate that language is a dynamic socio-biosemiotic system. We rejected the separation between language performance and language competence (E and I language if you like) and have argued in a manner akin to usage-based approaches. For us to borrow terms from Saussure 'parole' is what individuals hear and it is 'parole' that requires attention: 'langue' after all as an immanent and never arriving system can only be studied once it has been idealised and it is not our intention to study idealisations.

We proposed in Chapter 1 that there are a number of mechanisms which we claim underpin language and its use and here we have illustrated a number of them at the phonemic level:

1   Prospection in the formation of syllable onset systems;
2   Articulation;
3   Redundancy;
4   The logic of the A-curve.

We also briefly mentioned the notion of language as an ecologically situated stratified system.

We have introduced the notion of embodiment and illustrated that the capacity for language within the brain is a network. We have argued that language emerged as a result of Darwinian selectional pressures, but that once interacting organisms were equipped with language ready brains cultural evolution became the driver of language evolution and language change. At the phonemic level, we have demonstrated that the vowel system is a self-organising one which adheres to the three criteria proposed by Barbieri (1985:169–170) and Maturana & Valera (1980:93–94). We have shown in relation to syllable onset systems that prior articulatory gestures increase the possibility of following articulatory gestures occurring, and so enable fast and efficient, though imperfect, word recognition and production.

In the next chapter we will argue that it is the stratal nature of language which allows for the creative redundancy necessary for language to be a complex adaptive and dynamic system. In this chapter we have focused only on what Hjelmslev (1961 [1943]) dubbed the 'expression plane of language', which is the lowest level of abstraction described in Chapter 1. In subsequent chapters we will illustrate that the mechanisms explicated here are equally applicable to the content plane. In other words we are not simply describing formal patterning but meaningful relations produced by languaging humans.

Chapter 3

A systemic and stratal account of language and society, as told by three t-shirts, a urinal and a karaoke machine

3.1   INTRODUCTION

Building on the discussion of embodiment in Chapter 2, in this chapter we will look at the relationship between *distinction*, as an embodied process, and *systematicity*, as an emergent property of language. While we maintain that these are universal features of language, we compare partial systems from English and Scottish Gaelic to demonstrate that categories within individual languages are a function not of universal distinctions, but of language-internal constraints and affordances and the impetus to systematise the differences that arise from historical drifts. We then discuss *articulation* and the emergence of systems of meaning at higher levels of abstraction (or *strata*). Finally, we will consider the multiple indeterminacies involved when speakers produce utterances in response to an overdetermined and multiply-layered context and present synchronic and evolutionary evidence for an optimum balance between predictable (or criterial) language features and non-criterial features. As the latter group provides a reservoir for the emergence of new criterial features, we refer to it as *serviceable noise*.

3.2   DISTINCTION

In Chapter 2, we discussed the *phylogenetic* processes of genetic adaptation that provided humans with a natural selection advantage in the form of a language-ready brain. In this section we expand upon this idea from the *ontogenetic perspective* in terms of the cognitive skills that the individual must develop in order to break into language and the ways in which linguistic ability, once attained, feeds back into this skill set. For the purposes of this chapter, we focus specifically upon the ability to distinguish between elements, which we defined above in terms of the biological perception of difference, the cognitive interpretation of materially significant difference, and a potential socially motivated evaluation of difference. Tomasello (2003:58) talks of three sets of processes involved in word learning at different stages of development, though these processes are clearly also relevant for larger structures (e.g. Wray 2008, 2014):

1   Prerequisite processes: segmenting speech; conceptualising referents;
2   Foundational processes: joint attention; intention reading; cultural learning;
3   Facilitative processes: lexical contrast; linguistic context.

According to Tomasello (2003:59) prerequisite processes begin to work prelinguistically. This is not surprising if we compare them to those phylogenetic developments which are seen as both the necessary precursors for language and the means by which 'our individual and social cognition is doomed to achieve the fulfilment of its purposes' (Pennisi and Franzone 2016:178). However, on their own these processes are necessary but 'not adequate for acquiring a linguistic convention. The child must also be exposed to that convention in the context of social interaction in which she and the adult find some way to share attention – or perhaps she discerns shared attention between other persons from the outside' (Tomasello 2003:67; see also Corballis 2017:9). The necessity of the social element and context in making learning relevant echoes the perspective taken by Vygotsky (1978) and Wertsch (1998), that language is first learnt in interaction, as part of the irreducible triad, and only subsequently internalised as a means of individual thought (*pace* Reboul 2017). The foundational processes, then, while they still represent the workings of innate cognitive abilities, mark a significant shift from individual conception to social communication and shared understanding. Tomasello claims such processes are (almost[1]) unique to humans, that these, rather than any universal grammar, are essential to 'jump start' language, and that it is the time it takes for these to mature in infants that delays the onset of speech.

In line with our discussion in Chapter 2, joint attention sharing refers to the ability of humans to focus on those areas of context that are relevant to the ongoing interaction and to relegate other aspects of context to peripheral attention (*cf.* Hasan's 2013:279 concept of the linguistic construal of *relevant context*). Connected to joint attention is intention reading – a child's ability to discern what interacting adults are aiming to achieve by means of the joint interactional frame. While

---

1   Hare (2013) and Hare and Tomasello (2005) say that dogs share attention frames, though with humans, rather than conspecifics. And in his later works Tomasello accepts that monkeys share attention frames to a greater degree than he had previously suggested (see also Benson and Greaves 2005).

this is an area of some debate, Tomasello (2003:67–72) presents a wide range of experimental data to demonstrate that infants respond to adult behaviour according to the intentions behind it.

Prerequisite and foundational processes, then, provide the bases for an infant to develop elementary linguistic understanding and production. However, there is also a need to account for the acquisition of more complex words and structures at the point when, as Tomasello (2003:92) puts it, 'all the easy ones are taken'. To this end, Tomasello proposes the facilitative processes that bootstrap on the linguistic and social capacities already developed. The first of these is lexical (and we would add, by extension, structural) contrast, which in itself depends on both intention reading (from the foundational processes) and an appreciation of context (which is thus a facilitative process in itself). In Tomasello's (2003:72) account, once infants have learnt to interpret both adult intentions and the symbolic conventions by which they are realised, then, when faced with a similar but not identical context in which a novel word (or structure) appears where a known word (or structure) might have been expected, children will attempt to figure out, from a consideration of the context, the minor difference in intention that prompted the selection of the alternative – a further manifestation of the *will to semiosis*. In this vein, Corbetta and Shulman (2002) describe a largescale network or networks in the brain, the dorsal attention network (DAN), which controls attentional selectivity and provides a top-down orientation towards predictable events. In novel situations, however, DAN is supplemented by the ventral attention network (VAN), also known as the salience network, which allows for a bottom-up reformulation and for the incorporation of unpredictable but relevant stimuli. This echoes Pennisi and Falzone's (2016:191) suggestion, referred to in Chapter 1, that 'unexpected cases "oblige" the central structure by reincorporating them within our knowledge...creating new algorithms' and the possibility of 'innovative types of behaviour'.

The significance of this complex interaction of language and context, of the previously-experienced and the newly-encountered-but-familiar, cannot be stressed enough with regard to the picture we will be building up here of the *language dynamic* as it unfolds from morpheme to ideology. Sticking with the acquisition of words and structures for now, Tomasello's (2003:75) summary can nonetheless provide a promissory note for the importance of these interpretative tendencies at all levels:

> Children's broad application of contrast suggests that it is not just a linguistic principle but rather a more general pragmatic principle for interpreting communicative behavior. The important theoretical point is that lexical contrast is a natural outgrowth of children's attempts to

understand adult communicative intentions, in the context of their understanding that people may have many symbolic options for construing the immediate situation in whatever way they wish for their immediate communicative purpose, and that they make these choices for pragmatic reasons.

While we take issue with the exuberance of 'in whatever way they wish', we do agree with the importance of the range and delicacy of behavioural options this contrastive facility opens up, which we see as the basis for the speaker's building up of language as a *system* of meaningful contrasts motivated by the *relevant features of context* (an interpretation that fits squarely with the idea that the contrasts in the language system cross-couple with social and material differences). This description also suggests limitations in models of functionality, acquisition and development, such as Kirby (1999), which are based purely on the facility of parsing of decontextualised linguistic structures. As Tomasello (2003:87) puts it, such a limited perspective:

> ...radically underestimates the informational richness of the social-interactive environment in which children learn language. In social-pragmatic theory, in contrast, the focus is on two inherently constraining aspects of the word-learning process: (1) the structured social world into which children are born – full of scripts, routines, social games, and other patterned cultural interactions; and (2) children's social-cognitive capacities for tuning into and participating in this structured social world – especially joint attention and intention reading (with the resultant cultural learning).

This idea is developed from within the field of Systemic Functional Linguistics (SFL) by Painter (1999; 2017), who provides a detailed case study of an individual child's language development and the emergent systematisation of the choices available to them as they learn to interact within the sociomaterial world they inhabit.

While Tomasello's reasoning is based on experimental studies with children, and Painter draws on observational data, their findings tally with the neurolinguistic and evolutionary perspectives that connect embodied language acquisition and use to the external environment. In humans, foetal development continues beyond birth and:

> ...[t]he brain wiring that occurs in the last phase of foetal development provides the neurological basis for the mental models that the organism is going to use throughout its life. If that phase occurs in the highly stable and reproducible environment of the uterus, the operations of brain wiring follow a pre-established sequence of steps and

generate a cognitive system that has been highly conserved in evolution. In our species, instead, the last phases of foetal development have been progressively displaced outside the uterus, in a radically different environment, and that created the opportunity for a radically new experiment in brain wiring. That was the precondition for the evolution of a uniquely human cognitive system, but let us not forget that a precondition for language was not yet language. It was only a potential, a starting point.

> Barbieri (2015:135; see also Corballis 2017:7; and *cf.* Reboul
> 2017:106)

Hagoort (2005; see also Hagoort et al. 2004; Feldman Barrett 2017:168) suggests that Broca's area, far from being the site of an autonomous language module, is responsible for integrating linguistic and contextual information. This idea extended by Hald et al. (2007) to explain the acquisition of new semantic concepts through 'comparison with the phrasal context and, above all, with knowledge of the world' (Pennisi and Falzone 2016:159).

Reboul (2017) approaches language ontogenesis and phylogenesis from a (highly nuanced and enriched) formalist perspective and sees individual cognition as the precursor to inter-individual communication. She, therefore, generally opposes a Vygotskian account of language development and takes issue, in particular, with Tomasello's predominantly sociocultural account. Nonetheless, she agrees with Tomasello in seeing the ability to make contrastive generalisations as a fundamental feature in the evolution of human cognition. Reboul (2017:101–104) cites evidence that only chimpanzees and humans (as far as present research allows us to surmise) are capable of 'bypassing details in favour of global shape' (Reboul 2017:103) and to develop working distinctions between *basic-level concepts* (e.g. classes of animal, such as bird, as opposed to either specific species, such as a hawk, or to animals as a more general category). The ability to generalise at this intermediate level, she suggests, is connected to humans' and chimpanzees' shared ability to make and use tools and the need 'to adapt their tool-using behaviours to their current needs'.

Reboul (2017:107–108) goes on to say, however, that there is a fundamental difference between chimpanzees and humans in that, even in their use of tools, chimpanzees are still attending to the affordances of the context in relation to their current bodily states and their immediate survival needs, while humans are able to scan the environment for features not related to their immediate needs but which may serve them on future occasions – what Reboul (2017:107) labels *endogenous attention* as opposed to the *heterogenous attention* of chimpanzees. This suggests that humans have developed not only the ability to generalise, in common with chimpanzees, but also the ability to extend this generalising capacity from comparing the current situation with past experience to *decoupling* their thoughts from present needs and to form displaced representations of entities and events, a capacity not shared by other animals (*cf.* Hockett 1960 on displacement, and Maturana and Varela 1980:51 on recursive representations). Corballis (2017:74, 78), who shares Tomasello's general approach, refers to this capacity for cognitive decoupling as mental time (and space) travel and extends the concept to include the human capacity to generalise and compare not just between individual instances, but across a range of spatiotemporal scales. Corballis (2017:78) cites an experiment by Collin, Milivojevic and Doeller (2015) in which subjects were shown a series of four videos with the accompanying narrative initially focusing on the individual details of each video before gradually generalising across the videos, first in pairs and then all together. Results showed that 'as the people processed these narratives, activation in the hippocampus progressed from the rearward end to the forward end as the scale of the narrative shifted from small and detailed to larger and more global' (*cf.* Eagleman 2015:28)[2].

So, whereas humans and chimpanzees share, as tool-users, a capacity for basic-level categorisation and generalisation, humans are alone in the ability to decouple representations from the here and now. Reboul (2017:105) relates this distinction to the idea that chimpanzees are niche specialists, well-adapted to their habitual environment, while humans are a *generalist* species, able to adapt to a wide variety of environments. Humans are not the only generalist species, however, notably sharing this facility with rats (Reboul 2017:105). As suggested by Rogers (1989:821), and discussed further below, rats' abilities to thrive in diverse contexts is down to a high degree of risk-taking. However, this strategy only succeeds in species that reproduce quickly and in great numbers and can therefore afford the high mortality rate that risk-taking entails, as discussed by Reboul (2017:105–106), or in species with in-built armour, as with the three-spine sticklebacks referred to in Chapter 2. Humans, in contrast, are soft-skinned souls that reproduce slowly and in small numbers. In order to thrive as a generalist species, therefore, humans have been able to:

> ...adapt to an extremely wide array of environments by devising new artefacts, including tools, and habitations with widely different features, and by being able to form representations of their new environments very quickly through their conceptual abilities...

> Reboul 2017:106

---

2   See Taverniers 2021 for a detailed discussion of the various spatiotemporal domains of context in relation to the language system.

In other words, humans are able to make generalisations about environment conditions and to consider these *in absentia* from the conditions themselves across various spatiotemporal scales – and ultimately to pass on this information through displaced language, so allowing for more judicious risk-taking. In this way humans have been able to overcome both the limitations of hard-wired niche specialism and the pitfalls of situated trial, error and social learning that demands a high fertility rate for its success. We will develop the idea of judicious risk-taking below.

To summarise the ideas here, we can say that phylogenetically and ontogenetically, the embodied human capacity for language is dependent on a capacity for distinction and is built up, at least in part, in terms of contrasting features and the association of these with contextualised behaviour. So far, these ideas have been described from the perspective of the individual person and their socialisation. In the next section we consider how these ideas can be represented with regard to the language system itself before taking the ideas developed in that section and considering them in relation to social interaction, materiality and contexts of use on the one hand and to bioevolutionary forces on the other.

3.3   LINGUISTICS IN THREE T-SHIRTS: SYSTEMS THINKING

Figure 3.1 is a picture of a t-shirt Tom saw on a trip to Amsterdam in 2014. As a linguist, he was immediately interested in the design, which was not only a decent language game but also suggested a level of metalinguistic awareness from the designer and an assumption on their part of a similar level of awareness from the observing public. The basic joke, which we would imagine was immediately obvious, is that the t-shirt wearer is suggesting that they are the sort of person who takes action rather than dreaming of it and who therefore has a rich biography of memories rather than a series of what-might-have-beens and excuses. We get this point

Figure 3.1 Systemic contrasts to a tee

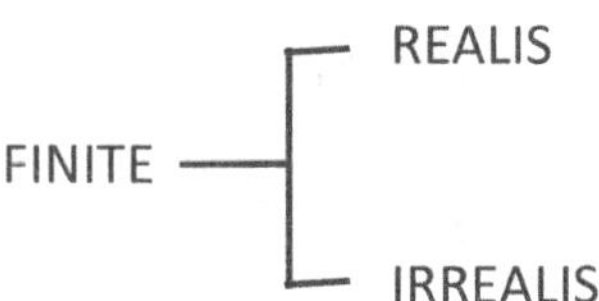

Figure 3.2 A basic system: Meaning as contrast

not from the undeleted 'did' on its own (though that might also have worked, with a bit more effort from the reader), but from the contrast between that 'did' and the three deleted words, which is the difference between actions in the real world (or *realis* in linguistic terms) and hypothetical (or *irrealis*) actions that exist only as possibilities. This is the first linguistic axiom that is captured in the t-shirt: Saussure's central claim that meaning is made through contrasts, with individual items gaining their meaning, or *valeur*, as a function of the place they hold within a set of related but contrastive meanings. This contrast can be represented by the basic system (i.e. the set of meanings which are defined in opposition to each other) in Figure 3.2.

In Figure 3.2 the square brackets indicate an either/or choice, meaning that (according to the figure) whenever we have a finite clause then the linguistic choice at that point is between realis or irrealis, one and only one of which must be selected. And the important point here is that the item selected gets its value from those items which were available but were not selected – as represented by the deleted words on the t-shirt. If a language has no set of irrealis meanings[3] then the meaning of realis is radically changed or even disappears as a meaning in its own right within that language system.

The observer will probably get this point from the picture on the t-shirt, though Figure 3.2 is clearly different from that picture, and not just in terms of the technicality of the terminology. The crucial difference is that Figure 3.2 represents the opposition in terms of semantic categories, whereas the t-shirt had the specific lexical items that the observer will recognise as *realising* these meanings in concrete physical form (either as sounds or writing). So, the second linguistic principle captured on the t-shirt is that abstract semantic categories must be made *sensible* (in the meaning of being sensed) in order to be communicated (and, following Tomasello, for infants to respond to them). Figure 3.3 captures this idea in the same notation as the previous figure but with the addition of a slanting arrow from the semantic concept to its realisation in form. The row of dots signifies that not all possible realisations have been included.

---

3   A highly unlikely scenario, but the general point stands.

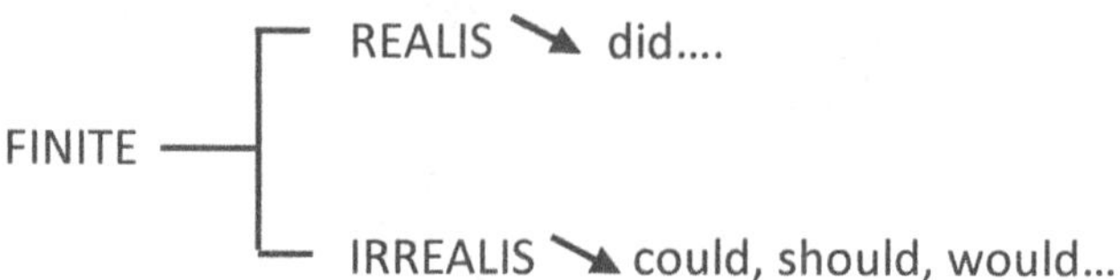

Figure 3.3 Value and realisation in linguistic systems

To improve the coverage, accuracy and explanatory power of this means of representing systemic contrasts and relations, we need to add a few more features. For example, while Figure 3.3 captures the contrastive opposition *between* the realis and irrealis forms, it doesn't capture the idea that *within* each of these semantic categories there are contrastive oppositions, as between the meanings of *could*, *should* and *would*, etc., which all carve out their own meanings within the irrealis space, as well as between *did* and *does*, etc., within the realis space. In other words, once an individual distinction, or choice, has been made (a term which, in its technical sense, does not imply conscious deliberation), this potentially opens up another series of what are called more *delicate* choices. This is represented in Figure 3.4, where more delicate semantic choices appear to the right of less delicate choices, with the forms through which these choices are realised once again included after the slanting arrow and a series of dots once again representing that not all options have been included.

There are a couple of further alterations and additions included in Figure 3.4. The first is that realisation rules have been added to REALIS and IRREALIS as well as to the more delicate options. Secondly, *do* and *did* have been replaced with the generalised English present tense and past tense morphology (Ø means add nothing to the base form). On the Amsterdam t-shirt the word *did* is already morphologically marked in order to narrow down its range of meanings to past realis, suggesting the wearer has really done stuff, while still teasing us with the question of what the wearer actually got up to, as *did* can be used to refer to any activity.

The notion of delicacy represented here illustrates an interesting concept that we will return to at various points as we explore the dynamics of meaning making at different levels: what connects the more delicate meanings within the area of irrealis is their distinction from the meanings in the area of realis. That is to say, in lumping these items together, the differences between the individual irrealis items can be temporarily overlooked as these are less important than their shared difference from the category REALIS or, to put it in the language of critical theory, the label irrealis *underspecifies* the meanings of the individual terms within the category and so renders them *equivalent* in respect of their common *opposition to* the REALIS category. This means of creating distinctions is referred to in critical theory as the *logic of equivalence* (Laclau and Mouffe 1985), and it is a powerful conceptual

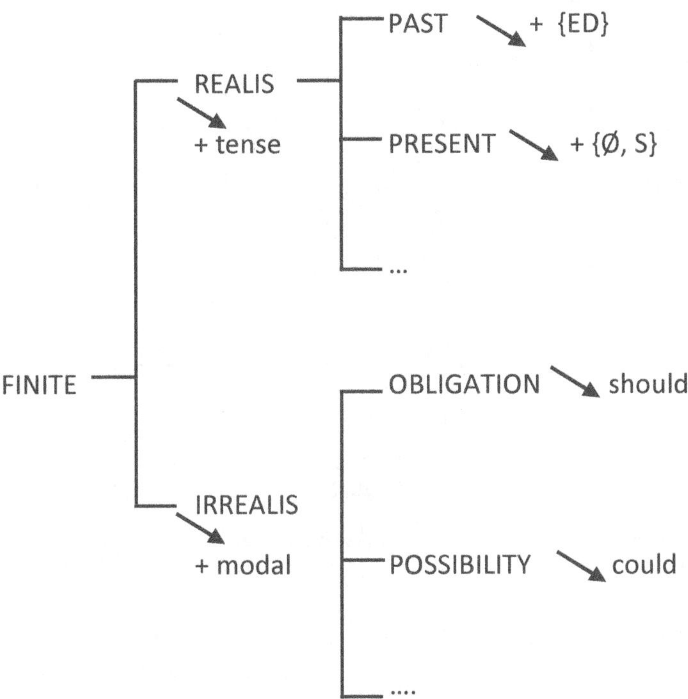

Figure 3.4 Value, realisation and delicacy in linguistic systems

tool that is used in meaning-making practices from linguistic description to political manipulation, as we will explore in various ways as the book proceeds.

The figures so far have introduced the concept of systemic oppositions in terms of EITHER/OR options (represented by the square brackets): a finite clause in English is EITHER realis OR irrealis, not neither or both of them. The selection of one or other opens up further EITHER/OR options at a more delicate level, and so on until no more options are available and a specific form or word is available to realise the meaning of the sum chain of the options taken until that point.

As well as EITHER/OR options, however, there are some sets of options that are available simultaneously. This is exemplified in Figure 3.5, where we see that there are simultaneous options within BOTH the mood AND the polarity systems, with the choice of indicative in the mood system leading to further options. This BOTH/AND relationship is represented by the curly brackets. Note that every simultaneous system must end up as an EITHER/OR option if it is to have any meaning (or contrastive *valeur*, as discussed above).

We can unpack what this *systems network* is saying, for a specific version of English, bit by bit:

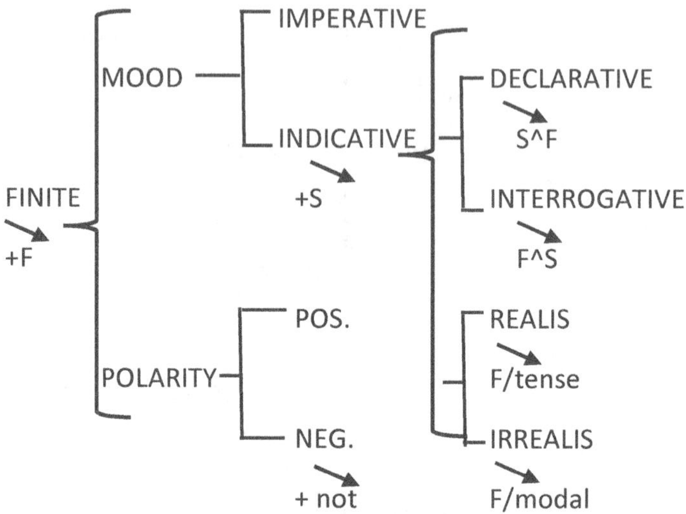

Figure 3.5 Value, realisation, delicacy and simultaneous systems for English MOOD and POLARITY

- Finite clauses are realised/recognised by the inclusion of a finite verb (+F).
- Once you have a finite clause, you need to choose for BOTH polarity AND mood.
- Within MOOD, you must choose EITHER indicative OR imperative.
- If you chose indicative, you need to include a subject (+S).
- If you choose indicative, you then have to make two simultaneous choices: BOTH (declarative OR interrogative) AND (realis OR irrealis).
- If you choose declarative, you put the subject before the finite (S^F).
- If you choose interrogative, you put the finite before the subject (F^S).
- If you choose realis, then the finite verb will be marked for tense (F/tense).
- If you choose irrealis, then the finite verb will be a modal auxiliary (F/modal).
- Within POLARITY, you must choose EITHER positive OR negative.
- If you choose negative, you must include a form of *not*.

Traversing this systems diagram leads to ten different grammatical outputs: (i) the positive imperative; (ii) the negative imperative; (iii) the positive realis declarative; (iv) the negative realis declarative; (v) the positive irrealis declarative; (vi) the negative irrealis declarative; (vii) the positive realis interrogative; (viii) the negative realis interrogative; (ix) the positive irrealis interrogative; and (x) the negative irrealis interrogative. These correspond to the clauses below (note an extra complication, not represented in Figure 3.5, that the finite becomes *do* when realis clauses are negative and or interrogative):

3.1   Go!
3.2   Don't go!
3.3   She goes.
3.4   She doesn't go.
3.5   She should go.
3.6   She shouldn't go.
3.7   Does she go?
3.8   Doesn't she go?
3.9   Should she go?
3.10   Shouldn't she go?

One fundamental point to stress here is that the options and their realisations represented in Figure 3.5 are descriptive and not prescriptive: that is to say that the diagram is meant to represent the distinctions called upon by speakers in the act of meaning making and not a normative statement about what constitutes good grammar. Moreover, the distinctions captured in the diagrams may not be those utilised by all speakers or by any speaker in all situations. Rather, contrasts captured in such networks represent, in idealised form, the distinctions that are operative over specific spatiotemporal scales – that is, at particular times and in specific places. They are not supposed to be taken as universally true, and even within specific spatiotemporal scales there may be differences in use depending on variables in the nature of the situation. In other words, the linguist's description of language is a form of *imaginary*, an idealised depiction, an abstraction from complex concrete reality in order to 'make sense of' language through ignoring, isolating and recombining elements as necessary. For Thibault (1997:40), Saussure's celebrated lecture notes (1957, 1960) are an operator's manual for just such an exercise: the theoretical linguist's attempt to impose order on chaos – or better said, on unfathomable complexity. This is not to say, however, that such distinctions do not exist and that the concept of distinction is a structuralist imposition, but rather that such distinctions are always permeable and are fixed only to the extent that users recognise them as such. This corresponds with Derrida's (1973; 1982:21) concept of *différance* in post-structuralism, with the meaning of items being both defined in terms of their *difference* from other items, but with their ultimate meaning always being *deferred*, or put off till a never-arriving point in time. The concept of deferral is inherent in related concepts such as *emergence*, a term that captures the constant (re)creation of systematicity, and *unfinalisability* (Bakhtin 1984:53, 61) and *undecidability* (Torfing 1999:62), terms from literary theory and sociology respectively, that capture the idea that perfect systematicity will never be attained. Referring back to the irreducible triad, we should add that these concepts can be (and are) applied to the person and to society as much as to the language system. There is no such thing as a fixed or fully-coherent person, only a continuous process of *subjectification* (e.g. Foucault 1982) or *identification* (Torfing 1999:149–152), which takes place through language in social interaction; and there is no such thing as a fixed or fully-coherent society, only the imperfect sharing of conventionalised behaviours by interacting individuals, primarily through language, across different spatiotemporal scales (e.g. Blommaert 2015).

We will return to these central idea of scales, différance, emergence and unfinalisability when we discuss the concept of metaredundancy below. Before that we will demonstrate how such variability applies between languages, as well as within them, and illustrate with reference to Scottish Gaelic how the grammatical distinctions relevant to a specific language are not necessarily those that are relevant to other languages, and that such differences are not merely formal but relate to significant functional distinctions.

3.4   CONTRASTING MOODS: LANGUAGE SPECIFIC SYSTEMS

To a native English speaker, and possibly even to linguists operating in an Anglocentric discipline, the systems network in Figure 3.5 very possibly seems to make 'intuitive' sense as 'the way language works'. However, if we turn our attention to a different language – Scottish Gaelic, one of the Celtic languages of Europe – we can see that the systemic distinctions marked out by the grammar of the language are quite different (and see Bartlett 2021a for a much fuller treatment). These distinctions appear in the following examples, with the relevant elements in bold:

> 3.11   ***Rach dhan*** larach-lin seo.
> **Go (sg.)** to this website.
>
> 3.12   ***Rachaibh*** *dhan larach-lin seo.*
> **Go (pl./respect)** to his website.
>
> 3.13   ***Na rach*** dhan larach-lin seo.
> **Don't go (sg.)** to this website.
>
> 3.14   ***Na rachaibh*** *dhan larach-lin seo.*
> **Don't go (pl./respect)** to this website.
>
> 3.15   ***Chaidh*** *mi dhan larach-lin seo.*
> I **went** to this website.
>
> 3.16   ***An deach*** *thu dhan larach-lin seo?*
> **Did** you **go** to this website?
>
> 3.17   ***Nach deach*** *thu dhan larach-lin seo?*
> **Didn't** you **go** to this website?
>
> 3.18   ***Cha deach*** *mi* dhan larach-lin seo.
> I **didn't go** to this website.
>
> 3.19   ***Feumaidh*** *gu'n* ***deach*** *e* dhan larach-lin seo.
> He **must have gone** to this website.

3.20   ***Feumaidh nach deach*** *e* dhan larach-lin seo.
He **mustn't have gone** to this website.

3.21   ***Thuirt e gu'n deach*** *e* dhan larach-lin seo.
He said that he **went** to this website.

3.22   ***Thuirt e nach deach*** *e* dhan larach-lin seo.
He said that he **didn't go** to this website.

The important thing in drawing systems networks for individual languages is that, rather than imposing the logic of your native language or of a dominant language, such as English or Latin, you must respect the distinctions – that is the meaning/ form relations – that are present in the language itself and that capture the distinctions made by speakers of the language collectively over the longue durée. As a corollary of this, it is also necessary to consider the functionality of the structural distinctions the language displays.

So, for example, we see from Examples 3.11 to 3.14, in comparison with the other examples given, that there is a distinctive form in Gaelic that we can call the imperative, as it is typically used to function as a directive. We can also see, comparing 3.11 and 3.13 with 3.12 and 3.14, that there is a distinction between the form used when addressing a single familiar person on the one hand and more than one person, or a single person who is due respect, on the other. Likewise, we see that the negative forms, what we can call prohibitives rather than directives, as sub-categories of imperatives, include an additional particle *na*. All this information is captured in Figure 3.6, where we see an initial split between imperative and indicative forms, and then, with the imperative, as more delicate options, simultaneous choices for singular vs plural/respect and directive vs prohibitive.

To this point, the distinctions marked in Gaelic grammar do not seem so different from those of English. When we begin to look at the systemic contrasts within the indicative, however, we begin to notice systematic differences. The most immediate difference is that in Example 3.15, the form of the verb, *chaidh*, is very different from the form in Examples 3.16 to 3.21. The form in 3.15 is traditionally called the *independent* form of the verb, and the form in 3.16 to 3.21 is traditionally called the *dependent* form. The forms given for illustration here are for the past tense, but similar distinctions hold for different tenses. The reason for these traditional labels is that the independent form stands alone, whereas the dependent form follows after clitic particles such as *an*, *nach* and *cha*, as shown in Figure 3.6. Following the logic of the Gaelic grammatical marking, therefore, we see that indicative clauses are primarily divided into the independent versus the independent forms and, at a further level of delicacy, according to the addition of the distinctive particles. This is very different from the split into declarative and interrogative in English and we need a different label to capture the different range of functions realised by each form. In Bartlett (2021a) the terms *assertive* and *non-assertive* were (provisionally) chosen to label the primary distinction, as clauses using the independent form of the verb without a clitic particle are typically used to make unmitigated statements, whereas the forms with the dependent form and a clitic particle all mitigate the clause in some way. This is not the same distinction as the declarative/interrogative distinction in English, as the non-assertive form realises not only questions, but also negative forms and propositions (i.e. putative statements) after modal verbs and verbs of reporting. The non-assertive form, therefore, brings together some aspects of the English interrogative and irrealis into a single category, while not including other aspects of English interrogatives (Bartlett 2021a). Similarly, distinctions at the more delicate level within the non-assertive forms correspond in a straightforward way neither to a negative/positive distinction nor to an interrogative/distinction, but to a three-way distinction between propositions, denied propositions and denied statements (or negative assertions, if you like).

Notice, also, that the particle used to distinguish directives from propositions, *na*, is not the same as that used to distinguish between assertive and denied forms. For this reason it would not be appropriate to combine the two forms within a single category of negative as an option within an independent system of POLARITY.

Figure 3.6, therefore, seems to capture the distinctions made in Gaelic grammar in the most straightforward way, while the labels given to the distinctive features correspond to the range of functions carried out by each, rather than to the traditional labels of Latin- or English-based grammar. To highlight this point, the systems network in Figure 3.7 demonstrates the extent to which imposing Latin- or English-based labels on Gaelic grammar would distort the systematic contrasts proper to the language itself.

As can be seen from the complexity and repetition of information in Figure 3.7, such a representation fails to capture the *natural economy* of Gaelic grammar. In contrast with Figure 3.6, the independent form cannot be introduced until [declarative] and [positive] are chosen simultaneously, while the dependent form has to be introduced and motivated separately for [interrogative] in the mood system and for [negative] in the polarity system. This representation, therefore, fails to capture the idea of a single – if ineffable (Halliday 1984) – meaning for the dependent form. And, by extension, the systemic connection between the three particles *an*, *cha* and *nach*, which comprise a single system of oppositions in Figure 3.6, is lost in Figure 3.7. Moreover, as regards the labelling of the distinctions according to the functions the different forms realise, notice that the system network in Figure 3.7 would necessitate ad hoc expansion of the function of interrogatives to include non-assertive propositions as in Example 3.19 and 3.21. What we see, therefore, is that, whereas the system of mood *that has emerged* in English is functionally and structurally organised around distinctions relating to statements and questions (the primary function of declaratives and interrogatives respectively), the system of mood in Scottish Gaelic is organised around distinctions related to degrees of surety and

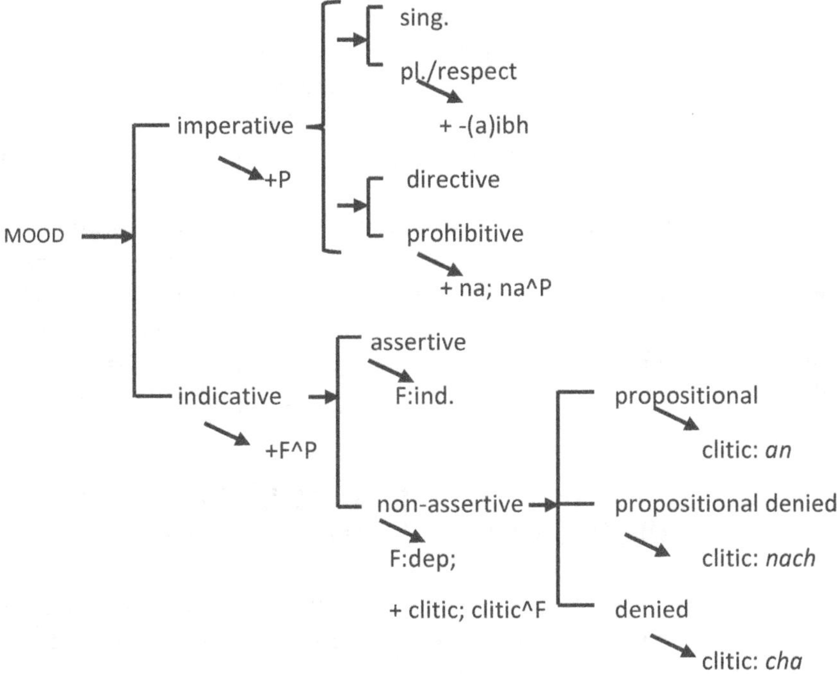

Figure 3.6 Provisional mood network for Gaelic. F:dep means the finite is in the dependent form; na^P means the Predicator (lexical verb) follows na

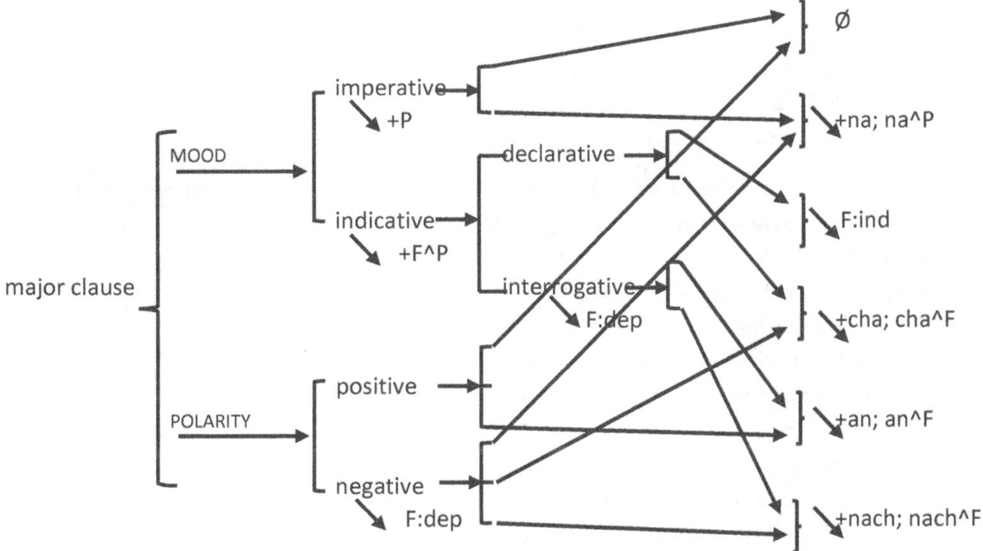

Figure 3.7 Rejected MOOD network for Gaelic. Arrows leading to curly brackets indicate where forms are only realised as the outcome of necessary simultaneous choices

contrasts between mitigated versus unmitigated statements. This is not to say that there is no distinction between statements and questions in Scottish Gaelic, nor that English does not distinguish between assertive and mitigated statements. These distinctions are, of course, possible, but they are not directly indexed by the lexico-grammatical systems of the respective languages and will have to be realised by other means (which we return to below).

To conclude, we would state that attempting to impose systemic distinctions from English (and other languages) onto the grammar of Gaelic leads to a situation where, in the first place, the system of structural contrasts proper to Gaelic itself is not appropriately represented and, as a consequence, the functional range of the structural distinctions is misrepresented and the specific character of Gaelic as a social semiotic is sacrificed on the altar of cross-linguistic generalisation.

3.5   INTERROGATIVES OF THE WORLD UNITE; YOU HAVE NOTHING TO LOSE BUT YOUR QUESTION MARKS

We can take a little excursus here to illustrate how the processes of distinction formalised within the language system and the strategic idealisation that underpins language description are more general socio-semiotic phenomena with repercussions that stretch as far as ideological distinctions. To illustrate, we can imagine the different ways in which the following four clauses can be split into two groups according to grammatical criteria.

3.23   *Have you got a light, boy?*
3.24   *I don't like Mondays.*
3.25   *Don't you love me, baby?*
3.26   *All you need is love.*

One option would be to put 3.23 and 3.26 in one group and 3.24 and 3.25 in the other on the basis of their contrasting polarity (positive vs negative); another option would be to oppose 3.23 and 3.25 with 3.24 and 3.26 on the basis of their contrasting moods (declarative vs interrogative); and a third possibility would be to contrast 3.26 with the other three on the basis that 3.26, a simple statement, is straightforward (or unmarked) compared with the rest.

The point we are making here is that there are many overlapping ways of categorising linguistic elements, each of which depends on focusing on specific features in preference to others (i.e. underspecifying) and ignoring, or at least putting on hold, the differences within categories, including the range of ways they interact with other elements and the ways they function in context.

Extending these operations into other realms of social meaning-making, we can consider what happens if we substitute grammatical categories for other simultaneous options such as gender, race or class. Focusing on these categories alone (and bypassing for now further complications brought in when we move beyond fixed and binary categorisations), there are eight possible combinations of individuals, though focusing on only one variable at a time would divide these into two groups in three possible ways, with different memberships each time. Here again we have the logic of equivalence, where differences *within* groups are overlooked in order to define that group *in opposition to* another group, the internal divisions within which are similarly overlooked and categories made on the basis of strategic underspecification. This is a powerful social force, as is evident if we consider how people who display a vast range and mix of different characteristics come together around one or two of these variables at different times. This is an evolutionary survival mechanism (Pagel 2012; Everett 2012; Edwardes 2010; Hart 2010:9) – the herd mentality providing safety in numbers as well as the opportunity to reproduce – but like many such mechanisms, it can have both its positive side, in acts of solidarity, and its negative side, in acts of discrimination and repression. And just as children learn to discriminate between meanings on the basis of sensible differences, so it takes least effort to discriminate against a particular grouping on the basis of easily distinguished physical features such as race, gender or way of speaking. This is evidenced in a study by Kinzler et al. (2009) showing that children prefer the company of other children who sound like them. There are less obvious but still *sensible* bases for discrimination – such as when we hear negative things of people and categorise them on the basis of this knowledge. In such cases, the sense involved is more cognitive than perceptual, a form of both semantic and social discrimination that is only available at a higher evolutionary level.

We might also categorise people on the basis of where they are from and, if this area has a bad reputation, we can stigmatise the individual by association. And if, for example, we have a situation where two different variables coincide, so that a particular area is associated with a particular race or we have schools segregated according to religion, then our discrimination may become easier and hence reinforced. Multiple causes reinforcing a single effect is known as *overdetermination* or *redundancy*[4]. By this meaning, being working-class, female and black are all causes of discrimination, while being a working-class black woman would entail suffering discrimination to a higher degree that any of the individual categories would entail. The term *overdetermination* is also used when multiple distinctions react together to create a single effect that no single cause alone would produce. In these terms, being a working-class woman would entail having a special array of problems that is not solely the result of being a woman, working class or black. And in relation to language evolution, overdetermination means that we need not look for

---

4   The term *intersectionality* is increasingly being used to refer to the ways in which multiple factors combine to produce social differences (and especially deep-rooted disadvantage).

Figure 3.8 T-shirt 2. Underspecification and imaginaries

a single distinction between humans and other species that led to the emergence of language in humans alone. The difference can just as easily and much more feasibly be explained in terms of a unique combination of features, such as Donald's (2001) *executive suite* of cognitive capacities, none of which need be exclusive to humans. We will return to the concept of overdetermination in Chapter 6.

We can take the analogy one stage further. In English grammar, the positive realis declarative is taken to be the unmarked or canonical form while the use of the negative interrogative form is overdetermined by a conjunction of different semantic features. This categorisation is, in general, based both on frequency and simplicity of form. However, we have to ask if there is equally good reason to take the white middle-aged, middle-class, Anglo-Saxon male as the unmarked case in society. The answer is that it all depends on how we systematise our variables. Which takes us to our second t-shirt.

What is of interest here is that the wearer is defining themself, or creating an identity, in opposition to, what **they** are not. In this case the concept of 'boy' becomes a *constitutive outside* (Mouffe 2000:12), an undifferentiated alien that is everything that the wearer is not. Through this act of identity, therefore, the wearer simultaneously renders all 'boys' equivalent while setting up an alliance with all other 'not boys'. And in doing so, we would suggest, they are also indicating that gender is a socially constructed and harmful imaginary – or, returning to our discussion of Saussure in Chapter 1, that traditional gender labels are not the only way of semantically carving up the material world.

Having considered systemic relations in their own terms, in the following section we examine how individual system networks operate at different scales of meaning and the relationships between systems at different scales.

3.6   LINGUISTICS IN A URINAL: ARTICULATION

The physicist Geoffrey West, in an overview of his work on urban science, writes that in the latter half of his career, he 'began to speculate that networks form the fundamental scaffolding for understanding how our bodies, our cities and our companies work' (West 2017:265). He presents this realisation as a critical moment in his thinking, a moment at which he began to translate ideas from computer science, in which 'something miraculously powerful and "complex" emerged' from a 'very few simple modular units connected by wires and connected in clever and complicated ways following very simple rules', into the fields of first biology and then urban science. And, in particular, he is referring to the concept of *scale*, which predicts the relative ratios of such diverse features as petrol stations, infectious diseases, body organs and new patents between organisms of different sizes, be these natural (such as mice and elephants) or sociocultural (such as villages and cities). The concept of scales itself derives in large part from the more basic concept of *fractality*, which captures how, within biology and beyond, smaller units repeatedly organise themselves into patterns that replicate their form at a larger scale, thereby allowing for growth without loss of stability – a process which, just as with the computer, is based on a few simple rules interacting in complex ways on the basis of multiple feedback loops. Here we will be considering scale and fractality from a semiotic perspective to demonstrate how smaller units of meaning combine to make larger units, which themselves form the building blocks of still larger units on the basis of the same mechanisms by which they themselves were formed, and so on. For the first of these ideas we turn to the concept of *articulation* as the basic mechanism, or 'simple rule', by means of which elements recursively combine to create higher-order meanings while renovating the stock of raw materials available for future combinations.

The philosopher Daniel Dennett, in his book *From Bacteria to Bach and Back: The Evolution of Minds*, (2017:7), cites as one of the critical moments of evolution the collision two billion years ago between two different prokaryotes, single-celled entities which had evolved their own 'competences and habits'. Dennett explains:

> Collisions of this sort presumably happened countless numbers of times, but on (at least) one occasion, once cell engulfed the other, and instead of destroying the other and using the parts as fuel or building materials (eating it, in other words), it let it go on living, and, by dumb luck, found itself fitter – more competent in some ways that mattered – than it had been as an unencumbered soloist.
>
> This was perhaps the first successful instance of *technology transfer*, a case of two different sets of competences, honed over eons of independent R&D (research and development), being united into something bigger and better.

This process of 'technology transfer' is no more and no less than a primitive process of *articulation*, the process by which different elements, each with their own functions, combine in such a way that they are no longer operating simultaneously, or in parallel, but as interconnecting and interdependent nodes in a higher order system that is, in its turn, dependent on such articulations for its own survival. One of the principal purposes of this book is to demonstrate how such 'technology transfer' occurs in semiotic systems as meaningful units combine to create higher order meanings, from the structure of the phoneme to the structure of discourses and cultures. From this perspective, it is interesting to juxtapose the quote from Dennett above, describing the most primitive instance of articulation, with the following lines from Carpentier (2017:273), in which he describes the process of articulation at an advanced evolutionary scale, as theorised in political theory (Laclau and Mouffe 1985; Chouliaraki and Fairclough 1999):

> ...all social phenomena and objects obtain their meaning(s) through discourse, which is defined as 'a structure in which meaning is constantly negotiated and constructed' (Laclau 1988:254). The concept of discourse is also described as a structured entity which is the result of articulation (Laclau and Mouffe 1985:105), which is in turn viewed as 'any practice establishing a relation among elements such that their identity is modified as a result of the articulatory practice'. As these definitions indicate, the articulation of discursive elements plays a vital role in the construction of the identity of objects as well as of individual or collective agents. The articulation of these elements produces discourses that gain a certain (and very necessary) degree of stability.

As we can see then, the combination of existing entities, or meanings, can lead to the creation of something new and potentially enduring – though the conditions for both the coming together and the success (both of which are necessary elements of articulation) are not pregiven. In Darwinian terms, we can assume that how long the structures resulting from articulation last is dependent, at least in part, on the degree to which they fill a functional niche within the system as a whole, irrespective of whether this niche had existed previously to the novel form that filled it (Barbieri (1985:169–170); Maturana and Varela (1980:93–94)

In the previous section we illustrated the concept of system as it applies to the basic semantic building blocks of language, and in this section we will build on this systemic conception of language to describe articulation as the process of reproduction and mutation that leads to rescaling, diversity and innovation – not just in language, but in all systems of cultural semiosis (e.g. Bateman and Allori 2014). To do this, we will start in an unusual place.

In Figure 3.9 we see some objects that will be very familiar to at least a significant number of readers: urinals in a gents' toilet. Taken on their own terms, these are

Figure 3.9 Urinals

functional objects that have been designed to serve a specific purpose efficiently and, no doubt, with some degree of aesthetic style. Starting from the idea that function equates to meaning in a social semiotic system, we can claim that those of us who are familiar with men's public toilets will know the 'meaning' of these objects, as well as a little about their likely use, and the norms and evaluations surrounding their use in our own cultures (*cf.* Durkheim 2002 [1925]) – such as the unwritten rule in the UK that if, on entering the toilet, a gent is using the urinal on the left and the other two are free, you should use the urinal on the right, not the one in the middle.

Leaving the gents' for a while, let us consider another cultural artefact. Figure 3.10 is my signature (and culture vultures will have worked out where we are going with this by now).

A signature is basically the representation in orthographic form and in their own distinctive handwriting of a writer's name. If it is someone else's name, or not in the distinctive handwriting of the producer, then it is not what we conventionally think of as a signature. And it is this functional combination that lends a signature a second-order function, as a mark of authenticity on legal documents and works of art (though there are of course exceptions, such as the *X* of the illiterate or the computer-generated signature of electronic documents, which, nonetheless derive their power from the functionality of a signature proper). In terms of Austen's (1961) felicity conditions for a successful speech act, we can say that the formal qualities of a signature make it suitable as a performative, a first-person warrant or promise of authenticity that is fulfilled at the moment of enunciation and is recognisable as coming from a particular 'speaker' and no other. This performative aspect is often further indexed by the date accompanying the signature, marking that the act took place at

Figure 3.10 Signature

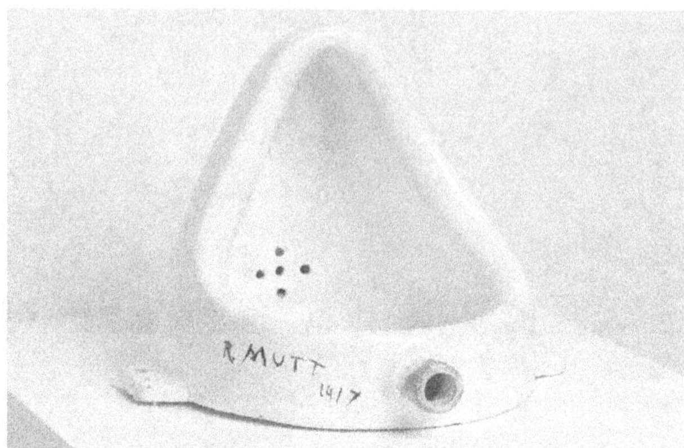

Figure 3.11 *Mutt's Urinal* or Duchamp's *Fountain*. © Association Marcel Duchamp / ADAGP, Paris and DACS, London 2023

a particular moment and that at the moment the necessary actions for declaring the artefact genuine were performed. In this way a signature has already developed distinctive cultural functions as a result of fit between its physical and semiotic properties and an emergent social need. The difference between the signature and the urinal is that the urinal was specifically designed to fit a specific cultural need, whereas the signature represents a refunctioning (or exaptation) of an existing form. We thus see in the signature and the urinal two functional objects, each with their own histories of meaning. But what happens when we combine the physical properties of the signature and the urinal, as in Figure 3.11?

Figure 3.11 is a picture of what is known as *Mutt's Urinal* or Duchamp's *Fountain*. It was presented at an exhibition organised by the American Society of Independent Artists by Marcel Duchamp, an influential member of the group, using the assumed name of Richard Mutt (Belsey 2002:84–87)[5], and was titled '*Fountain*'. Despite the expressly avant-garde nature of the society, which was open to any artist of any nationality and which avowedly refused to follow academic restrictions on what counted as art, the committee refused to exhibit the 'piece', a move which led to Mutt's resignation. The following month, Duchamp's journal *The Blind Man*, carried an unsigned (!) editorial defending the would-be exhibit, accompanied by a photograph by Alfred Stieglitz, a gallery owner who had exhibited Rodin, Matisse, Cézanne and Toulouse-Lautrec. In the ensuing years, the work has become an icon of post-structuralism, though all that remains of the original is Stieglitz's photograph – what Belsey (2002:85) labels 'a signifier of a signifier'. However, reproductions of *Fountain* are on display, as shown in Figure 3.12. As these were no

---

5   For an alternative attribution see https://www.theguardian.com/books/2019/mar/29/marcel-duchamp-fountain-women-art-history

Figure 3.12 *Mutt's Urinal* on display

doubt inspired by Stieglitz's picture, we can say they are the signifiers of signifiers of signifiers (and the picture here a fourth order signifier, with meanings accruing with each new order).

Examining *Mutt's Urinal* not from the position of post-modern art but from the dynamics of meaning-making, there are some central points to be made regarding semiotic systems in general. With regard to the meaning of the signature, we can see that this has progressed from being a personal warrant applied to genuine existing works of art by the author in order to index their authenticity to being a device by which an everyday object is elevated to the status of art. The process of artistic production and warranty is thus reversed, with the warranty producing the art. And this despite the fact that the signature was of a person who was not a person, let alone an artist. The placement of the name on the object in a particular way and in a particular context (Duchamp's journal, or the art gallery in Figure 3.12) is enough for previous significations to be evoked and reinterpreted. Such a move, then, relies on the previous semiotic function of the signature but reproduces it in a mutated form, in this case through a knowing and reflective second-order act of meaning-making. The semiotic processes involved here (whether reflective or automatic) are what we have been calling *articulation*, the joining together of multiple existing meanings to create a single meaning with two defining characteristics: (i) it is greater than the sum of its parts, or elements; and (ii) it alters, or *perturbs*, the meaning of the original elements themselves.

With regard to *Mutt's Urinal*, the first defining characteristic has been demonstrated for the meaning of a signature in general (and not just Mutt's pawprint), which no longer signifies merely the warrant of an artistic piece, but now also the means by which art can be created out of non-art. As for the urinal itself, Duchamp/ Mutt's creative articulation has playfully ignored certain features (its usual function, and the plumbing that makes this possible) while retaining others (the fact that it is a human artefact), and hence given to the urinal and, by extension, to everyday objects in general, a new meaning as potential works of art, as demonstrated by Figure 3.13.

Figure 3.13 A tin of Campbell's tomato soup and a picture of Andy Warhol's picture of a tin of Campbell's tomato soup[6]

Figure 3.14 Art subject to gaze

After the original articulation, a new semiotic object is available for our gaze (Figure 3.14), becoming an element with potential for further articulations, as wittily captured in Figure 3.15, a metaplay on Duchamp/Mutt's original game with its implication that the meaning of urinal has been perturbed to such an extent that it is now necessary to distinguish between urinals-for-the-pissing-in and urinals as *objets d'art*. The two urinals, side by side and suitably labelled, are thus a variant of the systems diagrams above and the pairs of contrasting *valeurs* each carrying a single *sensible* difference.

The various levels of meaning represented in this history of *Mutt's Urinal* correspond to Silverstein's (2003) *orders of indexicality* with regard to linguistic production. For Silverstein, a word or signifier has a first-order meaning in terms of its sense or referential value. On top of this, these signifiers accrue a second-order indexicality when a word, or the way it is uttered, is associated with a particular subgroup of speakers, and a third-order indexicality when the use of these signifiers evokes evaluations associated with that group. A fourth order is reached when producers knowingly use signifiers in a certain way so as to provoke such connotations, as in Figure 3.16, which takes us back to t-shirts. Here the Cardiff habit of adding an *-s* to first person present simple forms is redundantly marked on the t-shirt (it is not usually marked for third person forms with the heart symbol) in order to draw attention to the (supposed) fact that the wearer is themselves from The 'Diff (the affectionate word for

---

6   Thanks to Saerah Dewi Suyasa for the metareproduction.

Figure 3.15 A system

Figure 3.16 I Loves the 'Diff t-shirt

Cardiff) and therefore worthy to bathe in the affection that the city evokes. And at a further level of meaning, it should be noted that a basic joke behind the I ♥s the 'Diff t-shirt is in terms of its valeur in relation to the globally recognisable I ♥ NY t-shirt.

To finish this section we should emphasise that the purpose of this urinary excursion has not simply been to introduce the concept of articulation in an entertaining way, but to show from the outset that the process is not restricted to the language system (for which we will produce a fuller description below), but pervades social semiosis in general and at multiple levels, or orders, of meaning.

3.7   STRATA IN GRAMMAR – REDUNDANCY, METAREDUNDANCY, CRITERIALITY AND NOISE

In Sections 3.3 and 3.4 we gave an overview of the systemic organisation of language and, using illustrations from English and Scottish Gaelic, demonstrated how this follows similar principles but takes on different forms in individual languages. In this section, we draw on and expand upon the concept of articulation, as we reconnect the systematicity in language to social interaction, materiality and contexts of use on the one hand and to bioevolutionary forces on the other. To do this we draw on the concepts of *redundancy* and *metaredundancy*, which relate to the associations speakers are socialised into making between signs and meanings and between sign-meaning relations and context. We go on to show that such associations are not absolute but operate to a degree of consistency that allows meanings and contexts to be recognised, while leaving room for innovation. We relate this balance between consistency and innovation – what we labelled above as *judicious risk-taking* – to the adaptation of *Homo sapiens* as a highly mobile species and suggest mechanisms by which *ad hoc* innovations might become the new normal in certain contexts (see also Bartlett 2018a, 2021b).

Taken together, the concepts of redundancy and metaredundancy allow us to consider linguistic ontogenesis as a process of associating language form and function, and of associating such pairings with their contexts of use (in line with Tomasello's descriptions of ontogeny in Section 3.2). To illustrate, we can start with some of the systemic distinctions illustrated with reference to the language system in Section 3.3. In Figure 3.5, we saw that one of the MOOD options in English is the declarative, and that this grammatical function is realised through the linguistic structure S^F (Subject followed by Finite element). In terms of ontogeny, we can say that language learners note a strong association, in context, between this form and the social (or semantico-pragmatic) function of *presenting a piece of information as potentially needing no further input*. Over time, such associations are strengthened in the child's mind as they are socialised into their speech community, and the linguistic structure and the social act are said to be in a *redundancy* relationship. That is to say, there is a *mutual expectation* between information being presented as potentially needing no further input and the use of the declarative form, with each predicting the other strongly but not absolutely. In contrast to this we have the interrogative structure (F^S in English), which is in a redundancy relationship with the social function of *presenting information as needing further input*. On this basis, we can say that declarative and interrogative clauses represent a contrastive pair within the lexicogrammatical system of MOOD (as in Figure 3.5) and that they are in redundancy relations with the contrasting pair of semantico-pragmatic acts of *presenting a piece of information as potentially needing no further input* and *presenting information as needing further input* respectively.

If we now turn to the parallel system of TONE (O'Grady 2010; Halliday 1967; Tench 1996) we can say that, for English at least, a falling intonation across an utterance is associated with *speaker certainty* while a rising intonation is associated with *speaker uncertainty*. Or, to put it another way, falling tone is speaker-centred, while rising tone is directed towards the hearer (Cruttenden 1997). We see, therefore, that there is a *natural association* between the declarative and falling tone, as the social functions of presenting information as needing no further input and presenting information as certain fulfil similar though non-identical social functions. There is, therefore, a higher than average probability of their co-occurrence (see Matthiessen 2015). The same point can be made for the interrogative mood and rising intonation. In other words, roughly equivalent, or overlapping, functions can be achieved by both syntactic and phonological means, while the combination of the two will intensify the force of the overlapping functions. There is a degree of overlap between the basic functions of the two structures, and it is this *redundancy of information* that is made relevant within the context of a statement, while the excess, or non-redundant, meaning of each form is temporarily backgrounded

However, while the association between such choices in mood and tone (and beyond) may be 'natural' or well-motivated, the non-redundant meaning of the two structures means such associations are not absolute. This has two significant repercussions. On the one hand, it opens up the possibility that *marked* combinations of lexicogrammatical features can be employed to realise novel speech functions. This idea will be developed in the present section. And, conversely, it suggests that 'the same' speech function can be realised by more than one combination of lexicogrammatical features, both within and across languages. We will return to this second point below.

The possibility of marked combinations of features realising novel speech function is illustrated in Example 3.27, in which a declarative structure is uttered with a rising tone:

3.27   *You're leaving?*

Simplifying things greatly, the combination of associations in Example 3.27 function together as neither fully a statement nor a question. On the one hand, the declarative form suggests that the information is complete and accurate; while, on the other hand, the rising tone signals speaker uncertainty (see O'Grady 2020b for a more precise discussion). And the resultant combination functions to present the information as tentatively complete and accurate but still in need of further confirmation, a semantic complex we can label as a *check* (Hasan 1996:120). This specific combination of features is a *marked* form, in that the two component elements of declarative and rising tone have a lower degree of shared meaning potential (redundancy of information) and so, *in general*, predict each other relatively weakly. The degree of association will vary, however, according to the communicative demands of different situation types and the linguistic registers associated with these, a point to be developed below[7].

Notice also that the semantic functions emerging from such combinations are more than the sum of their parts in two distinct ways. Firstly, they amplify the redundant information indexed by their component parts while backgrounding the excess of information of each; and, secondly, the semantic structure as a holistic unit will develop its own set of (non-absolute) associations with social functions,

---

7   It is worth noting here that rising intonation is a continuum rather than a unitary phenomenon and that the different degrees of tone may carry distinct meanings (in articulation with other grammatical features).

filling functional niches in accordance with, but not determined by, the communicative affordances of the individual parts. Therefore, while lexicogrammatical structures and intonation contours are meaningful in their own terms, we can consider the semantics of utterances that arise from the synergies between these units as being of a higher order of meaning, and entering into systems of contrast with other structures at that same level. As suggested above, the general term for this process is *articulation*, defined as 'any practice establishing a relation among elements such that their identity is modified as a result of the articulatory practice' (Laclau and Mouffe 1985:105). Articulation is a core concept in language adaptation and development, as it not only increases the number of meanings that can be made from a finite set of resources, given the various possible combinations of these individual elements but, in doing so, it also gives rise to the emergence of higher orders of meaning which develop into systems of contrast in their own right. This is in line with Barbieri (1985:169–170) and Maturana and Varela's (1980:93–94) requirement that an adaptation must simultaneously fill a useful function in its own terms and find a place within an existing system of relations if it is to survive and be reproduced[8].

The example above of the *check* falls within interpersonal meaning in the framework of Systemic Functional Linguistics, and this is the area where the great majority of work in this area has been carried out (n.b. Hasan 1996). However, we can also see this phenomenon at work for ideational meanings, where the lexicogrammatical properties of punctual verbs and continuous aspect are articulated in order to express the semantic concept of iterativity, as in Example 3.28[9]:

3.28   *He was banging his head against a wall.*

---

8   There is a dispute between two schools here, with Barbieri (1985, 2015, 2019) explaining away the function in the new system in terms of codes, or arbitrary transformations, while Maturana et al. (2016:651–652) prefer to explain this process in terms of molecular behaviour. Something comparable happens within different versions of SFL, where Halliday connects the lexicogrammatical and semantic strata according to the meanings made at both, while Fawcett (2001) prefers to present the semantics as realised directly by lexicogrammatical structures without reference to their inherent properties as such. In relating higher-order meaning to both the system at the higher level and to the meanings of the component parts at the lower level, we are firmly alongside Halliday in Maturana's camp. However, it should be noted that Fawcett's approach may better capture the reality of language use, in which the histories behind the codes are not necessarily relevant (or even knowable).

9   This spread of lexicogrammatical forms to cover a range of semantic constructs and the variability of these over time and between languages is viewed from a cognitive perspective in Construction Grammar, where mind maps are developed to show the encroachment of a language-specific (emic) lexicogrammatical structure over what are considered to be universally (etically) adjacent cognitive categories (Croft 2001)

Within the textual metafunction, which we take to include tense and aspect as deictic relations, we can see how the perfect aspect (roughly, the past seen as present experience) articulates with simple and continuous aspect, along with various circumstances of time, to provide higher order temporal concepts. This is illustrated in Examples 3.29 to 3.32.

> 3.29   *You've been crying.*
> 3.30   *I've finished my dinner.*
> 3.31   *I've known him for four years.*
> 3.32   *I've never been to Disneyland.*

It is also possible for articulation to cross metafunctional boundaries. In Example 3.33, for instance, a popular parody of everyday Scottish talk, we see how the articulation of ellipted interrogatives (interpersonal metafunction) and verbs of perception (ideational metafunction) can be used to progressively thematise and focus in on specific elements of the clause (textual metafunction).

> 3.33   *See me? See my man? See mince? Loves it!*

And to take an example from Gaelic and the lexicogrammatical structures discussed above (see Figure 3.6), we have the example below of the propositional denied form, with the particle *nach* and the dependent form of the verb, performing the contrasting semantico-pragmatic acts of a question pre-supposing a negative response, when articulated with rising tone, or making a polite request, when articulated with a falling tone:

> 3.34   *Airson barrachd fiosrachaidh mun phròiseact, nach cuir sibh fios*
> *gu Niall Somhairle?*
> For more information about the project, won't you contact Neil
> Sorley?
> For more information, please contact Neil Sorley.

What we see in all these examples is that increasingly abstract, or higher-level, layers of meaning are composed out of more concrete forms. Or, to put it in reverse, that more concrete, lower-order meanings are *articulated* to create higher-order meanings. We refer to this property of language, the outcome of articulatory processes, as *stratality*, but it has been developed to different degrees and under a variety of different names in a number of linguistic theories. Martinet's (1960) concept of *double-articulation*, which states that the physical variables of the vocal organs are articulated to produce meaningless phonemes which are in turn articulated to make meaningful words, demonstrates the idea in its most basic form. Similarly, Hockett (1960) cites *duality of patterning* as a distinctive property of human language. These concepts are extended by Hjelmslev (1961 [1943]), whose elaboration of *form, substance* and *purport* as cyclical levels of abstraction provided the basis for the stratal organisation of language developed in Systemic Functional Linguistics (Matthiessen

2007, 2022; and see Taverniers 2011, 2019, for a comparison of Hjelmslev's and Halliday's approaches).

We have suggested to this point that novel articulations represent marked forms. However, this is only the initial case and we now develop the idea that what are marked forms in general terms may be the unmarked options in certain contexts. This introduces the concept of *metaredundancy*. In his 'unitary biosemiotic account' of meanings and feelings, Lemke (2015), following Peirce (1998[1907]) via Bateson (1972), describes semiosis in terms of sets of associations between phenomena and introduces the concepts of redundancy and metaredundancy as general adaptational properties of biological organisms. In terms of redundancy, he states (Lemke 2015:597) that:

> As we interact in the world we encounter a lot of perceptions, actions, phenomena, doings and happenings, processes and things, places and occasions. For some of them to count for us as signs of others, there has to be some set of associations (our nervous systems seem good at producing these), such that there is not, for us, an equal likelihood that anything can go with (i.e. follow closely in time, or appear nearby in space) anything else... Mathematically, this means that there is some degree of 'redundancy' or informational order: some things are more likely to go with (predict) some other things. Not absolutely, not 100% of the time, but more than by mere chance alone.

While the capacity to recognise and respond to such co-occurrences provides an evolutionary advantage, in associating a specific smell with the presence of a specific source of food, for example, it remains a relatively blunt tool, restricted to those highly constrained environments in which such associations reoccur with a high enough degree of frequency to improve the chances of survival and reproduction. In order to improve adaptability to a greater range of environments, therefore, a higher level of semiotic capacity is necessary: one that varies the strength of associations according to distinctions in the context in which they occur. At this higher level of capacity, a sensate organism recognises a distinctive context X and predicts that, within this specific context rather than any other, A and B are likely to co-occur. The converse is also true, in that an organism, on recognising the co-occurrence of A and B, can predict that it is operating within a specific context X. Thus, context X can be said to be in a redundant relation with the redundancy relationship between A and B, as each predicts the other. This is the concept of *metaredundancy*, or the ability to 'recognize, classify, and respond to the same difference differently in different contexts' (Lemke 2015:599, drawing on Bateson's 1972 concept of *metalearning*). To give a simple example of such adaptive behaviour, we can note that the same physical reaction of heightened nervous activity is related in some contexts to the presence of danger and results in flight or fight, while in other contexts it is associated with sexual attraction, with quite different behavioural consequences in terms of survival and reproduction (Wilson 2002:101; see also Feldman Barrett 2017).

At the level of lexicogrammar we talked about redundancy in terms of there being a strong association between the declarative and falling tone. Expanding on this, we talked about a higher level of meaning in which the articulation of these two elements realises the semantic-pragmatic act of a *statement*, whereas the marked articulation of a declarative and rising tone realises the semantico-pragmatic act of a *check*. That is to say, in the semantico-pragmatic context of a statement, we expect the articulation of a declarative and a falling tone, while the articulation of declarative and a falling tone is associated with the semantico-pragmatic context of a statement. We therefore have a *metaredundant* relationship between the lexicogrammatical and semantic systems: the context of presenting information as a statement is redundant with the redundancy relationship between the declarative and falling tone, while the context of presenting information as a question is redundant with the redundancy relationship between the interrogative and rising tone. This is not the whole story, however, and in this section we develop and expand on the concept of metaredundancy in order to demonstrate its generative power.

Starting, then, with the relationship between the semantics and the lexicogrammar, the following examples illustrate how the general semantico-pragmatic act of requesting information may be realised through various articulations of lexicogrammatical and intonational features:

3.35   *Are you going to the shops?*
3.36   *You going to the shops?*
3.37   *Going to the shops?*
3.38   *Going to the shops, are you?*
3.39   *You're going to the shops, are you?*
3.40   *You're going to the shops, aren't you?*
3.42   *You're not going to the shops, are you?*

and even, in some dialects of Scottish English:

3.42   *You're going to the shops, aren't you no?*

These variations will have arisen organically, drawing on the redundancy of meaning in the lexicogrammatical and intonation systems in different ways but to similar effect. There is not, therefore, a one-to-one correspondence between strata, but interrelations between *zones of meaning* (see Taverniers 2019 for a full discussion). As we communicate across contexts, however, we can expect that our collective *will to semiosis* will act as a centripetal force (Bakhtin 1981), imposing systemic order and assigning mutually agreeable distinctions to each of the structural variations. Such distinctions may be either semantic or distributional. A semantic distinction was suggested for the marked question form in Example 1, above, which was said to have appropriated a distinctive function as a *check*. Such a process of semiotic stabilisation can never be complete, however, given the vast number of contexts in which language operates and which act as centrifugal forces. It should not be assumed, therefore, that a specific structure has the same function in different contexts. Conversely, it should not be assumed that a specific function is realised in the same way across contexts. In other words, distinct articulations of lexicogrammatical features might relate not to different semantic functions but to 'the same' semantic function as it is realised across different sub-populations or situation types (a distributional distinction). As an illustration of this we can consider the characteristic lack of any mood at all for statements within the specific context of the radio shipping forecast, as in Example 3.43:

3.43   *Hebrides gale force 8 backing northeasterly soon, backing north-westerly and increasing severe gale force 9 later.*

In instances such as Example 3.43 we see, therefore, a further level of metaredundancy in that the specific context of the shipping forecast is in a redundant relationship with the already metaredundant relationship between the clause semantics and the individual lexicogrammatical features that realise the semantics, and it is this set of relations that defines the language of shipping forecast as a distinctive register. Generalising, we can say that within a specific register, we can predict that a specific semantico-pragmatic function will be realised by a particular combination of lexicogrammatical features.

This relationship is not absolute, however, and what we find is that, as long as there enough of the expected redundancy relationships available to help us identify the register, we can live with the background noise that does not go along with the dominant melody. In fact, as demonstrated by Kretzschmar (2015:8–9), there seems to be a healthy ratio – somewhere in the region of 80:20 – between what we might for now loosely call norms and exceptions at all levels of linguistic activity. In order to develop the idea that such indeterminacy is a force for the creative good in language (and, also, by our logic, for the persona and for society), we can take a brief excursus to consider the emergence of this phenomenon as an evolutionary advantage.

In a paper entitled *Does biology constrain culture?*, Rogers (1989) considers the relative advantages of cultural versus acultural learning (i.e. dependence on social transmission rather than individual trial and error) in the evolution of the adaptive behaviour captured in the principle of metaredundancy. He begins with the hypothesis that individual learning leads to greater variability of response and an increased habitat, while social learning is safer if more constrained:

...the value of individual learning reflects a tradeoff between the benefit of a broad diet and the cost of occasional poisoning. A rat that learned his diet socially, by copying an elder, would be less often poisoned, but would be unable to use novel foods. Thus, cultural transmission of diet reduces the risk of being poisoned, at the cost of a narrower diet.

Rogers 1989:821

Building on this idea, Rogers conducts a thought experiment, mathematically modelling the results of different behaviours for an imaginary creature, the 'snerdwump' (Rogers 1989:820). His conclusion is that both individual learning and social learning are necessary, with a happy balance to be struck between the two. The exact balance, however, in words that echo the concept of metaredundancy, are liable to vary according to the behaviour type and the environment even for a single species. In highly stable environments, consistent behaviour and social learning provide the surest means of long-term survival, while in rapidly changing contexts – in other words, in situations where the need for context-sensitive or metaredundant associations is increased – individual learning is useful in increasing the range of responses and therefore the chances of finding a more successful behaviour. Nonetheless, even in rapidly changing environments, *imitation based on observation* provides a safeguard for individuals and hence the species.

Roger's original thought experiment was taken up by Pennisi (2010) in considering the strategies individuals might adopt when they find themselves in unfamiliar environments: *Do you copy or innovate? And if you copy, who do you copy?* These questions were then tested through a computer tournament (Rendell et al. 2010) in which competitors were challenged to design the computer programmes with the most successful mix of individual and cultural learning strategies in response to beneficial information randomly provided by a 'multi-armed bandit'. At each turn, the individual programmes could carry out one of three possible moves: innovate ('pull a new arm' on the bandit to discover the 'payoff' of a particular behaviour); observe (watch a different programme's move to see what the payoff is); or exploit (carry out a move from the programme's existing repertoire). Random changes were introduced into the environment as the tournament progressed. Players were also able to update their strategies and to observe how other contestants changed theirs. When these programmes were run against each other inside a supercomputer, it was found that the winning strategy had relied exclusively on copying others, while a strategy that relied almost entirely on innovation came 95th out of a field of 100. There are two further findings of note, however, in that when the winning strategy was run in isolation, it performed very badly; and when the highest performing programmes were removed from the competition, the average payoff across the population increased. There are three provisional conclusions to be drawn here: (i) that a tendency to imitate others is more likely to prove successful than taking risks; (ii) that this is only the case in an environment in which innovation and novelty are present in sufficient numbers; and (iii) that society as a whole prospers more when the most 'parasitic' members are removed. However, as Rendell et al.'s results presently contain figures only for the ratio of observe to innovate for individual programmes, they do not make any predictions as to what represents the most effective balance of innovation to novelty in terms of the distribution across the population as a whole.

A relatively precise empirical answer to this question is, however, suggested by research into complex dynamic systems. Kretzschmar (2015:8–9), for example, observes that within natural complex systems, such as ant colonies, entirely deterministic responses to external stimuli such as attacks by intruders would leave the colony vulnerable. Rather than every ant rushing to defend the colony, therefore, some act to protect the queen while others continue to forage for food. Importantly, it is not the case that the same ants perform the same task each time, but that the population as a whole has evolved to display such regular variation. And the ratio of behavioural variation found repeatedly throughout such systems hovers somewhere around the 80:20 mark, whereby 20% of variation accounts for 80% of the total activity while the remaining 80% of variation accounts for only 20% of the total activity[10]. Kretzschmar refers to this skewed distribution as an *A-curve* (as introduced in Chapter 2) and demonstrates its relevance for linguistic phenomena, presenting detailed evidence to show that lexical and phonetic variation consistently shows such a distribution across different groups of speakers. In other words, rather than there being an absolute correlation between groups of speakers and the linguistic variables with which they are identified, there is rather a tendency towards a norm (the predominant 20% of variants), while the 'tail' of the A-curve (the 80% of variation doing only 20% of the work) is composed of old dominant forms that have fallen out of use, of novel forms, and of minor more localised variation.

Combining Kretzschmar's findings with Rogers' and Rendell et al.'s work, we have the beginnings of an evolutionary explanation for the rise and functionality of the A-curve in the suggestion that a ratio *somewhere in the region of* 80:20 of normative to marked behaviour provides the optimal environment for the informed risk-taking necessary to protect the system from senescence and vulnerability to unexpected risks. We are less interested than Kretzschmar in the exact figure, and will interpret his findings more in terms of a predominance of a small number of items and a tailful of assorted extras. Either way, as Pagel (2014) says, 'The sobering truth is that far from being highly creative and innovative, most of us are just glorified "karaoke singers" in most aspects of our lives, using things others have made.' But to balance this, we have some degree of innovation and unpredictability. Bergman (2009:156-157) makes a similar point in his Peircean theory of communication:

---

10   As such, Kretzschmar's work is an elaboration and refinement of Zipf's theorem.

> We should not complain about the fact that symbols are never com-
> pletely determined, because if they were, there would be no semiotic
> growth or change; as Brock boldly states, 'vagueness is the mother of
> invention'. (Brock: 1981:136)

However, while an A-curve distribution is a regular feature, its specific make-up is neither synchronically uniform nor diachronically stable. From the synchronic perspective, Kretzschmar demonstrates that, although the A-curve distribution holds stable at different scales and across different population sets, the specific features that occupy the head and the tail of the curve may vary. So, for example, at the national level, a small handful of lexical variants may dominate for a specific referent; however, if we look only at men, or only at women, or at different age groups, we see different selections of lexemes dominating for each category. And, from the diachronic perspective, we see that for each subgroup of the population, different features will occupy the head and tail of the A-curve at different times, while new features enter and existing features disappear. Within stable environments, such as an ant colony or an isolated social group, the rate of change within the system is slow as the existing balance in behavioural variation is sufficient to counter or accommodate external intrusions without undermining group cohesion. Within rapidly changing environments, such as a superdiverse city, however, the system must respond more rapidly in order to survive. In such cases, the rate of movement up and down the A-curve is greatly accelerated and, if there is not the time for adaptive behaviour to even out slowly across the system, fractures will appear in the form of an increased variability of context-specific behaviours. The result of increased risk-taking in such contexts is therefore increased diversity and the disappearance of established registers and genres rather than the untimely death that awaits overly adventurous rats and which, phylogenetically, requires rapid and plentiful reproduction rates.

Following Kretzschmar, then, we can predict that, across all contexts, a statement will be realised by a small number of constructions, and predominantly the declarative and a falling tone, the vast majority of the time. However, within different registers, as with Kretzschmar's subpopulations, different constructions will be at the head of the A-curve, as with the moodless form that typifies with the shipping forecast. We can therefore distinguish between the *criterial features* of a text, those that contribute to defining its register and hence its association with a situation type (generally at the head of the curve, but also including regular functions within the tail), and the *background noise*, those elements in the tail of the A-curve that neither typify the register nor undermine the overarching activity. As we have suggested, however, the dynamic equilibrium between criterial features and noise is more than an abstract statistical tendency. Within any given context there will be a centripetal pressure towards the norm in terms of those features that are most salient as indicators of what activity is being carried out any time (*cf.* Zuraw 2006). In terms of evolutionary metaredundancy, these are the features with the highest degree of redundancy, or mutual association, within a specific context and which therefore carry the greatest chance of success, or survival, within that context. In the terms of Rendell et al.'s evolutionary mind games, these criterial features are once innovative responses that have been imitated and taken up wholesale by generations of speakers. These criterial features are motivated by the redundancy of meaning that associates a register with a specific situation. This is not to say, however, that the noise is unmotivated, but rather that it is motivated by the excess of information that is generally backgrounded. Generally, as they represent centrifugal forces, these innovative or marked features will have only a fleeting existence. Others, however, will fill an unforeseen (or previously non-existent) functional niche within the context of situation and will be therefore taken up by the imitators, without the risk that innovation entails, when such functionally equivalent contexts are next encountered. And, as success breeds success, these features will move up the A-curve, accelerating ever more rapidly until they become the criterial features of a reconstructed register (*cf.* Zuraw 2006). And so the cycle continues, maintaining an A-curve distribution, but with the features at the head and the tail of the curve in constant flux and the occasional intrusion of entirely innovative features. For this reason, we refer to such elements of the tail as *serviceable noise*. In the terms of evolutionary biology, such non-criterial features are the equivalent of *genetic debris*, or what Pagel (2012:128) calls 'the raw materials of our differences'; and just as evolutionary biology sets out to establish the conditions and mechanisms by which such debris becomes criterial to different species, in the present book we will set out to explain the contextual conditions and embodied mechanisms by which non-normative behaviour is replicated and becomes dominant. This process will be illustrated in more detail in Chapter 6.

3.8 CONCLUSION

In this chapter we have outlined a model of language as a fractal system, defined as the recursive application of self-similar mechanisms of articulation across different scales to produce meaningful units of ever higher orders of abstraction. This entails that the relationship between criterial features and noise on the one hand and innovation and systematisation on the other holds between all strata of language and beyond, as illustrated by *Mutt's Urinal*/Duchamp's *Fountain*. This is an idea that is captured, in brief, by Pennisi and Falzone (2016:96–97), who describe the development of the language capacity from a Darwinian biolinguistics perspective as a 'species-specific bodily technology applied to symbolic needs' and state that:

> ...language produces a system of articulations of first, second and third level allowing a virtually infinite combinatorial technology based on sound units (phones, phonemes, syllables), morphology (morphemes), semantics (lexemes, words, sentences, discourses, texts) from a finite number of dedicated physiological elements.

However, while we argue that we are genetically disposed to use language, to internalise and reproduce associations of form and function, the combinatorial technology that Pennisi and Falzone refer to is a property not of the embodied mind, but of the language system as an external, distributed and transmittable resource. This property of language does, however, rely on the existence of embodied mind capable of utilising this property, and it is this symbiotic interplay between the internal and external, the now and the not-now, that has made it possible for the human species to 'throw off the yoke of its genes' and to conquer and flourish in new niches through adaptive learning rather than genetic adaptation (Pagel 2012:4; *cf.* Reboul 2017:106; Everett 2012).

According to the description we have developed in this chapter, language is at once systemically structured and fluid. That is to say, that the systems of structures that comprise it are always *emergent* (Hopper 1987) or, as Kretzschmar (2015:58) puts it, grammar 'never exists as such but is always coming into being'. Hopper took the idea of emergence from James Clifford's work in anthropology and we see clear resonances with Derrida's concept of *différance*, introduced above. Despite this link to meanings beyond the language system per se, the idea of emergence has been largely limited in linguistics to the study of forms and meanings of grammatical and semantic items with the clause as 'the level of existence...of interest' (Beckner et al. 2009:15). In the present chapter we have extended on existing concepts of language as a complex adaptive system to present a metaredundant model of language that connects the concepts of redundancy, articulation and indeterminacy as the essential ingredients for creativity across strata, from the morpheme up to ideology. We have, however, only hinted at the conditions under which such novel articulations arise. This is an idea we will return to in Chapter 6, where we take a closer look at the dynamic processes of language production.

Chapter 4

Stratification, redundancy, the mechanism of change

4.1 INTRODUCTION

In this chapter we will build on the concept of stratification in order to illustrate the importance of redundancy as a mechanism through which language self-organises into a dynamic and adaptive system. In Chapter 3, we illustrated Halliday's well known view that language has evolved to be a stratified system where higher order meanings are realised through lower order strata. In other words, language does not consist of sound meaning pairs directly linking meaning with sound. It is instead a stratified system with stratified content and expression planes.

We will demonstrate in this chapter through illustrative text analyses that a stratified model of language provides a model of how the prelinguistic purport i.e., the flux of formless and amorphous sensations, is formed into meaningful language. As meaning making animals our interactions with the purport form it into meaningful substance. As noted by the contrast in Mood choices between English and Gaelic in Chapter 3, semiosis makes the non-linguistic sensible and there is no natural or objective way to slice up the prelinguistic cake. It is rather our will to semiosis coupled with our shared biological capacity and the affordances/constraints found in individual languages that allows humans to function in an appropriate and relevant manner within the diverse social and material contexts in which they find themselves.

Halliday and Matthiessen (2014:25) state that it is the stratification of the content plane into semantics and lexicogrammar which expanded the power of language and enabled human mental creativity, and that this stratification is the foundation of how we construct knowledge. They further note that the relationship between strata is one of realisation, with the higher strata being realised by the lower and the lower realising the higher strata. Briefly put, meaning is realised by wording which itself is realised by composing which itself is realised by sounding.

When we talk of meaning, we have to distinguish between the latent meanings in the *environment*, the sociocultural setting in which interaction takes place, and the actualised meanings in the *context of situation*, the specific activity which speakers attend to through their semiotic acts (see Bartlett 2013, 2017 for a fuller discussion of the distinction). This making relevant (Hasan 2013:279) of specific aspects of the environment as the context of situation is realised by the semantic stratum[1], and in the following move from meaning to wording the semantics is realised by the lexicogrammatical stratum.[2] In the move from wording to composing, we move from the content plane to the expression plane. The expression plane is itself stratified into phonology and phonetics. By phonology we refer to how speech sounds are organised axially into formal structures and systems. The wording is realised by the phonology. Finally, the move from composing to sounding is realised by the phonetics. The realisational relationship between content and expression is chiefly arbitrary (see also de Saussure 1957, Harris 1987) though Halliday and Matthiessen (2014:27) acknowledge some exceptions such as sound symbolism which was discussed briefly in Chapter 2. We interpret arbitrary relations, perhaps idiosyncratically, as agreed conventions. Thus, for us there is no reason why all signs, including icons and indexes, cannot be classed as arbitrary conventions. Hence, English dogs go 'woof woof' while Japanese ones go 'wan wan' and the human representations of the canine sounds are arbitrary signs within the respective languages.[3] Conversely, the realisational relationships between meaning and wording, and composing and sounding are fundamentally motivated. This is a point we will visit in Chapter 5 when we examine sequential ordering in language.

First however, we will look in more detail at the meaning of realisation and develop the description of redundancy set out in Chapter 3. This will give us the necessary tools required to make sense of the linguistic choices we will meet in a short spoken extract. In earlier work, O'Grady and Bartlett (2019) and O'Grady (2020a), we proposed some revision to the content and expression planes and

---

1   In our description of the model we adopt a speaker's point of view. Receptively the moves would proceed in the opposite order.

2   In this view grammar and lexis are not distinct, with lexis representing the most delicate grammar (Hasan 1987). Nor in this view are syntax and morphology classed as belonging to different strata, though clearly they differ in terms of rank.

3   Saussure, himself, discusses barking as a form of onomatopoeia. He argues that a French dog's *ouaoua* and a German dog's *wauwau* once introduced to a system are subject to the rules of the system and hence not fully natural. This explanation for us is problematic in that it reifies the difference between synchrony and diachrony. We, though agree that at the current moment in time both construals of barking are accepted social facts to French and German speakers as they have a conventionally agreed value in the respective languages.

argued that that the higher elements of the phonological rank scale and the systemic choices that accrue to them are in and of themselves meaningful, and hence part of the content plane. We will test this claim in the spoken extract. We do this in order to demonstrate the materiality not only of the expression plane but also of the content plane.

4.2   WHAT IS REALISATION?

As the term realisation is open to misunderstanding we need to expand on our previous discussion and spend some time explicating what is meant in Halladayian linguistics by realisation. It means more than 'actualisation', or 'bringing into being'. Instead, following the work of Lemke (1984), Halliday (1992/2005) redefined realisation in terms of a redundancy relationship. Redundancy is itself a technical term and does not merely convey its dictionary meaning of excess, expendability or unnecessariness. Halliday notes that for language to be a truly open and dynamic system the relationship between strata is not determined but predictive. So a form on a higher stratum does not actualise a form on the lower stratum; rather it predicts it. Halliday explains:

> Consider a minimal semiotic system, such as a protolanguage — a system that is made up of simple signs. When we say that contents $\mathbf{p}$, $\mathbf{q}$, $\mathbf{r}$ are "realized" respectively by expressions $\mathbf{a}$, $\mathbf{b}$, $\mathbf{c}$, what this means is that there is a redundancy relation between them: given meaning $\mathbf{p}$, we can predict sound or gesture $\mathbf{a}$, and given sound or gesture $\mathbf{a}$ we can predict meaning $\mathbf{p}$. This relationship is symmetrical; "redounds with" is equivalent both to "realizes" and to "is realized by". (2005:356)

However, language is not a minimum semiotic system comprising form/meaning signs; instead, in Halliday's terms, it is multistratal, i.e., consisting of an additional stratum of 'content form' and so expressions are realised as wordings which are themselves realised as soundings. Thus, a wording redounds and makes possible a sounding. Lemke (1995:168–169), whose work was influenced by the anthropologist Gregory Bateson,[4] describes this as a redundancy of redundancy or a *metare-*

---

4   Bateson (1972:405–416) outlines a theory of metacommunication where animals recognise that their own communicative activities simulate and hence refer to other (absent) activities. Indicatively, we as dog companions are drawn to the activity of play fighting where non-present activities such as feeding practices and relationships such as temporary disruptions to dominance are activated and referred to in the ritualistic act of negotiated play fighting (see Bekoff 1995). Bateson argued that the ability to engage in metacommunicative activities enables the comprehension that an activity can have multiple referents.

dundancy. In other words, the predictable connection between two things can itself be redundant. To illustrate, when seeking a specific response from a hearer a speaker could produce any of the following utterances:

- What's your name?
- Please tell me your name?
- And your name is?

The thought or message predicts the possibility of any of the three forms (which of course in turn predict the thought and the form if not the content of the response) – though one can imagine contextual variables which would make some of them less or more likely. So, in our account, we can say that the context predicts the meaning, which is realised by the semantics as an utterance seeking information which is either not known or not confidently known. The semantics predicts the wording realised by the lexicogrammar itself composed by the phonology into one or more tone groups with relevant tone choices. Finally, the sounding is realised by the phonetics and the speaker produces the utterance. For instance, the context may be a concierge checking a list of names for a reservation and so the wording chosen is 'And your name is?' This predicts that the most common sounding will be [ə̃ jɔː /ne͠ɪmz] articulated in a single tone group with a tonic syllable on *names* with a rising tone. Though the speaker could produce the utterance as [ə̃ jɔː ne͠ɪm \ɪz]. The less natural combination with a falling tone, as will be shown below, results in a slightly different meaning; one where the speaker is perhaps clarifying an ambiguity or an absence on the list.

Yet, one can easily imagine a famous TV performer who greets contestants on a popular gameshow using the same wording. However, she sounds it as [ænd jɔː / ʜne͠ɪm ɪz] with high rising intonation. One could well imagine such a variant form spreading and leading to a change in the concierge's articulation as a result of a game show host's initial greetings to a contestant. The cultural capital accrued by the TV performer is sufficient to lead to at least a temporary change in the concierge's and others' use of language. We use this made up example to illustrate an important point – that recombinations of features can lead not only to new ideational meanings but also to novel interpersonal ones.[5] We will revisit the concept of voice in Chapter 6. For now, though, our important point following Halliday – and indeed usage based approaches such as Bybee (2002) – is that instances of language used in context or tokens are the drivers of localised, though perhaps transient, change. However, it is worth noting that people interact within contextually delimited social

---

Redundancy in Bateson's words 'creates communication' (ibid:412) by constraining the choices available to the communicator and by ensuring robust transmission of the code.

5   For instance, the catchphrase 'nice to see you, to see you nice' indexes the late British TV host Bruce Forsyth.

spaces, and thus the language of the classroom is very different from the language of the pub.[6] Thus, the potential for new meanings if they occur are restricted, at least initially, to specific registers and even to restricted groups of users of these registers with the novelty potentially spreading further, subsequently fossilising and so indexing that subgroup or gradually falling out of use.

While it is, of course, impossible to read the thought processes of another individual, it is possible to parse an individual's lexicogrammatical choices in the context in which they occur in order to predict the speaker's communicative goals on a turn-by-turn basis, while at the same time using what is known about the wider social environment to predict the speaker's motivation for construing the context of situation in the way that they do across the text as a whole.

In the following section, we will examine a short speech produced by the then UK Prime Minister, Tony Blair, from the G8 summit in Gleneagles on the morning of 7 July 2005 in response to a series of terrorist bombings in London that had occurred earlier that morning.[7] We do this in order to demonstrate the stratification hierarchy and to shed some light on the speaker's motives by showing that only a stratified semiotic system is sufficiently nimble to enable a speaker to produce the subtle meanings, we as languaging animals produce effortlessly all the time. Without stratification meanings would be tied to forms, and hence new meanings would require new forms, and the system would rapidly become unbounded resulting in inefficiencies in learning. In other words, the system would not be human language. Then in the following section, we shall add prosody to our examination in order to discuss how redundancy has the potential to be a powerful meaning making device, and suggest some revisions to the content expression boundary.

4.3   THE WRITTEN STATEMENT AND THE CONTEXT IN WHICH IT WAS PRODUCED

On 7 July 2005 Britain, which was basking in the afterglow of the previous day's news that London had been selected as the host for the 2012 Olympics, woke up to the shocking news of a series of major incidents on the London Underground. After a period of initial confusion, when the first reports of explosions on the Underground were blamed on a power surge, it became clear within an hour or so that the cause was a terrorist attack. The Metropolitan police initially reported that just

---

6   This is obviously an enormous simplification because we are ignoring dialect, age and gender among many relevant variables.

7   We have previously analysed this text in O'Grady (2010, 2020a) and Bartlett (2014). As our thoughts have matured we have slightly changed our analysis.

before 9 o'clock perhaps as many as 6 bombs[8] had been exploded on the London Underground and that an hour later a further bomb had exploded on a double-decker bus in Central London resulting in numerous fatalities and casualities. At the time of the bombing the UK Prime Minister, Tony Blair, was hosting the 31st G8 summit in Gleneagles in Scotland from 6–8 July. The aim of the summit was to explore ways to reduce poverty in Africa and to combat climate change by moving beyond the Kyoto protocols. Blair was informed of the incident while in a meeting with the then Chinese President, Hu Jintao. About two and a half hours after the initial Underground bombings, with the situation still somewhat confused, Blair made a short televised statement which he (2010:566) later described as the most important of his political career. The text is reproduced in Text 4.1.[9]

Text 4.1 Short statement produced by Tony Blair on morning of 07/07/2005

> I am just going to make a short statement to you on the terrible events that have happened in London earlier today, and I hope you understand that at the present time we are still trying to establish exactly what has happened, and there is a limit to what information I can give you, and I will simply try and tell you the information as best I can at the moment.
>
> It is reasonably clear that there have been a series of terrorist attacks in London. There are obviously casualties, both people that have died and people seriously injured, and our thoughts and prayers of course are with the victims and their families.
>
> It is my intention to leave the G8 within the next couple of hours and go down to London and get a report, face-to-face, with the police, and the emergency services and the Ministers that have been dealing with this, and then to return later this evening.
>
> It is the will of all the leaders at the G8 however that the meeting should continue in my absence, that we should continue to discuss the issues that we were going to discuss, and reach the conclusions which we were going to reach. Each of the countries round that table have some experience of the effects of terrorism and all the leaders, as they will indicate a little bit later, share our complete resolution to defeat this terrorism.

---

8   There were actually only three suicide attacks on the Underground.

9   The audio statement is available at https://www.youtube.com/watch?v=5MzKDH4wNyI [last accessed 2 Feb 2021]. An archive version of the written statement is available at http:// webarchive.nationalarchives.gov.uk/20121005153058/http://www.direct.gov.uk/en/Nl1/ Newsroom/DG_10020708 [Last accessed Feb 2 2021]

It is particularly barbaric that this has happened on a day when people are meeting to try to help the problems of poverty in Africa, and the long term problems of climate change and the environment. Just as it is reasonably clear that this is a terrorist attack, or a series of terrorist attacks, it is also reasonably clear that it is designed and aimed to coincide with the opening of the G8. There will be time to talk later about this.

It is important however that those engaged in terrorism realise that our determination to defend our values and our way of life is greater than their determination to cause death and destruction to innocent people in a desire to impose extremism on the world. Whatever they do, it is our determination that they will never succeed in destroying what we hold dear in this country and in other civilised nations throughout the world. Thank you.

Halliday in a series of works e.g. (1969, 1973, 1975, 1978; Halliday & Hasan 1985) has shown that meaning in and between clauses has evolved to serve a number of highly generalised functions to do with how we construe our experience, enact social relationships and build up sequences of text into a cohesive and coherent whole. These strands of meanings are known as metafunctions, and they serve to present the clause as a representation of an event, an exchange and as a message. A fourth strand of meaning presents the relationship between clauses. These are known as the experiential, interpersonal, textual and logical metafunctions respectively. All meaning is of course, as de Saussure (1957) noted, oppositional and relational. In the discussion below we will focus on oppositional meaning with our discussion of relational meaning deferred until the following chapter.

As described above, a series of violent events in London provoked Blair to make a televised address to the British public and international community. In semiotic terms the unformed, amorphous, ephemeral flux of the external event was perceived by Blair and integrated into his existing knowledge base. This is, of course, a bit of a cheat in that he did not directly perceive the events but received them as second order mediated impressions from the media and relevant informants. However, Eagleman (2015) demonstrates that second order representations of events result in the same cognitive realignment as first order sensory impressions. Prior to forming his response he knew that: (i) intentional human actions had caused the violence; (ii) the G8 meeting he was attending was occurring in the UK; (iii) British troops were fighting as part of coalition forces in Afghanistan and Iraq, and that their deployment, especially to Iraq, had been controversial and was opposed by large sectors of the population; (iv) he was vulnerable to claims that the violent events were blowback for his policies; (v) violent actions frequently spark retaliations aimed at members of communities considered sympathetic to or similar to the protagonists; and (vi) he must have strongly suspected the identity or provenance of those he construed as terrorists. Blair's talk occurred behind a dais and in front of microphones and cameras with his audience distant, and hence he received no immediate feedback. While his briefing may have seemed to be an informational briefing, his purpose was persuasive. In his own words he stated that the purpose of the statement was 'about defining the feeling so that the reaction can be shaped and the consequences managed' (Blair 2010:566). Blair's communicative goals were realised by very different lexicogrammatical choices than would have been produced had his aim been to advocate for a military reprisal or for a crackdown on a religious community or political grouping. Thus, in the description below, the meanings realised are to be understood as the sum of all the meanings that were not realised.

4.3.1   Experiential meanings

Experiential meanings are particulate and based on the principle of constituency. By this we mean that meanings related to how we model experience as configurations of phenomena are perceived in terms of an event which is formed out of discrete parts. We have noted earlier the claim that human brains are in some way doomed to interpret input in terms of syntactic structures, which is probably itself the result of the fact that our brains 'are doomed' to interpret events in terms of patterns formed out of discrete actions themselves grounded in bodily actions (see Calvin and Bickerton 2001 for an evolutionary account).

Experiential meanings construe speakers' experiences of the world in terms of configurations of processes encoded in verbal groups and attendant participants and circumstances. There are six process types in English[10] which are sketched in Table 4.1 with the verbal group underlined. The process types are recognisable in terms of different structural potentials with – in English, for instance – material processes (related to doing) occurring in unmarked form in the present continuous while mental processes related to cognition, emotion and perception occur in the unmarked form in the present simple. The fact that the process types are recognisable in terms of different structural potentials indicates that within particular languages meaningful and distinct patterns emerge and solidify because of frequency of use; itself the consequence of human localised socialisation.

In Text 4.2 we have underlined the verbal groups and labelled the processes and participant roles in Blair's speech.

---

10   For a complete description of process types and the grammatical probes used to identify them see Halliday and Matthiessen (2014: Chapter 5).

Table 4.1 The process types

Process type	Participant roles	Example
Material	Actor ^ Goal/Scope	John (Actor) <u>is baking</u> a cake (Goal)
		John (Actor) <u>is crossing</u> the street (Scope)
Mental	Sensor ^ Phenomenon	John (Sensor) <u>loves</u> the city (Phen) – emotive
		John (Sensor) <u>knows</u> the answer (Phen) – cognitive
		John (Sensor) <u>wants</u> the answer (Phen) – desiderative
		John (Sensor) <u>hears</u> the explosion (Phen) – Perceptive
Relational	Carrier ^Attribute	John (Carrier) <u>is</u> English (Attribute) – Intensive Attributive
		John (Token) <u>is</u> the team captain (Value) – Intensive Identifying
		John (Carrier) <u>has</u> many houses (Attribute) – Possessive Attributive
		The house (Carrier) <u>is</u> on top of the hill Circumstantial (Attrib: Circ)
		On a hill top (Carrier) <u>is</u> number 9 (Circumstantial Identifying
Verbal	Sayer ^ Verbiage	John (Sayer) <u>reported</u> his rage (Verbiage)
	Sayer ^ Recipient ^Verbiage	John (Sayer) <u>told</u> Jim (Recipient) his name (Verbiage)
	Sayer ^ Target	John (Sayer) <u>slandered</u> Jim (Target) to Mary (Receiver)[11]
Existential	^ existent	There <u>was</u> an explosion (Existent)
Behavioural	Behaver	John <u>belched</u>

---

11   Slander is an example of what Matthiessen, Martin & Painter (1997:126) dub 'judgemental verbal processes'. This sub-class of process type could be analysed as a behavioural e.g. *behaver ^ process ^ range ^ receiver*. However, as *slander* is a semantic action where words are produced we consider it to be verbal.

Text 4.2 Terrorist/ism – reference chain and prominence choices

A/ I [Actor] <u>am just going to make</u> [Material] a short statement [Range] to you [beneficiary]on the terrible events that have happened in London earlier today, [Circumstance of Matter] /
// and I [Sensor] <u>hope</u> [Mental – desiderative] you understand that at the present time we [Actor] <u>are still trying to establish</u> [Mental cognitive] exactly what has happened [Phenomenon], //
// and there <u>is</u> [Existential] a limit to what information / I [Actor] <u>can give</u> [Material] you, [Goal] / [Existent] //
and I [Sayer] <u>will simply try and tell</u> [Verbal] you [Recipient] the information [Verbiage] as best I can at the moment /.

B // It [Carrier] <u>is</u> [Relational Intensive Attributive] reasonably clear that there <u>have been</u> [Existential] a series of terrorist attacks in London. [Existent] / [Attribute] //
/ There <u>are</u> [Existential] obviously casualties [Existent] /
/ both people [Behaver] that <u>have died</u> [Behavioural] /
/ and people [Carrier] (who <u>are</u>) [Relational Intensive Attributive] seriously injured, / [Attribute]
/ and our thoughts and prayers [Carrier] of course <u>are</u> [Relational Circumstantial Attributive] with the victims and their families. [Attribute] /

C It [Token] <u>is</u> [Relational Intensive Attributive] my intention (I) [Actor] <u>to leave</u> [Material] the G8 [Scope] / within the next couple of hours / [Value] //
/ and (I) [Actor] <u>go down</u> [Material] to London [Circumstance] /
/ and (I) [Actor] <u>get</u> [Material] a report, [Goal] face-to-face, with the police, and the emergency services and the Ministers that have been dealing with this /
and then (I) [Actor] <u>to return</u> [Material] later this evening. /

D//// It [Token] <u>is</u> [Relational Intensive Attributive] the will of all the leaders [Attribute] at the G8 / however that the meeting [Carrier] <u>should continue</u> [Relational Attributive Circumstantial] in my absence, [Attribute] / Attribute //
/ that we [Sayer] <u>should continue to discuss</u> [Verbal] the issues [Verbiage] / that we [Sayer] <u>were going to discuss,</u> [Verbal] / [Verbiage] ////
/ and [Behaver] <u>reach</u> [Behavioural] the conclusions / Phenomenon which we [Behaver] <u>were going to reach</u> [Behavioural]. / //

/ Each of the countries round that table [Carrier] <u>have</u> [Relational Possessive Attributive] some experience of the effects of terrorism [Attribute] /
/ and all the leaders, [Carrier] {as they [Sayer] <u>will indicate</u> [Verbal] a little bit later}, <u>share</u> [Relational Possessive Attributive] our complete resolution / (G8 leaders) [Actor] <u>to defeat</u> [Material] this terrorism. [Goal] / [Attribute] //

E/// It [Carrier] <u>is</u> [Relational Intensive Attributive] particularly barbaric [Attribute] {that this <u>has happened</u> on a day} / when people [Actor] <u>are meeting</u> / [Actor] t<u>o try to help</u> [Material] the problems of poverty in Africa, and the long term problems of climate change and the environment. [Goal] ///

// Just as it [Carrier] <u>is</u> [Relational Intensive Attributive] reasonably clear [Attribute] / that this [Carrier] <u>is</u> [Relational Intensive Attributive] a terrorist attack, or a series of terrorist attacks, [Attribute] //

/// [Carrier] it <u>is</u> [Relational Intensive Attributive] also reasonably clear [Attribute] / that it [Scope] <u>is designed</u> [Material (passive)/causative] and (It) [Scope] <u>(is) aimed [Material (passive)/causative]</u> to coincide [Relational Circumstantial Attributive] with the opening of the G8. [Attribute] /// [Attribute]
/ There <u>will be</u> [Existential] time to talk [behavioural] later about this. [Existent] /

F//// It [Carrier] <u>is</u> [Relational Intensive Attributive] important [Attribute] / however that those {engaged in terrorism}[Sensor] <u>realise</u> [Mental Cognitive] / that our determination {to defend our values and our way of life} [Carrier] <u>is</u> [Relational Intensive Attributive] greater {than their determination to cause death and destruction to innocent people in a desire to impose extremism on the world}. [Attribute] / [Phenomenon] ////

J/ Whatever [Goal] they [Actor] <u>do</u> [Material] /,
/ it [Carrier] <u>is</u> [Relational Intensive Attributive] our determination [Attribute] /that they [Actor] <u>will never succeed in destroying</u> [Material] {what <u>we</u> [Carrier] hold [Relational Intensive Attributive] dear in this country and in other civilised nations throughout the world} [Goal]. / [Attribute] //

Thank you.

The short statement contains mostly processes of doing, behavioural processes and processes of being and cognition. Blair construes himself, either singularly or collectively as a political leader, as agentive. In this way he succeeds in construing cognitive behaviour as a doing rather than as a thinking. However, the actions he construes that he is or will be doing are themselves rather restrained and cautious. In the opening line the doing is in fact semantically a report that he is speaking! Overall he construes himself as a cautious figure: one who will not be rushed into hasty and perhaps misjudged responses. Instead he will wait until the facts of what has occurred emerge before committing himself to any definite action. In paragraphs C and D Blair represents himself as a leader capable of balancing competing priorities – his hosting of the G8 summit and his need to return to London to assume control of the investigation. He will return to London to be briefed before resuming his hosting duties. Simultaneously, though, he indicates that the G8 meeting can continue in his absence as its telos has been previously determined; the leaders will reach the only conclusion that can be reached. In other words, his linguistic choices implicitly convey that the bombings have not impacted upon the political dialogue.

It is noticeable that in Blair's construal the bombers, with one exception, are not construed as being agentive. The effect of this is again to bring calmness to the chaotic flux of the news. The sole process in which the bombers are represented as Actor is DESTROY, but the process itself is contained in a rankshifted clause, which itself functions as the attribute of the matrix clause, and the presence of the adverb *never* further construes the futility of the bombers' actions. In paragraph E, the causative processes DESIGN and AIM impute cognition to those responsible for the bombing. It is noticeable, though, that the target of the bombing is the international community. The bombers are construed as external to the UK. In paragraph D, the G8 leaders, the representatives of the international community are represented as Actor for the process DEFEAT but the process itself is non-finite. Thus, Blair construes a world where there is no temporal indexing of when the bombers will be defeated: he suggests that it is likely to be a long hard struggle. Had the thought been to construe a world where he was a war leader (which he actually was!), rather than a cautious civilian politician, the realised linguistic choices[12] would have been rather different.

Within the statement in the opening two paragraphs the event of the bombing, and its effect, is construed as a series of Relational and Existential processes. Blair informs that the bombing exists and, with it, casualties. One effect of presenting the bombing as an entity rather than as a process is to supress discussion of the reason as to why the bombing occurred, and to remove it from a historical timeline of cause and effect. Furthermore, Blair construes the murder of the civilian commuters as a

---

12   Presumably he would have chosen other non-linguistic signs to signal his belligerence such as flags, uniforms etc. The absence of such signs is itself a redundant signal predicting that Blair's message would be one of caution and moderation.

behavioural process, i.e., *they are 'people that have died'* and, by not directly ascribing blame for the deaths, the effect is not to increase emotion but rather to signal calmness. Again the lack of processes attributing direct causation to the terrorists predicts that the communicative purpose of the speech is not to exact retribution, though Blair clearly assigns sole blame for the crime to the terrorists

Blair construes the relationship between the international community and the effects of terrorism as a Relational possessive process. This construal represents a world where terrorism is a widespread fact of life and, once again, backgrounds discussion as to potential motivation for the bombings. The relational construal further represents the bombing as part of a wider whole, and hence as an event which does not necessarily require new or innovative responses.

4.3.1.1 *Summary of experiential meaning*

To sum up, the experiential meanings construed by Blair redound with a real world where terrorism is an intractable problem, and one where terrorist acts should be responded to in a measured and considered manner once the full facts have been gleaned. And this thought predicts, but does not obviously determine, his lexicogrammatical choices. It is not hard to imagine a different politician[13] whose response would have been to construe himself as a decisive actor through the employment of more concrete material processes; one who would, for instance, extirpate the virus of terrorism. In this alternate construal we could predict that this different thought would redound with a designation of the bombers as extremists whose actions were formed by their religious beliefs.

Blair though is not, at least overtly, that politician. In paragraph A he represents himself as the Senser of the Mental desiderative process HOPE with the public as the intended audience. The effect is to indicate his desire that the public respect his wish to balance transparency with the need to find out what occurred. In this construed real world politicians should be calm, cautious but resolute in pursuing their goals, and they can expect their publics to be calm and to trust in their leaders' actions. In the next section we will examine the interpersonal meanings enacted in the text of the short statement.

4.3.2   Interpersonal meanings

Interpersonal meanings are prosodic-like and saturate a text. The most significant interpersonal systems comprise Mood, Modality and Evaluation and, in this section,

---

13   We wrote these words in the immediate aftermath of Trump's failed coup, so it is likely that our imagined other politician is at least to some extent Trumpian. You of course are free to imagine an alternate politician.

we shall examine the short statement in order to explicate the significance of the Interpersonal choices in order to show how these choices redound with the context of situation in which Blair enacts his social relationship with his audience.

We will first briefly describe the Mood system of English where the chief cut is between Indicative and Imperative Mood.[14] Indicative Mood contains a subject + finite, and itself is more delicately divided into Declarative mood signalled by Subject ^ Finite order, and Interrogative signalled by Finite ^ Subject order, with the optional presence of a Wh question element. In a clause, the Subject/Finite is the Mood element and the remainder of the clause is known as the Residue. Speakers produce acts semiotically concerned with goods and services known as proposals and those semiotically concerned with information known as propositions. Speakers may choose to give or demand. And this leads to the following classification of speech function (Halliday 1978; Halliday & Matthiessen 2014; Andersen 2017)

	Proposal	Proposition
Give	Offer	Statement
Demand	Command	Question

Speakers may wish to assert that their assessment of the probability of a proposition or the necessity of a proposal occurring is somewhere between 0% and 100%. In relation to propositions they may signal their assessment of the probability or usuality. Assessments of probability and usuality may be expressed in the following ways: (i) by a finite verbal operator such as *can, may, must* etc.; (ii) by a Modal Adjunct e.g. *probably, usually* etc.; (iii) by a comment adjunct such as *it is possible that*; or (iv) indirectly and metaphorically by expressions such as *I think*. In relation to proposals speakers signal their assessments of degrees of obligation and inclination. They do so through (i) a finite verbal operator such as *will, should, must* etc.; (ii) through the expansion of the verbal group e.g. *need to do X, would be happy to do X*; (iii) through an active or passive verb e.g. *you are required to*; or (iv) by an adjective such as *keen, willing, determined*.

A further way speakers signal their attitude or stance towards their utterance is by producing evaluative language (Biber and Finegan 1989; Hunston 2010; Hunston and Thompson 2000). In our view the most rigorous and complete schema of evaluative language is the Appraisal framework (Martin and Rose 2007; Martin and White 2005; Oteíza 2017; Hood 2019 etc.). Within this framework there are three interacting subsystems ATTITUDE, ENGAGEMENT and GRADUATION. ATTITUDE itself comprises 3 subsystems: affect, appreciation and judgement. Affect signals the

---

14   This, while similar in many languages – e.g. French, German, Mandarin, Japanese – may not be the case for all languages (see the chapters in Cafferel, Martin and Matthiessen (2004) especially the chapter by Prakasam (2004) on Telugu). See also the discussion of Mood in Gaelic in Chapter 3.

speaker's evaluation of a target's emotions and is segmented into the three pairs: *happiness/unhappiness, security/insecurity* and *satisfaction/dissatisfaction*. The *happiness/unhappiness* distinction refers to emotions related to affairs of the heart. The *security/insecurity* distinction refers to emotions to do with well-being. The *satisfaction/dissatisfaction* distinction refers to emotions to do with the pursuit of goals and dreams. Appreciation signals a speaker's aesthetic evaluation of natural and semiotic phenomena. Judgement signals a speaker's attitude towards a target's behaviour either in terms of social esteem or social sanction. The second system ENGAGEMENT comprises a choice between heterogloss and monogloss which refer to whether or not the speaker/writer includes other voices and opinions within the text. Within heterogloss there are further delicate choices related to whether the speaker wishes to open up or close down the proposition. GRADUATION is the resource for up-scaling or down-scaling ATTITUDE as seen in the contrast between: *she is very nice, she is nice* and *she is kind of nice*. In Text 4.3 we have marked up the short statement for Mood, Modality and Appraisal.

Text 4.3 The statement analysed for Mood, Modality and Appraisal

A

- I am [Mood] **just** [-Graduation -Force, intensity counter expectation] going to make a short statement to you on the **terrible** [Inscribed Judgement: social sanction -propriety] events that have happened in London earlier today, / [Residue] Declarative/Proposition – Statement (unmodalised))

- and I hope [Mood] you understand that at the present time we are **still trying** [inscribed Judgement +tenacity] to establish exactly what has happened, [Residue] Declarative/Proposition – Statement (Unmodalised but optative mood in process HOPE)

- and there is [Mood] a limit to what information I **can** give you [Inscribed Judgement: social esteem -capacity], [Residue] Declarative/Proposition – Statement (Unmodalised but rankshifted proposal median inclination in finite operator CAN)

- and I will [Mood] **simply try** [inscribed Judgement + Tenacity with-Graduation -Force, intensity counter expectation] and tell you the information **as best I can** at the moment [Inscribed Judgement: social esteem +capacity]. [Residue] Declarative/Proposal – Offer (Modalised high inclination finite operator WILL plus median inclination in construction AS BEST I CAN and)

B

- It is [Mood] reasonably [Graduation Force – intensification] clear that there have been **a series of** [Graduation +Quantification upscale] **terrorist** [Inscribed Judgement: social sanction – propriety] **attacks** [Inscribed: Affect: – Security] in London. [Residue] Declarative/Proposition – Statement (Explicit objective median)

- There are [Mood] **obviously casualties**, [inscribed affect -security with modal adjunct obviousness] both people that have **died** [inscribed affect -security] and people **seriously injured**, [inscribed affect -security with Graduation Force +intensification] [Residue] Declarative/Proposition – Statement (Implicit objective probability high)
- and our thoughts and prayers of course are [Mood] with the **victims** [inscribed affect -security] and their families [evoked affect -happiness]. [Residue] Declarative/Proposition – Statement (Implicit objective probability high)

C

- It is [Mood] my intention [Inscribed affect + inclination] to leave the G8 within the next couple of hours and go down to London [Residue] Declarative/Proposition – Statement (Explicit objective inclination medium)
- and (I) get [Mood] a report, face-to-face, with the police, and the emergency services and the Ministers that have been dealing with this, and then to return later this evening. [Residue] Declarative/Proposition – Statement (Unmodalised)

D

- It is [Mood] the will [Inscribed affect: +inclination] of **all the leaders** [Inscribed Judgement social esteem + capacity with Graduation, Force + Quantification] at the G8 however that the meeting **should** continue in my absence,[Residue] Declarative/Proposition – Statement (Unmodalised but high median obligation in finite operator SHOULD in rankshifted clause – proposal/offer)
- It is [Mood] the will [Inscribed affect: + inclination] of **all the leaders** [Inscribed Judgement social esteem +capacity with Graduation, Force + Quantification] that we **should** continue to discuss the issues that we **were going** to discuss, [Residue] Declarative/Proposition – Statement (Unmodalised but high median obligation in finite operator SHOULD in rankshifted clause – proposal/offer)
- and (that we) reach [Mood] the conclusions which we **were going** to reach. [Residue] Declarative – Declarative/Proposition (Unmodalised)
- Each of the countries round that table have [Mood] **some** [Graduation Force – Quantification] experience of the effects of **terrorism** [Inscribed Judgement: social sanction -propriety] [Residue] Declarative/Proposition – Statement (Unmodalised)
- and **all the leaders**, [Inscribed Judgement social esteem +capacity with Graduation, Force + Quantification] as they **will** [Mood high probability] indicate a little bit later, share our **complete resolution** [Judgement: Social Esteem +capacity with Graduation Force +intensification] to defeat this **terrorism** [Inscribed Judgement: social sanction -propriety]. [Residue] Declarative/Proposition – Statement (Unmodalised)

E

- It is [Mood] **particularly barbaric** [Inscribed Judgement: social sanction – propriety with Graduation Force +intensification] that this has happened on a day when people are meeting to try to help the problems of poverty in Africa [Inscribed Judgement: social sanction + propriety], and the **long term problems of climate change and the environment.** [Inscribed Judgement: social sanction + propriety with Graduation Force +intensification] [Residue] Declarative/Proposition – Statement (Unmodalised)

- Just as it is [Mood] **reasonably** [Graduation Force – intensification] clear that this is a **terrorist** [Inscribed Judgement: social sanction] **attack** [Inscribed: Affect: -Security], or a **series of terrorist** [Inscribed Judgement: social sanction -propriety with Force + Quantification] **attacks,** [Inscribed: Affect: -Security] [Residue] Declarative/Proposition – Statement (Explicit objective inclination medium)

- it is [Mood] also **reasonably** [Graduation Force – intensification] clear that it is **designed and aimed** [Inscribed Affect + inclination] to coincide with the opening of the G8. [Residue] Declarative/Proposition – Statement (Explicit objective inclination medium)

- There will [Mood high] be time to talk later about this. [Residue] Declarative/Proposal – Offer (Modalised objective– High inclination in finite operator WILL)

F

- It is [Mood] **important** [Inscribed appreciation + valuation] however that those engaged in **terrorism** [Inscribed Judgement: social sanction – propriety] realise that our **determination** [Inscribed Judgement: social esteem + tenacity] to **defend our values and our way of life** [Inscribed Judgement: social sanction + propriety] is greater than their **determination** [Inscribed Judgement: social esteem + tenacity] **to cause death and destruction to innocent** [Inscribed Judgement: social sanction + propriety] people in a **desire to impose** [Inscribed Judgement: social esteem + tenacity] **extremism** [Inscribed Judgement: social sanction - propriety] on the world. [Residue] Declarative/Proposition – Statement (Unmodalised objective)

- Whatever they do, it is [Mood] our **determination** [Inscribed Judgement: social esteem + tenacity] that they will never [modality high probability with negative polarity usuality] **succeed in destroying** [Inscribed Judgement: social sanction – propriety] what we **hold dear in this country and in other civilised** [Inscribed Judgement: social sanction + propriety] nations throughout the world. [Residue] Declarative/Proposition – Statement (Unmodalised)

Thank you.

The short statement consists of Declarative mood utterances, primarily propositions. Blair has situated himself as the authority figure with sole access to the knowledge, and the modality encoded within his utterances is primarily of the explicit objective kind. In other words, the modality is used to project what is packaged as common sense reasoning. He assumes the role of the primary knower (see discussion in Berry 2016, Muntigl 2009, and O'Grady 2020b). Knowledge is a resource to which people may claim access. Thus, we define a primary knower as a speaker who claims primary epistemic rights or is positioned by another speaker as having these rights. A speaker can signal a greater or lesser claim to knowledge. One way[15] in which speakers can signal a lowering of a claim to knowledge is through their modality choices. In the unmodalised propositions Blair does not use modality to signal a lowering of his epistemic rights: his claims that the international community has the will to fight and defeat terrorism, and that the bombings were designed to coincide with the G8 summit, are presented as non-contestable.

In the statement there are two modalised proposal/offers both of which contain the finite operator *will*. In proposals speakers do not signal their assessment of their access to knowledge but rather their access to action (Berry 1981a, 1981b). Blair presents himself as the primary actor which we define as a speaker who claims primary action rights or is positioned by another speaker as having those rights. As with knowledge, speakers can lower their claim to action. By choosing the finite operator *will* Blair lessens his actional claims. He signals a high inclination to tell what he knows though this is naturally lower than an unmodalised telling. Similarly, his future promise to talk more is also modalised, and signals a high degree of inclination to discuss his claim that the bombings were somehow connected with the G8 summit. In other words, he does not provide a 100% warranty that he will be able to perform the promised actions.

Within the statement there are a number of modals which are found in the Residue. Consequently, they have more limited scope. In the opening paragraph Blair post modifies the nominal *information* with the finite operator *can*. This has the effect of narrowing down his ability to perform the embedded offer of proffering information on the bombings. Similarly, in the next clause the construction *as best I can* signals his assessment of his inclination or ability to perform the offer. The finite operator *should* occurs twice in the Residue in paragraph D. It signals a median obligation towards the proposal/offer of the uninterrupted continuation of the summit and the discussions which are themselves embedded within two unmodalised propositions. Blair, on the one hand, asserts his rights to claim knowledge, but

---

15   Tag questions, evidentials and prosodic choices also play a role in how speakers signal a raising or lowering of the claim to knowledge. As there are no tag questions in the statement they will not be discussed further. Evidentials however, will be discussed under the Appraisal system of Graduation and prosody will be discussed in Section 4.5.

on the other hand acknowledges that he does not have sole actional rights sufficient to warrant the uninterrupted continuation of the summit.

We noted in fn 14 that Mood and Modality as a semiotic resource differs in its scope and realisation across languages. In paragraph A the subject ^ Finite *I hope* realises Declarative Mood but this is not the complete story. The process HOPE lexicalises a meaning choice that is expressed in other languages by Optative Mood. For example Teruya (2017: 221) describes the presence of the suffix *tai* as indicating Optative Mood which he labels as a subtype of Imperative mood in Japanese.[16] Blair, while asserting his role as primary knower, simultaneously signals his dependence on his hearers' understandings of the difficult situation he finds himself in and thus indicates that his access to knowledge is to an extent contingent on fast moving external events.

The short statement contains a number of attitudinal lexical items and their presence presents Blair's stance towards the bombings and the bombers. The lexical items *terrible, terrorist, terrorism* and *barbaric* signal negative judgement of the propriety of the bombers and of those who have engaged in similar actions. With the exception of paragraph D the short statement contains no reference to other voices: Blair neither reports security nor medical assessments of the ongoing and unfolding situation. In short, Blair presents himself as the sole source of information and by so doing signals his wish to close down the discourse space. In paragraph D, he presents himself as part of a larger group, namely as a leader of a G8 country and he aligns himself with the propositions expressed by his peers. This strategy results in a further contraction of the dialogue space and no room is made available for alternative voices and chimes with Blair's representation of his statement as enacting common sense.

As evaluations are inherently gradable, speakers may either turn up or turn down the strength of their evaluations. In the Appraisal framework this can take two forms

---

16   For instance, if we compare Japanese and English we see that translated pairs may have different Moods:

私	は	今	本	を	読んでいる	Declarative Mood (Japanese)
Watashi	wa	ima	hon	o	yondeiru	
I		now	book		am reading	
I am reading a book now						Declarative Mood (English)

今	本	を	読む	Imperative Mood (Japanese)
Ima	hon	o	yomu	
Now	book		read	
Read a book now				Imperative Mood (English)

今	本	を	読んでみたい	Imperative-Optative Mood (Japanese)
Ima	hon	o	yondemitai	
Now	book		read/want	
I want to read a book now				Declarative Mood (English)

(i) Focus and (ii) Force. Focus refers to the resource that boosts or scales down the prototypicality of an experiential category in an evaluation. Force is the resource that boosts or scales down the intensity or quantification of an evaluation. In the short statement there are 13 examples of Focus. In four cases Blair intensifies the prototypicality of the experiential category. For instance, people are not injured but are *seriously* injured, acts are not barbaric but are *particularly* barbaric, leaders do not share a resolution but rather a *complete* resolution and the bombings resulted not only in casualties but it is implied that the bombings were so heinous a series of actions that they resulted in *obvious* casualties. The sole down-scaling of the prototypicality of the evaluated experiential category *terrible* events indicates Blair's horror at what has occurred in London and by so doing implicates a negative judgement of the bombers and their supporters.

In the short statement force is used to downscale the strength of some claims: allowing some wiggle room if facts change. Blair states that it is *reasonably* clear that there has been a terrorist attack on two occasions. In this statement his caution seems unnecessary but at the same time he also claims much more controversially that it is *reasonably* clear that the attack was aimed to coincide with the G8. But again his downscaling provides him with some wiggle room. He indicates an upscaling of his *trying* on two occasions and thus succeeds in smuggling in a means of boosting his own face and signals an expectation that his audience will judge his diligence and perseverance in a positive manner.

4.3.2.1 *Summary of Interpersonal meanings*

To sum up, the interpersonal meanings enacted by Blair redound with a real world where terrorists and their supporters are to be judged as evildoers of barbaric acts. The use of explicit objective modality, articulated with evaluative language, presents Blair's viewpoint as common sense. World leaders responding to terrorists are to act in a restrained but forceful manner: their views are to be listened to and respected. They are not to be challenged but rather trusted and admired for their efforts in trying to keep their country safe. In this 'real' world Blair is not open to accusations that his policies contributed to radicalisation and resulted indirectly in events such as the bombings. The articulation of the interpersonal meanings in Blair's statement in total realise higher-order meanings which are not simply the accretion of the lexicogrammatical choices. Blair's thoughts enact a relationship with his audience; one in which he is positioned as the primary knower. This positioning is realised not, as would be expected, by unmodalised propositions alone, but rather through the judicious use of modality and evaluative language.

There is an opposition between terrorists and word leaders with the former being barbaric, violent, and unreasonable while the latter are civilised, restrained and cautiously determined. This opposition not only has the effect of othering the terrorists but also of creating two mutually exclusive groups. Blair presents all terrorists as equivalent and hence the world leaders with public support must unite against them in defence of civilised values. Yet, as noted, the required response is presented as temperate and cautious.

Were the leader making the televised address a more overtly bellicose one we would expect the speech to be formed out of directive proposals likely realised with imperative mood. Furthermore, we would expect the speaker to signal their assessment of the situation by signalling (i) a high degree of obligation on them and their audience to respond to the attack, and (ii) their own high inclination to act. Depending on whether the politician wished to be seen as a leader or as part of the collective we would expect the modality to be realised subjectively by finite verbal operators or objectively by expansions of the verbal group or through the use of passive voice. We would also predict the presence of modality realised by adjectives such as *keen, determined* etc. Our bellicose leader would likely deploy highly evaluative language signalling negative social sanction of the terrorists perhaps contrasted with positive social esteem of us. Blair himself employs some highly evaluative lexis such as *barbaric* but, as noted above, is relatively restrained especially in his representation of the victims. All of these hypothetical choices would have resulted in a different relationship between leader and public with very different real world consequences. Once again we see that meanings are as much about the potential unused choices available as they are about the choices made.

4.3.3   Textual Meanings

Language as wave is organised as a series of prominence peaks which weave texture throughout the unfolding spoken or written language. Within an English clause there are two sites for prominence: the first of which is located at the beginning, the other is usually located towards the end of the clause. The prominence peak at the beginning of the clause is Theme and the other one is New (see Forey & Thompson 2008, Halliday 1967, Halliday & Greaves 2008, Halliday & Matthiessen 2014, Hasan & Fries 1995 and O'Grady 2017). New, as will be discussed in the following section, is primarily signalled by the phonological system of Tonicity and hence, in this discussion of the written short statement, we will focus on Theme.

In Declarative Mood, Theme extends from the beginning of the clause and continues until the first element that functions in transitivity, which is usually but not always also the subject (Halliday and Matthiessen 2014).[17] It is known as the Topi-

---

17   The concept of Theme emerged first in the work of the Prague School scholar Vilem Mathiesus, and was further developed – in terms of the element which carried the lowest degree of communicative dynamism – by scholars such as Daneš and Firbas (see Mathiesus 1975; Daneš 1972, 1974; and Firbas 1987, 1992). Functional schools other than SFL have adopted from Prague scholars the similar concept of Topic and Comment (see Gómez-

cal Theme and is realised by either participant (subject or complement) or by a circumstance. If the Topical Theme is not subject it is labelled as a Marked Theme e.g. 4.1 is unmarked and 4.2 is marked.[18] In all examples the Theme is underlined. The * indicates that the examples are our own creations.

> 4.1   *The terrorists bombed the underground in London.
> 4.2   *In London the terrorists bombed the underground.

Prior to the Topical Theme there may be additional textual and interpersonal elements. Textual Themes are elements which expressly link the Theme to the cotext and are realised by elements such as continuatives, conjunctions or conjunctive adjuncts. Interpersonal Themes are elements which set up the speaker's/writer's assessment of the clause operating in its local context and are realised by elements such as vocatives, comment adjuncts and modal adjuncts. Example 4.3 illustrates.

> 4.3

And	now	people	sadly	in my opinion	this country	is	facing	an existential threat from terrorism
Conj Stru	Conj Adj	Vocative	Modal	Comment Adj	Subject	fin	Pred	Comp
Textual		Interpersonal			Topical			
Theme						Rheme		

In examples such as 4.4 and 4.5 the Theme is predicated on the Rheme with the Theme equating with the value and the Rheme as the variable (Halliday and Matthiessen 2014:122).

> 4.4   *It is the terrorists who bombed the underground
>   Theme (Value)   Rheme (Variable)
> 4.5   *It was the underground that the terrorists bombed
>   Theme (Value)   Rheme (Variable)

In these examples there is a single point of focus in the clause. In 4.4 it is the terrorists, while in 4.5 it is the Underground. The variable is presented as information which is recoverable while the value reveals the identity of the variable (Van Praet and O'Grady 2018). In 4.4 it is the terrorists and no one else who caused the bombing. In 4.5 the situation is reversed: the variable terrorist bombing is presented as

---

Gonzàles 2001). We have written elsewhere on the relationship between Theme and Topic (Bartlett and O'Grady 2019).

18   Within SFL there are scholars such as Fawcett (2001) and Berry (1995) who argue that, in English, the subject is always contained within the Theme. So those scholars would analyse Example 4.2 as having a theme with two experiential elements.

known but what they bombed is presented as the focus of the clause. In 4.6 we have what Halliday and Matthiessen (2014:92) label a thematic equative; the Theme = the Rheme.[19]

4.6   *<u>What the terrorists did</u> was to bomb the London Underground,

In examples such as 4.7 the speaker projects a thought or desire[20] and the projecting clause is the Theme or stating point of the integrated complex.[21]

4.7   *<u>I expect</u> that we all will rally around to defeat the terrorist threat

Similarly in 4.8, where the dependent and the following independent clause form into a tight nexus, the initial dependent clause is the Theme of the complex.

4.8   *<u>If we are vigilant and united</u> we have nothing to fear from these
terrorists

Theme is an enabling resource which functions to orient and locate the clause in its context and, as such, it enables the logogenetic growth of experiential and inter-personal meaning within a text (Halliday & Martin 1993:244; Matthiessen 1995; and Halliday & Matthiessen 2014). It is not simply a unit of clause structure but the result of a choice which is sensitive to context. In Text 4.4 we have notated the Thematic choices and we will discuss below. Within the figure any ellipted Themes which we have reinserted are contained within round brackets.

Text 4.4 Theme analysed in statement

1   **I** am just going to make a short statement to you on the terrible events that have happened in London earlier today,

2   **and I hope you understand that at the present time** we are still trying to establish exactly what has happened,

3   **and there** is a limit to what information I can give you,

4   **and I** will simply try and tell you the information as best I can at the moment.

---

19   Predicated theme and thematic equatives are more commonly known in the literature as clefts and pseudo-clefts respectively.

20   The same point naturally applies for a projected locution; but as the short statement contains no projected locutions we will illustrate the point through a mental rather than a verbal projection.

21   *I expect* could be analysed in certain contexts as an interpersonal Theme – in which case *we* would be the topical Theme. In theory at least the tag question test could disambiguate the structures e.g.,
   • *I expect that we will all rally around the flag don't I?* = <u>*I expect* is Theme</u>
   • *I expect that we will all rally around the flag won't we?* = *I expect that we* is Theme,

 5 **It is reasonably clear** that there have been a series of terrorist attacks in London.
 6 **There** are obviously casualties, both people that have died and people seriously injured,
 7 **and our thoughts and prayers** of course are with the victims and their families.

 8 **It** is my intention to leave the G8 within the next couple of hours
 9 **and (I)** go down to London
10 **and (I)** get a report, face-to-face, with the police, and the emergency services and the Ministers that have been dealing with this,
11 **and then (I)** to return later this evening

12 **It is the will of all the leaders at the G8** however that the meeting should continue in my absence,
13 (**It is the will of all the leaders at the G8**) that we should continue to discuss the issues that we were going to discuss,
14 **and (that we)** reach the conclusions which we were going to reach.
15 **Each of the countries round that table** have some experience of the effects of terrorism
16 **and all the leaders, as they will indicate a little bit later**, share our complete resolution to defeat this terrorism

17 **It is particularly barbaric** that this has happened on a day when people are meeting to try to help the problems of poverty in Africa, and the long term problems of climate change and the environment.
18 **Just as it is reasonably clear** that this is a terrorist attack, or a series of terrorist attacks ,
19 **it is also reasonably clear** that it is designed and aimed to coincide with the opening of the G8.
20 **There** will be time to talk later about this

21 **It is important however that those engaged in terrorism realise that our determination to defend our values and our way of life** is greater than their determination to cause death and destruction to innocent people in a desire to impose extremism on the world.
22 **Whatever they do**, it is our determination that they will never succeed in destroying what we hold dear in this country and in other civilised nations throughout the world.
Thank you.

One of the most interesting aspects of the Thematic structure of the short statement, as alluded to earlier, is that Interpersonal themes are found only in projecting clause themes such as *It is reasonably clear* which allows Blair to thematise his evaluation of what the likelihood of what has happened being a terrorist attack. By deploying explicit modality with the phrase *it is reasonably clear* Blair removes everything but the modalised evaluation from the Theme which hence is made prominent. This has the effect of suggesting that Blair's assessment is common sense and serves to close down the discourse; albeit that the addition of the adverbial *reasonability* signals only a median probability. It further presents his assessment as an agreed upon starting point for the clause which he will then develop in the Rheme. While the information presented as New in the Rheme in clauses 5 and 18 is uncontroversial that in clause 19 is not!

The opening Theme selection is *I* which Berry (2013) notes is the most frequent theme choice in dialogue – see also clauses 8, 9 10 and 11. Thus Blair orientates his message deictically in himself as an interlocutor in a conversation with his audience; though, as noted above, he very much enacts a role where he is the primary knower. There is mostly a constant theme selection (see Fries 1995) and the propositions expressed are orientated to Blair. Blair chooses a Marked Theme in clause 2 which presents his projected desire of our understanding as the starting point of a clause informing us of the authorities intended actions. The next Theme selection is the dummy element *there* and this choice allows Blair to present the entire experiential content of the clause as News; the audience is informed of the limits of what can be told. He deploys the same theme construction in clauses 6 and 20.

In the second paragraph Blair's selection of *our thoughts and prayers* as Theme references the Rheme in the previous clause which presented the existence of a number of causalities as an unsurprising fact. It also moves the focus deictically away from an exclusive focus on Blair and orientates the statement towards a community that is presented as being united with Blair. The third paragraph as noted above thematises Blair. There is a change of focus in the Theme selection in the fourth paragraph where Blair angles his message through the lens of the international community. He thematises the absolute commitment and unity of the international community in both opposing terrorism and in not being cowed by terrorist acts. By so doing, Blair indexes his membership of two communities: one where he is united with his audience and the other where he is part of the international community. This has the effect of implying a dichotomy between the international community which includes the audience and the terrorists. This allows for Blair to orientate his condemnation of the bombings as *particularly barbaric* but not towards the victims as would be expected but rather as an attack on the norms of the international community. His final theme choice in the penultimate paragraph – the dummy *there* – is motivated by the prior co-text: Blair has set up his thesis that the bombings were an attack on international norms as a topic that he will develop in the future. The Theme choices in the final paragraph orientate towards the futility of the terrorists' actions: no matter what they attempt their actions will prove to be futile. The theme selections in the final paragraph further reify the contrast between the terrorists and the rest of us.

4.3.3.1 *Summary of textual meanings*

To sum up: the textual meanings enacted by Blair redound with a real world where terrorists and their supporters are to be judged as evildoers of barbaric acts who are outside the pale. Their attacks are aimed at the international community and not at any single nation. There is neither space nor need to reach out to the terrorists, who are enemies who must be faced down by greater determination. They exist outside the borders of the civilised community. In this real world there is nothing to be gained by attempting to explicate the terrorists' motivations, and hence no possible blame can be assigned to others whose actions may potentially have resulted in terrorist blowback. Once again we can see that Blair's thought is realised by lexicogrammatical choices which allow him to sound simultaneously personally and institutionally authoritative.

While it is, of course, not possible to predict how a thought is worded, we might expect a more bellicose and perhaps less subtle leader to have chosen some different options. For instance, had the leader wished to produce a text which more explicitly condemned the terrorists in order to stoke up tensions he/she could have chosen cleft structures where the terrorist's actions were explicitly equated with inhumane results. Similarly, our fictional leader would have had the option of producing modalised pseudo-clefts where the theme would present an obligation to do something as generally agreed.[22] We would also expect the victims, the country and perhaps the international community to be thematised in order to more explicitly oppose 'us' from the terrorists. Such choices would add to the condemnation and the promotion of alterity while also foregrounding a plan of confrontational actions.

4.3.4 Logical meanings

Now that we have seen the meanings realised by lexicogrammatical choices within clauses, it is time to examine the logical meanings realised by the sequencing of clauses. Halliday and Matthiessen (2014:443) state that the relation between clauses within a clause complex are based on two fundamental relationships: expansion and projection. The former refers to where the following clause expands the preceding clause through the systems of elaboration, extension and enhancement. The latter refers to the projection of the following clause as a wording or a thought. As

---

22 Though of course the same structure can be used to reduce tensions were that the intention. Compare 'What we <u>must/have to/are required to etc.</u> do is fight them' with 'What we <u>mustn't/can't shouldn't etc.</u> do is over-react'.

Table 4.2 Expansion and Projection based on H & M 2014

Symbol	System	Gloss
		Expansion
=	Elaboration	Restating, specifying in greater detail, commenting or exemplifying.
+	Extension	Adding a new element, giving an exception or stating an exception
x	Enhancement	Qualifying some circumstantial feature of time, place, cause or condition.
		Projection
"	Locution	The secondary clause is presented as a wording i.e., a direct or indirect quotation
'	Idea	The secondary clause is presented as a thought i.e., a direct or indirect thought.

Halliday and Matthiessen (ibid:443) state 'Expansion relates phenomena of the same order of experiences while projection relates phenomena of one order of experience (the processes of saying and thinking) to phenomena of a higher order (semiotic phenomena – what people say and think)'. The options are set out in Table 4.2

Text 4.5 illustrates the logical relations between the clauses within the text.

Text 4.5 The logical relations within the statement

1　1　　I am just going to make a short statement to you on the terrible events
　　　　　= [[that have happened in London earlier today]],
　　+2 α and I hope
　　　'xβ you understand
　　x'γ that at the present time we are still trying to establish x[[exactly
　　　　xγ1 what has happened,]]
　　+3 and there is a limit =[[to what information I can give you]],
　　+4 and I will simply try and tell you the information
　　　　as best x[[I can at the moment]].

....

2　1　　It is reasonably clear x[[that there have been a series of terrorist attacks
in London]].

3　1　1　　There are obviously casualties, =[[both people =[[that have died]]
　　　　and people seriously injured]],
　　+2 and our thoughts and prayers of course are with the victims and
　　their families.

....

4   It is my intention ⁺[[1 to leave the G8 within the next couple of hours
        ⁺2 and go down to London
        ⁺3 and get a report, face-to-face, with the police, and the emergency
        services and the Ministers =[[that have been dealing with this,]]
        ⁺4 and then to return later this evening.

....

5   1 It is the will of all the leaders at the G8 however
            ˣ [[that the meeting should continue in my absence]],
            +2 that we should continue to discuss the issues
            ˣ[[that we were going to discuss,]]
            +3 and reach the conclusions =[[which we were going to reach.]]

6   1   Each of the countries =[round that table] have some experience of the
    effects of terrorism
            ⁺2 α and all the leaders,
                ˣβ [[as they will indicate a little bit later,]]
            α share our complete resolution to defeat this terrorism.

....

7   1α It is particularly barbaric ˣ[[that this has happened on a day]]
        ˣβ when people are meeting
        ˣβ to try to help the problems of poverty in Africa,
        ⁺γ and the long term problems of climate change and the environment.]]]]

8   1   1 α   Just as it is reasonably clear
                ˣ [[that this is a terrorist attack, or a series of terrorist attacks,]]
            ⁺2 it is also reasonably clear
                [[1 that it is designed
                +2 and aimed to coincide with the opening of the G8.]]

9   There will be time to talk later about this.

....

10   1 It is important however,
            [[that α those =[[engaged in terrorism realise
            'β that our determination ˣ[[to defend our values and our way of life]]
                is greater than their determination ˣ[[to cause death and destruction
                to innocent people in a desire to impose extremism on the world]]]]

11   xβ Whatever they do,
     α   it is our determination
              ˣ[[that they will never succeed in destroying
              ˣ [[what we hold dear in this country
              and in other civilised nations throughout the world.]]]]

     Thank you

As can be seen, the written version comprised 6 paragraphs and was formed out of 11 clause complexes. The logical relationships mostly relate phenomena of the same order of experience to one another. There are exceptions. The first is the first paragraph, where Blair projects his inner mental activity of hoping, and his projected desire of his audience's mental activity as understanding his desire as wordings. It is the only occasion in the statement that Blair indexes his own mental activity and gives his audience insight into his thoughts. The second is in clause complex 10 and is contained in an embedded clause, which itself modifies a relational process. It refers to the mental activity of the terrorists, but only to impose an obligation on the terrorists' mental activity. They need to understand the strength of determination opposing them.

The remainder of the speech comprises relationships between extra somatic phenomena as they are construed by Blair. The first part of the statement unfolds as a sequence of extensions: subsequent clauses add to the assertion of the bombing by detailing the results of what has happened, stating Blair's plan of action, indicating how the G8 meeting will unfold and mentioning the experiences other countries and leaders have had with terrorism. The second part of the statement unfolds through a mixture of extension and enhancement. Blair not only adds new elements to his statement but also qualifies the extent of the barbarity through an implicit comparison of those who set off bombs against those who meet to resolve global issues. He illustrates the futility of the bombers' cause by qualifying the extent of our determination to resist their attempts.

While one could well imagine our alternate leader adopting a similar strategy in order to close down discussion and to rule out negotiation, we might also imagine that our leader would relate phenomena of a different order and hence his audience would be presented with a representation of this thoughts, predictions and words as to the way ahead. In order to stir up feelings our leader could project his shock and disgust or, indeed, he could project the imagined emotional states of victims and their relatives. Furthermore, he could project his and our determination to extirpate the terrorists and their supporters; construing a world where a violent reaction was the sensible and responsible response. For our fictitious leader the bombing was a declaration of war and not a crime. Once again we see that the possible choices not made are as significant as the choices made.

4.3.4.1 *Summary of Logical Relations*

To sum up, the realised logical relations in the statement construe a world where facts are extended and qualified by a leader. The projection of his mental activity redounds with a world where he, as a trusted and honest figure, has the right to anticipate that his audience will comply with his expectations. The imposition in the mental activity of the terrorists, coupled with the accretion of circumstances construing the determination to resist the terrorists, construes a world where the alterity of the bombers must be defeated. There is no room for discussion or negotiation. By not choosing logical relations which projected feelings and emotions, Blair attempted to calm down the situation by ensuring that his message was grounded in semiotic phenomena and divorced from somatic phenomena.

4.4 SUMMARY OF METAFUNCTIONAL RELATIONS

The combination of Blair's lexicogrammatical choices exist in a redundancy relationship with the semantic stratum and a metaredundancy one with the context, as illustrated by Figure 4.1.

The 'doings' that are realised is a world containing mutually opposing forces. Blair construes an 'us' and a 'them' who we are to resist and not treat as potential negotiable opponents. This has the effect of delegitimising the world view of the terrorists and, indeed, rendering them to be nothing other than a threat which must be dealt with. Political leaders such as Blair are deserving of trust and will act as reasonable and judicious proxies in achieving our assumed shared goal of defeating the terrorists. Citizens are passive and must wait for leaders such as Blair to clarify what has happened and what will happen. In other words, the recombinations of lexicogrammatical choices realise higher order meanings which allow Blair to construe the world and enact his social position with his audience. At the same time his lexicogrammatical choices perturb the meanings which are possible and, with overuse, may become trite. A possible example is the use of the lexeme *clear* which,

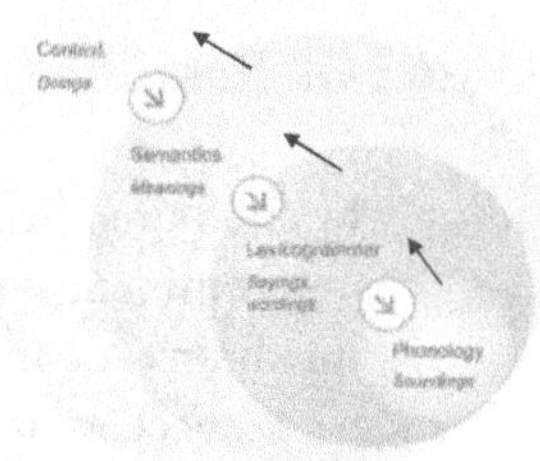

Figure 4.1 Summary of realisational relations

rather than enact objective and explicit authority, may through overuse become a discourse marker.

Blair's speech, itself the result of the articulation of his choices, is simultaneously an instance of a political speech. Its valuer is dependent upon its relation to all the possible speeches which could have been appropriately produced by a political leader responding to a terrorist bombing and the associations it evoked with other communicative acts such as relaying bad news, expressing sympathy, condemning violent acts and urging a cautious response. The speech itself is recognisable as appropriate as Blair's communicative intentions are realised by lexicogrammatical choices which are themselves organised in a way that matches expectations. Previous languaging events have (i) resulted in choices which have led to the emergence of self-organising patterns which trigger expectations, and (ii) constrained the appearance of other lexicogrammatical forms. Blair, in other words, deploys choices from a sub-potential of the language system (Halliday and Matthiessen 2014), and these choices split and then recombine through the resetting of the probabilities of what can and cannot be articulated (Lemke 2000:182). In other words, the choices that can be made are not free, but constrained by what has gone before, and by the mixing and ordering of lexicogrammatical forms. So, as the patterns emerge, the logic of the A-curve suggests that certain choices will do the majority of the work, and that the emerging system will be dynamic, with individual structures potentially increasing or decreasing in frequency. The circle in Figure 4.1 which presents meaning choice in terms of metaredundancy relations is thus not the complete story as it does no more than capture a synoptic moment. We will examine the expectations created by syntagmatic ordering in Chapter 5.

Up to this point we have presented Blair's speech as if it were an instance of written language. However, it was not, and in the next section we will examine the meanings realised prosodically in order to see if they are congruent with the lexicogrammatical choices, or to see whether they realise independent meanings which exist in a redundancy relation with the semantic stratum, and in a metaredundancy relation with the context. Simply put, we will investigate what, if anything, the prosodic choices added to the semiosis.

4.5   PROSODIC MEANINGS

Speakers make meaning prosodically by chunking their messages into tone groups. Each tone group contains one or more prominent syllables, with the final prominence being the locus for the major pitch or tone movement in the tone group. Perceptually prominent syllables are experienced as having higher pitch, and being louder, than non-prominent syllables. They are also likely to occur on a rhythmic beat (Ladd 2008). While tone groups may contain up to six prominent syllables, they are more likely to contain between one and three. The initial prominent syllable is the onset syllable, which sets the 'key' for the entire tone group; and it may be higher, around the same, or lower than the previous onset (Brazil 1997, Halliday 1967, Halliday and Greaves 2008). The approach to intonation that we adopt is known as 'British School Intonation'. For information as to how it compares and contrasts with other approaches to intonation, such as ToBI, see O'Grady (2017) and Westera et al. (2020). ToBI, unlike British School intonation, dispenses with tone movements and, instead, notates the speech signal as a series of transitions between tones, which are turning points of pitch, and are visualised as turning points on the F0 curve by software designed to analysis speech (see Pierrehumbert and Hirschberg 1990; Jun 2005; Arvaniti & Fletcher 2020). Like British School Intonation the approach transcribes the chunking of the speech signal – and the combination of the final prominent syllable, plus the following phrase and boundaries accents, are equivalent to British School tone movement. Cruttenden (1997) is an interesting descriptive comparison of the strengths and weaknesses of both approaches. Ladd (2008) and O'Grady (2013a) illustrate how to translate between both approaches.

Speakers parcel out their message, tone group by tone group. Each tone group presents a single piece of information or one idea (Halliday 1967; Chafe 1994; Cruttenden 1997). In speech, tone groups are often bounded by pauses and contain a single main tone movement. However, where there is no pause, the actual boundary between consecutive tone groups is difficult if not impossible to determine; see Barth-Weingarten (2018) for the fullest discussion in the literature of how to determine tone group boundaries. Yet, determining the actual placement of tone group boundaries is not of functional significance, as intonational meaning is projected by the *core of the tone group*[23], which is the part commencing with the first prominent syllable and continuing until the final prominent syllable – known as the tonic or nucleus (Brazil 1997; Cruttenden 1997; Crystal 1969; Greaves 2007; O'Grady 2010 etc.). Non prominent syllables signal to the hearer that the speaker projects that the meaning realised by the production of the lexical item is available either from the context or cotext. Prominent syllables signal that the lexical item realises a meaningful choice which is likely to be freshly introduced into the discourse. Hence the hearer is primed for the importance of the upcoming lexical item for the achievement of the speaker's communicative goal.

---

23   We have had to coin the very inelegant descriptor 'core of the tone group' because, unfortunately, in the literature there are numerous and competing descriptions of the part of the tone group commencing with the first prominent syllable and continuing until the final prominent tonic syllable.

Text 4.6 The structure of the tone group

> (non prominent syllables) (**prominent syllable <other prominent and non prominent syllables>) tonic syllable** (non prominent syllables)
>
> A (i) that **those engaged** in **ter**rorism
> (ii) with the po**lice and the e****mer**gency services
> (iii) and in other **civilised na**tions throughout the world
> Tone group with Onset and Tonic
>
> B (i) in **Lon**don
> (ii) **ear**lier today
> (iii) de**signed**

Tone group with tonic only Text 4.6 details the options, with optional elements enclosed in round brackets, and illustrates with examples taken from the short statement. The potential tone group core is in bold. Group A contains tone groups with more than one prominent syllable, while group B contains tone groups with a single prominent syllable.

It is immediately apparent that the intonationally meaningful part of the tone group can extend beyond the tone group core. Prominent and tonic syllables are themselves parts of lexical items and the meaning signalled by speakers' intonational prominences includes the lexical item containing the prominence. In group A we can see that there may be non-intonationally meaningful syllables prior to the first prominent syllable. The onset syllable, as we will see below, is the site of the key selection, while all prominent syllables represent a selection from an existential paradigm: the speaker signals that, out of the available senses that could have been chosen, the particular one was chosen (Brazil 1997). For instance in A(iii) 'civilised' has been chosen rather than 'unenlightened', 'uneducated', 'barbaric' and 'backwards', and contributes to the othering of the bombers. Had the speaker chosen not to make a syllable in the lexical item *civilised* prominent, the word would have been presented as previously available. Blair's message would have presumed that his audience did not need to be told that there are nations which were not civilised. Tonic syllables represent the focus of the message or, as Halliday and Greaves (2008:103) gloss it, as the portion of the message that the speaker is drawing particular attention to. It represents the Culmination of the New. New information is information that the speaker presents as if it is New to the hearer; and thus all the tonic syllables in A and B were presented as if they were freshly introduced into the discourse. Lexical items found after the Focal item are Given in that they are presumed to be shared by the speaker and the hearers. In A(iii) the burden of the message is on 'nations' signalling Blair's view that the world is divided into different types of nations rather than different types of people.[24] The post tonic and the pretonic lexical items 'throughout the world' and 'other' are presented as predictable and recoverable from context. Blair neither needs to emphasise that Britain is part of an ordered international community and that the international community is not confined to a particular region. New information, in most cases, includes all the lexical items contained between the tonic and onset unless the onset or other pretonic items are available in the context.

In the examples where there is only a tonic syllable, such as in the B examples, the tonic syllable usurps the function of the onset syllable, and if the tone group is not itself final it is the site of a key choice. The tonic syllable is the locus for the major pitch movements, which in English are: fall, rise, level, fall-rise and rise-fall. The functional significance of the tones will be described below.

Intonation, as conceptualised in this book, realises textual meaning through the systems of tonality (the choice of how to segment the speech signal into meaningful information units), and tonicity the prominence choices within tone groups. Tone movement realises two types of meaning: interpersonal meaning where it signals the speaker's certainty or lack of certainty; and also logical meaning where it signals the tactic relations between information units. Key choices signal both interpersonal and textual meaning.

Text 4.7 presents our intonational markup of the short statement.[25]

Text 4.7 Intonation in the short statement transcribed

1   – I am just going to (**H**) <u>make</u> a <u>short</u>
2   \ <u>statement</u>
3   \/ to you on the <u>ter</u>rible events
4   / that have <u>hap</u>pened
5   \ in <u>London</u>
6   \/ (**L**) <u>ear</u>lier today
     (.............)
7   \/ and I <u>hope</u> you under<u>stand</u>

---

24   This is, in reality, an odd projection as the bombers were British; a fact which was not determined at the time but one that was not unpredictable.

25   The conventions used are \ = fall (Tone 1); / = rise (Tone 2); – = level (Tone 3); \/ = fall-rise (Tone 4); and /\ = rise-fall (Tone 5). For reasons explained in O'Grady (2010, 2017) and also Tench (1990, 1996) we do not transcribe so called compound tones (13 and 53). The tone groups are presented on their own line. Salient or prominent syllables are underlined, with the final one being the tonic or nucleus. The **H** and **L** in tone group initial position signal key; and the **H** and **L** in final position signal termination (see Brazil 1997; O'Grady 2014, 2017). The functions realised by key and termination choices will be explained in the discussion of the text as and when needed.

```
 8   \ that at the (H) present time
 9   \/ we are still trying to establish exactly
10   \ what has happened
11   / and there's a limit
12   \ to what information
13   / I can (H) give you
14   \ and I'll simply try and tell you
15   – the information as
16   \ as best I (L) can at the moment
        ..............
17   \ it's (H) reasonably clear
18   \ that there have been a … a series of terrorist attacks
19   \ in (L) London
        ..............
20   – there are (H) obviously
21   \ casualties
22   \/ both people
23   / that have died
24   \ and people seriously injured
25   \ and our (L) thoughts and prayers of course are with
26   \ the (H) victims
27   \ and their families
        (..............)
28   \ it's my (H) intention to
29   \ leave the GEight
30   \within the next couple of hours
31   \ and [I] go down to London
32   / and get a report
33   \ face to face
34   \with the police and the emergency services
35   \ and the ministers that have been (L) dealing
36   / with this
37   – and then [I] to
38   – return
39   \ later this (L) evening
        ..............
40   \ it is the (H) will of all
41   \ the leaders at the GEight
42   / however
43   \ that the meeting
```

44   – should con<u>tin</u>ue
45   \ in my ab<u>sen</u>ce
46   \/ that we should continue to di<u>scuss</u> the is<u>sues</u>
47   \ that we were going to dis<u>cuss</u>
48   / and [that we] <u>reach</u> the con<u>clus</u>ions
49   \ <u>which</u> we were <u>go</u>ing to (**L**) <u>reach</u>
      ....
50   – (**H**) <u>each</u> of <u>the</u>
51   \ <u>coun</u>tries around that <u>ta</u>ble has some ex<u>peri</u>ence
52   \ of the (**H**) <u>effec</u>ts of <u>ter</u>rorism
53   \ and all the (**L**) <u>lead</u>ers
54   \ as they will in<u>dic</u>ate
55   \ a little bit <u>la</u>ter
56   \ <u>share</u> our <u>com</u>plete reso<u>lu</u>tion
57   \ to de<u>feat</u> this (**L**) <u>ter</u>rorism
      ....
58   \ it's (**H**) par<u>tic</u>ularly <u>bar</u>baric
59   \ that this has <u>hap</u>pened
60   \ on a <u>day</u> when
61   / <u>peo</u>ple are <u>meet</u>ing
62   – to <u>try</u> to
63   / <u>help</u> the <u>prob</u>lems of <u>pov</u>erty in Af<u>ri</u>ca
64   \ and the <u>long</u> term <u>prob</u>lems
65   \ of <u>cli</u>mate <u>change</u> and the (**L**) en<u>vi</u>ronment
      ....
66   \ just as it is (**H**) rea<u>son</u>ably <u>clear</u>
67   \ that this is a \/ <u>ter</u>rorist at<u>tack</u>
68   \/ or a <u>se</u>ries of terrorist attacks
69   \ it is also rea<u>son</u>ably <u>clear</u>
70   – that it <u>is</u>
71   \/ de<u>signed</u>
72   / and <u>aimed</u>
73   \ to coin<u>cide</u>
74   \ with the <u>open</u>ing of the GEight
      (..............)
75   \ there will be (**H**) <u>time</u> to
76   \ to <u>talk</u> (**L**) <u>la</u>ter about this
      ....
77   \ its (**H**) im<u>por</u>tant however
78   \ that <u>those</u> en<u>gaged</u> in <u>ter</u>rorism

79 / rea<u>lise</u>
80 \ that (**H**) <u>our</u> deter<u>mi</u>nation
81 / to de<u>fend</u> our <u>val</u>ues
82 \ and <u>our</u> (**L**) <u>way</u> of life
83 \ <u>is</u> <u>grea</u>ter
84 \ than <u>their</u> deter<u>mi</u>nation
85 \ to <u>cause</u> <u>death</u> and de<u>struc</u>tion
86 \ to <u>in</u>nocent <u>peo</u>ple
87 \ in a de<u>sire</u> to im<u>pose</u> ex<u>tre</u>mism
88 / on the (**L**) <u>world</u>
    (.............)
89 \ what<u>ev</u>er they (**H**) <u>do</u>
90 \ it is <u>our</u> deter<u>mi</u>nation
91 \ that <u>they</u> will never suc<u>ceed</u>
92 \ in de<u>stroy</u>ing
93 \ what <u>we</u> <u>hold</u> <u>dear</u>
94 \ in <u>this</u> <u>coun</u>try
95 \ and in other ci<u>vi</u>lised <u>na</u>tions throughout the world
    (.............)
96 \ (**L**) <u>thank</u> you

Table 4.3 details Blair's prosodic choices

Table 4.3 Tones and Key in the short statement

Tone	Number of
\	63
/	14
–	9
V	9
Λ	0
Key	
High	15
Mid	77
Low	3

4.5.1   Prosodic Textual meanings

The short statement comprises 96 tone groups/information units. Within the literature there is an expectation that if all things are equal then (i) a tone group will correspond to a clause e.g. (17); (ii) in the case of long clauses they will likely be segmented into two tone groups with the division corresponding to the Theme/Rheme boundary e.g. (82); (iii) non core clausal items such as circumstances are likely to be found within their own tone groups e.g. (45); (iv) embedded and rankshifted clauses are likely to be found within their own tone group e.g. (47) and (89).

What we would not expect to see are tone group divisions within grammatical constituents at the rank of group or phrase. Yet within the text we find examples of tone group divisions in nominal and verbal groups. For instance in (1) and (2) the nominal group *short statement* is presented in two tone groups. By so doing Blair ensures that the object, the *statement*, and its quality or length, *short*, are presented as separate chunks of information. In (15) and (16) the post modification of the nominal group is found within its own tone group where it signals that the limitation is of equal status to the noun it modifies. Similarly, in (40) and (41), the predeterminer *all* is separated from the remainder of the nominal group signalling that the mass – as well as the identity – of the people are of equal salience.[26] A similar effect is achieved in (50) and (51). (28) and (29) and (75) and (76) illustrate highly unusual tonality choices. Blair places part of a non-finite verbal group – the particle – in a different tone group from the process.[27]

The effect is to suggest that he is carefully searching for the most appropriate lexical item to construe the projected future actions. This presents the statement as deliberative and spontaneous. However, as we shall see in the following paragraphs Blair's key choices signal a different story.

The term key was first introduced into intonation studies by Henry Sweet and it referred to the general pitch height of the tone group which is signalled by the initial pitch level of the first prominent/salient or onset syllable. Key is a relative concept and can be high, mid or low as compared with the key of the previous tone group. The options and the functions they realise are outlined below. To illustrate, a high key can be followed by a further high key or a step down to mid.

---

26   (20) is also of interest even though, technically, the tone group/information unit boundary is between a post verbal adverbial and the nominal group. Nonetheless the effect is similar to make salient the 'obviousness' of what has occurred and present it as equally important to what has occurred. By so doing the audience are invited to reflect on what is obvious and to consider its import prior to Blair producing the prospected lexical items.

27   While it was noted earlier that it can be difficult if not impossible to determine the exact location of tone group boundaries, in these particular cases there was a long pause between particle and process.

Table 4.4 Key and its meanings

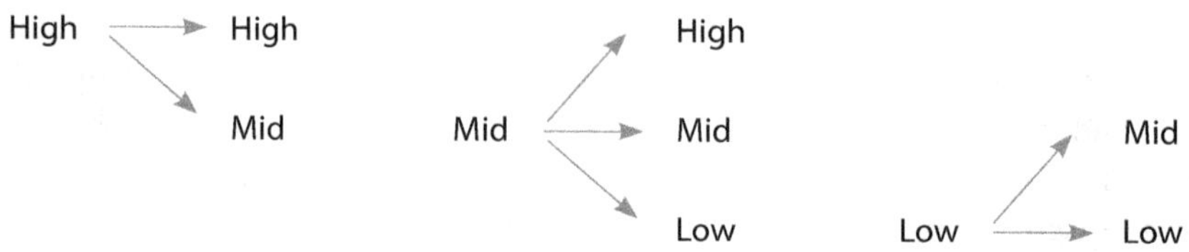

High Key	The speaker signals the proposition expressed in the following will be contrary to the previously created expectations.
Mid Key	The speaker signals the proposition expressed in the following will be accordance with the previously created expectations.
Low Key	The speaker signals the proposition expressed in the following will be equivalent to the previously created expectations.

Numerous scholars (e.g. Brazil 1997, O'Grady 2017, Tench 1996, Wichmann 2000) have proposed that a high key, that is usually preceded by an extended pause, and which follows an immediately prior fall to low in the speaker's pitch range signals, at least in prescripted read aloud text, a shift to a new topic. These units which may be considered a unit above the tone group have in the literature been labelled as paraphones, paratones (this is the name I shall use), pitch sequences and phonological paragraphs Tench (1996). Speakers use the resource of high key preceded by a low pitch to segment their messages into paratones. This has the effect of conveying the thought out and pre-planned nature of discourse and is something that is especially noticeable in radio and TV news broadcasts,

We used Praat (Boersma and Weenink 2021) to assist our auditory analysis of an audio file of the short statement. The software allowed us to visualise both the sound wave and the F0 curve which assisted us in identifying prominent and tonic syllables, pauses and pitch movements. We measured the Hertz values for the vowel centres of all onset syllables which enabled us to confirm our auditory impression of Key and final terminals. To illustrate with an example: the end of TU 16 was pitched at 81.35Hz whereas the following onset syllable was pitched at 150.1Hz with an intervening pause of 1.67 seconds. Thus, there was convincing evidence that TUs 16 and 17 were in different paratones. In Text 4.7 the dotted lines notate paratone boundaries while bracketed dotted lines indicate points in the text where one (but not both) of the high pitch reset or preceding low pitch were found at a point of possible syntactic completion. These are, in other words, points in the statement where Blair had the option of signalling the completion of a topic. In an investigation of the meaning potential of the short statement O'Grady (2013b) tasked 11 native speaking individuals with reading the same text and found that their selection

Table 4.5[28] The form and function of Blair's articulation of the short statement

Phase of the Text	Tone group numbers	Paratone	Tone group numbers
Abstract	1–6	1	
Orientation 1	7–16		1–16
Incident	17–27	2	17–19
		3	18–27[29]
Repercussions	28–39	4	28–39
Interpretation	40–49	5	40–49
Orientation 2	50–57	6	50–57
Evaluation	58–65	7	58–65
Incident Repeat	66–68	8	
Thesis	69–76		66–74
Deferral	75–76	9	75–76
Argument/grounds	77–88	10	77–88
Argument/conclusion	89–95	11	89–95

of paratones was distinct from Blair's.[30] Thus, paratone structure is not determined by the lexicogrammatical structure and Blair's decision to segment his text evidences careful pre-planned strategic choices.

Table 4.5, based on O'Grady (2013b), relates Blair's projected paratone structure with the various phases of the text (Labov 1972) in order to illustrate which phases of the text Blair presented as chunking together. This allows us to see how Blair foregrounded and backgrounded propositional information and created a listening pathway aimed to best get his message across.

As can be seen, with three exceptions, Blair's projected paratone structure correlates with the phases of the text. The first exception is that he chunks the Abstract and Orientation 1 into a single paratone. More significantly, he does the same for the Incident Repeat and the Thesis. The effect is to merge the stages into a single chunk so that the Incident Repeat and the Thesis represent a single proposition: one entails the other. In other words, the Thesis is not a point that needs defending or explaining: the fact that the international community was the target of the bombing

---

28   As tone group, 96 signals a polite closing; we have not included it within the phases of the text.

29   The paratone boundary here and between paratones 8 and 9 is not certain as there was no fall to low pitch signalling a closure of paratones 3 and 8. But there was an extended pause and a high key which suggested the opening of paratones 4 and 9.

30   It is further worth noting that, whereas Blair articulated the text in 96 tone groups, the other readers ranged from 68 to 93 with a mean of 83 and a standard deviation of 7.6.

requires no further justifications. Blair presents the incident as two paratones: the first states what occurred and where it happened, while the second reports on the damage caused and expresses the expected for sympathy.

Perhaps the most salient phonological feature of the statement is Blair's choice of tonic and pre-tonic prominences. We would predict that once a lexical item has been introduced into a discourse it becomes recoverable, and that it is likely to be articulated without a pitch prominence or as a pronoun for the remainder of the short statement. Yet if we trace the lexeme *terrorist* in the short statement we see that it does not follow the expected pattern. Text 4.8 details the occurrence of the lexeme in the short statement.

Text 4.8 Terrorist/ism – reference chain and prominence choices

18   terrorist attack (tonic)
    ↓ 18 tone groups
36   they (coreferential with Terrorists, non-prominent)
    ↓ 16 tone groups
52   terrorism (tonic)
    ↓ 5 tone groups
57   terrorism (tonic)
    ↓ 2 tone groups
59   this (coreferential with terrorists, non-prominent)
    ↓ 8 tone groups
67   terrorist attack (tonic)
    ↓ 1 tone group
68   terrorist attacks (non-prominent)
    ↓ 2 tone groups
70   it (coreferential with terrorist attack, non-prominent)
    ↓ 8 tone groups
78   terrorism (tonic)
    ↓ 11 tone groups
89   they (coreferential with terrorists, non-prominent – contrastive with us)
    ↓ 2 tone groups
91   they (coreferential with terrorists, pre-tonic prominence – contrastive with us)

The number refers to the number of the tone group where the lexical item is located. As can be seen, despite being prefigured by *terrible events* in tone group 3, the first overt mention of *terrorist* is in tone group (18) where, as a freshly introduced lexical item, it receives tonic prominence. However, what is unexpected is that 34 tone groups later *terrorism* is once again made prominent in tone group (52). As noted above, the choice of the high key signals that the content of the information unit is contrary to previously created expectations, and the selection of *terrorism* as the focal point of the tone group projects it as the lexical item with the highest news value. Blair ensures that the destruction caused by terrorism remains very much the nub of his discourse, and that a potential reconstrual involving marginalisation and alienation is prohibited.

Five tone groups later, *terrorism* is once more selected as tonic. Had it been ellipted from the context it is hard to see how the object of the material process *defeat* could have been misconstrued. But by being once again made focal, the semantic field of *terrorism* and all the associated negative consequences remain imprinted in the audience's consequences. Towards the end of his statement Blair's prominence patterns foreground the alterity of the terrorists, which has the effect of backgrounding discussion of the fate of the victims and of what may have caused the terrorists' actions. Thus, prosodic choices that initially appeared redundant are in fact creative and enable the speaker to produce subtle meaning through the recombination of lexico-grammatical and prosodic choices.

4.5.1.1 *Summary of Prosodic Textual meanings*

The interplay of the systems of tonicity, and the projected paratone structure, project the short statement as deliberative and thoughtful, while simultaneously signalling Blair's on-line processing. The effect is to construe a world where he is recognised as a thoughtful leader who represents civilised nations and opposes barbarity and threats that emerge from outside civilised space. This has the effect of conveying the partly reassuring impression that the bombings were not a completely unexpected event. His government had planned for – and presumably undertaken countermeasures against (albeit ones that proved ineffective) – the possibility of bombing. His tonicity choices especially foreground the alterity of the terrorists and of the ideas they embody.

4.5.2 Prosodic Interpersonal Meanings

There are two chief ways of representing interpersonal meaning prosodically. The most important system is tone.[31] Speakers choose falling tone when they wish to convey information and when they wish to add propositional content to their hearers' knowledge base. Rising and fall-rising tone signal that content is not assumed to add to their hearers' knowledge base. Falling tone is speaker directed whereas rising and fall-rise tone are hearer centred (Cruttenden 1997). Level tone signals an opt out of the immediate communicative situation; the speaker is perhaps focusing on assembling their thoughts or simply articulating routine information (Brazil 1997,

---

31   Tone is plurifunctional in that it signals logical as well as Interpersonal meaning. We will examine how Blair's tone choices projected logical meaning below.

Cruttenden 1997, Gussenhoven 2004, O'Grady 2010, Tench 1997). As would be expected in a statement comprising declarative mood utterances the overwhelming majority (66%) (see Table 4.3 above) of Blair's tone choices are falling. They signal that he is construing a world where he transmits information and his audience receives it. This reinforces his enactment of the role of primary knower. He neither expects nor requires his audience's input. His prosodic choices accordingly construe a hierarchical world where leaders speak and citizens listen. There are no examples of rise-fall tone; Blair does not intrude in his report by projecting his heightened commitment. Blair's choice on seven occasions of level tone construes two different meanings: the first of which is to signal that he is struggling to find the most accurate words to convey his intended meaning e.g. tone group (70); and secondly that the actions he reports are routine (Tench 2003), e.g. tone groups (37– 38), and are what would be expected of a leader in his position. The effect is to further construe a world where political leaders have and deserve trust.

Fall-rise tone is selected primarily in the earlier part of the statement in order to project a shared context between Blair and his audience; the implications he projects are common to his audience and himself. Rising tone is selected primarily to signal continuation within propositions e.g. tone group (63) – where the recombination of tone choice and the lexicogrammar is to signal that the information unit containing the rising tone contains incomplete information and is dependent on what follows, and this will be discussed more fully below. However, in tone group (13) the rising tone is hearer directed and signals that Blair is asking his audience to accept the reasonableness of his proposition. This is sole occasion in the text where the audience is directly invoked as a coparticipant in the semiosis. Lexically, Blair could have achieved a similar effect had he produced the tag *isn't there*.

We noted in the previous section that Blair uses the resource of high key preceded by a low pitch to segment his statement into paratones. Two high keys choices – tone groups (52) and (75) – however, do not signal the beginning of a new paratone. Instead they signal that the audience will find the content of Blair's proposition contrary to the expectations that the co-text has created. The first focuses attention on what is presented as surprising. Terrorism is a global problem and not one restricted to countries with active military engagements in the Middle East. The second signals that perhaps, contrary to expectations, there will be time to examine how the bombings and the summit were linked, which generates an implication that, as a responsible leader, Blair is withholding important and relevant information pertinent to his thesis until a more appropriate time. His use of high key on this occasion indexes his authority as a political leader.

4.5.2.1   *Summary of Prosodic Interpersonal meanings*

Blair's tone choices reinforce the construal of a world where leaders are to be trusted with speaking and getting on with the job at hand. The rising tone in (13) signals Blair's expectation that his audience will acquiesce with his projection of what has happened, why it has happened and how it is to be responded to. High key is used to reinforce Blair's message of a binary division between civilised nations which were the target of the London bombings and the others who committed the violence. In this world the bombings were not provoked or caused by the political and military activities of the civilised nations, but simply arise because the bombers and their backers are not members of the civilised nations. Accordingly they must be opposed, and neither appeased nor negotiated with.

4.5.3.1   *Prosodic logical meanings.*

Tone choices in concurrence with lexicogrammatical choices have the potential to knit stretches of speech into coherent propositions by (i) indicating the relative status of the propositional information contained within the individual tone group (Esser 1988); and signalling (ii) whether the proposition has been completed; or (iii) whether it requires a hearer's input to complete it. Tench (1996) also Halliday and Greaves (2008), O'Grady (2017) and Pierrehumbert and Hirschberg (1990) state that tone choice presents the content expressed by a tone group as signalling major vs minor information and whether or not the information is complete or not. The relationships are set out below:

> / ^ \ = Major Incomplete information ^ Major complete information
> \ ^ \ = Two separate pieces of major information
> \ or \/ ^ / = Major information ^ Minor information
> \/ = Major information + reservation/implication
> – ^ \ Speaker opt out.

A rising tone, or series of rising tones, followed by a falling tone, signals that a proposition is presented as a series of information units closed by the falling tone. The rising tone(s) signals that the message is as yet incomplete. Conversely, if the rising tone follows the falling tone it signals minor information which glosses the previous proposition. The lexical content of the tone group is usually a circumstance of time, place, manner etc. An independent fall-rise signals major information but adds an interpersonal gloss. Level tone signals that the speaker is either focusing on assembling his or her words, and is not focusing beyond the immediate tone group, or that the proposition expressed is routine and does not require linking with the rest of the speaker's message. A series of falling tones presents the tone groups as separate information units. Thus we would expect to see the following relations:

1   A falling tone signals the link between two paratactic clauses unless the first clause is completed by a circumstantial element. In that case the clause final tone group will contain a rising tone.

2   A rising tone signals the link between a hypotactic and paratactic clause and the paratactic clause is completed by a falling tone unless it contains a final circumstantial element.

3   A falling tone signals the link between a paratactic and a hypotactic clause which itself is signalled by a rising tone.

4   A fall-rise tone may substitute in final position for a fall, and otherwise for a rise, in order to project an implication or signal a greater degree of certainty.

The short statement, as detailed above, comprised 11 clause complexes. Table 4.6 lists the tactic links signalled by the lexicogrammar and the tone choices.

As can be seen on most but not all occasions, Blair's choice of tone is predicted by the tactic link created by the lexicogrammar and in line with the predictions set out above. However, there are occasions where Blair's lexicogrammatical and tone choices are not congruent: one does not predict the other; the redundancy relation is not 100%. On three occasions, despite the paratactic clause containing a final circumstantial element, it was articulated with a falling tone e.g.

4.9
14   \ and I'll simply try and <u>tell</u> you
15   – the in<u>form</u>ation as
16   \ as best I (**L**) <u>can</u> at the moment

Blair chooses to select a fall and not a rise on tone group 16. He chooses to present the final tone group as an independent chunk of information and not as an information unit which modifies the prior proposition. By so doing the final tone group is presented as representing the goal of his message (O'Grady 2016): the proposition is not concerned with the telling of information but rather with his ability at the time of speaking to tell the information.

4.10
77   \ its (**H**) im<u>port</u>ant however
78   \ that <u>those</u> en<u>gaged</u> in <u>terrorism</u>
79   / rea<u>lise</u>

In tone group 77 Blair neither places the circumstantial element 'however' in its own tone group nor produces a rising tone to signal that the preceding proposition is to be modified by the following information. The effect is that tone groups are presented as two independent pieces of information. And this subtly alters the meaning of Blair's proposition: rather than simply being a reflective remark targeted at

Table 4.6 Logical relations in the short statement: Prosodic and Lexicogrammatical

Clause	#TG	Link	Tone	Congruent
1	6	Paratactic + Circ	V	Yes
	10	Paratactic + Circ	\	No
	13	Paratactic + Circ	/	Yes
	16	Paratactic + Circ	\	No
2	18	Paratactic	\	Yes
3	24	Paratactic	\	Yes
	27	Paratactic	\	Yes
4	30	Paratactic	\	Yes
	31	Paratactic	\	Yes
	36	Paratactic	/	No
5	42	Paratactic + Circ	/	Yes
	46	Paratactic	V	Yes
	49	Paratactic	\	Yes
6	52	Paratactic	\	Yes
	57	Paratactic	\	Yes
7	60[32]	Paratactic	\	Yes
	61	Hypotactic	/	Yes
	63	Hypotactic	/	Yes
	65	Hypotactic	\	No
8	68	Hypotactic	V	Yes
	69	Paratactic	\	Yes
	71	Hypotactic	V	Yes
	74	Paratactic	\	Yes
9	76	Paratactic	\	Yes
10	77	Paratactic + Circ	\	No
	88	Paratactic + Circ	/	Yes
11	89	Hypotactic	\	No
	95	Paratactic	\	Yes

the TV audience, his words also serve to prefigure a warning targeting those who supported the bombers.

The rising tone in tone group 36 signals continuation. Blair presents the post verbal preposition phrase as the start of a sequence of actions which he will undertake. By considering the logical meaning produced by prosodic choices we can see

---

32   The tone group/information unit and clause boundaries do not fully coincide. The lexical item *when* is not chunked with the material preceding the β clause *when people are meeting.*

the motivation for what appears, at first glance, to have been an unusual tonality choice. Blair wishes to explicitly project his intended actions sequentially but also he does not wish to signal his meeting with the relevant ministers and their actions, prior to his projected meeting with them, as information dependent on his future actions. Despite Blair's physical presence in Scotland, at the time of speaking, his government is presented as a well-oiled machine and by implication he himself as the captain of a well-functioning ship.

4.11
35   \ and the <u>min</u>isters that have been (**L**) <u>dealing</u>
36   / with <u>this</u>
37   – and <u>then</u> [I] to

On two occasions Blair presents hypotactic clauses as if they were pieces of independent information.

4.12
58   \ it's (**H**) par<u>tic</u>ularly <u>bar</u>baric
59   \ that this has <u>happen</u>ed
60   \ on a <u>day</u> when
61   / <u>peop</u>le are <u>meet</u>ing
62   – to <u>try</u> to
63   / <u>help</u> the <u>prob</u>lems of <u>pov</u>erty in <u>Af</u>rica
64   \ and the <u>long</u> term <u>prob</u>lems
65   \ of <u>cl</u>imate <u>change</u> and the (**L**) en<u>vi</u>ronment

Here we can see that a hypotactic clause when people are meeting to try to help the problems of poverty in Africa and the long term problems of climate change and the environment has been produced as a sequence of 5 tone groups of which the last two contain falling tone. The effect is to present the hypotactic clause as dependent on the clause articulated in tone groups 58 to 60 but at the same time to signal a list containing two problems: the first poverty in Africa and the second the long term climate change problems.

This example also illustrates that tone choices occur at points within propositions where presumably speakers can be relatively confident that they will not be interrupted. In the stretch of speech which runs from tone group 58 to 65 the only point where a hearer might feel justified in intruding and competing from the floor is after tone groups 63 and 65. None of the remaining tone groups express a potentially complete proposition. Thus the status of the rising tones in tone groups (61) and (63) might not be identical. In (61) Blair presents the fact that *people are meeting* as minor information which retrospectively identifies the date of the meeting. But in (63) the proposition expressed by the tone group is prospective and the rising tone signals continuation. It is the first part of a list. The second part itself is presented as comprising two independent propositions of equal status.

The opening paratone of the short statement contains two propositions presented as a sequence of two paratactic clauses with the second extending the content:

(A) There are obviously casualties both people that have died and people seriously injured

(B) And our thoughts and prayers of course are with the victims and their families

But as the following example illustrates the two clauses were in fact articulated as 8 tone groups or information units.

4.13

1   – there are (**H**) obviously
2   \ casualties
3   \/ both people
4   / that have died
5   \ and people seriously injured
6   \ and our (**L**) thoughts and prayers of course are with
7   \ the (**H**) victims
8   \ and their families

There are a number of points where Blair could potentially have articulated a complete proposition, namely after tone groups 2 or 5 for the first proposition and 7 and 8 for the second. Therefore, the choice of non-falling tone in tone groups 3 and 4 is not dependent on a speaker's need to maintain the floor. Instead, the choices signal the backgrounding of propositional information: casualties implies that people have died. Logically, tone groups 3, 4 and 5 elaborate the proposition articulated in tone groups 1 and 2. The falling tone accompanying tone group 5 does not, in other words, only signal the completion of the proposition; it signals that the proposition itself is complete and does not require hearer intervention. The second proposition comprises three tone groups all with falling tone; thus presenting them as separate and equal pieces of information.

4.5.4.1 *Summary of Prosodic Logical Relations*

As is to be expected Blair presents his information mostly as a sequence of tone groups which are predicted by the lexicogrammatical choices. However, the exceptions illustrate that prosodic choices are not determined by the lexicogrammar and that speakers are free to disentangle the choices in order to produce subtly different meanings. Blair's choices allow him not only to reassure his audience but also manage to signal a warning to those he projects as supporting the bombing. His choices redound with a world where political leaders such as himself are both trustworthy reassuring figures and determined opponents of extremist views and actions. In other words the prosodic choices reinforce the meanings realised by the recombinations of lexicogrammatical choices and, in the vast majority of occasions, are fully predictable from the lexicogrammatical choices. But the exceptions illustrate that the prosodic choices which are not determined by the lexicogrammar result in recombinations that realise novel higher order meanings. In other words, they fill a function which may be copied and hence potentially in time being transformed from serviceable noise into criterial features.

4.6   A REVISED STRATIFIED MODEL

In this chapter we have examined the concept of stratification in order to illustrate the importance of metaredundancy as a mechanism through which language self-organises into a dynamic and adaptive system. We used a text to illustrate that higher order meanings predict, and are predicted by, choices in the lower strata. Many but not all of Blair's prosodic choices were predicted by the lexicogrammar; and the lexicogrammatical choices themselves were predicted by the semantic choices that could be articulated by a Prime Minister responding to a major terrorist attack. However, we have also seen that some of Blair's prosodic choices while in accord with the available semantic choices were not predictable from the lexicogrammatical choices. As noted here, and in the previous chapter, it is precisely the redundancy relations between strata which creates interstratal tension and that the emergent, less-predicted realisations add a layer of meaning that may itself be the engine of future semogenetic growth.

We have seen that speakers such as Blair have a degree of freedom which allows them to supplement their lexicogrammatical meanings and produce novel meanings. Textually, this arises from tonality, tonicity and paratone initial key choice; interpersonally, from tone and key choices; and, logically, from tone choices. As the prosodic choices are discrete and typological the meanings they create in combination with the lexicogrammatical choices redound with the allowable semantic choices, They can be summarised as follows:

- The chunking of the elements within the clausal core into separate tone groups/information units results in the clause having more than one focus and alters the distribution of information.
- Placement of a tonic focus on items which have been previously mentioned ensures that these items are re-presented as focal and that they are a goal towards which the message strives.

- Key choices may segment speech into paragraph type chunks, or signal the speaker's assessment of how the hearer will perceive the upcoming proposition.
- At clause boundaries tone choice signals: (i) the speaker's expectation of a response; and (ii) the speaker's degree of certainty of the proposition uttered.
- Within and between clauses tone choices signal logical meanings by signalling the tactic relations between tone groups.

The prosodic meanings combine with lexicogrammatical choices in real contexts to allow for the creation of novel meaning and also may result in stable meanings that spread through the system. Thus the relationship is not (a) below but rather (b)

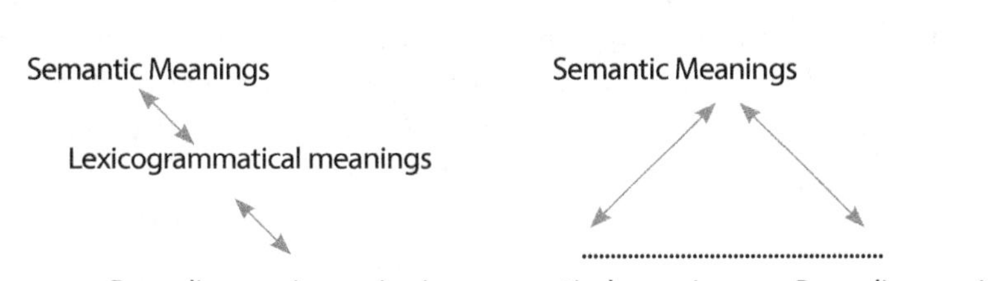

In (b) both lexicogrammatical and prosodic meanings are located as part of the content strata and both exist in a redundancy relationship with the higher semantic stratum and in a metaredundancy relationship with the non-linguistic context. The dashed line between the lexicogrammatical and the prosodic meanings signals that while there is no direct relationship between them, the fact that both redound with the higher semantic stratum ensures that they have developed in parallel, and thus in most cases converge, so that they appear to predict one another. For instance, expanding on a point made in Chapter 2, it is not simply the case that declarative mood predicts and is predicted by falling tone, but rather that the semantics of certainty and telling predict and are predicted by declarative mood and simultaneously by falling tone. Thus, declarative mood and falling tone converge and, were the system to reach stability, a fully redundancy relationship between the lexicogrammar and the prosody would emerge. But language as a living adaptive and dynamic system does not stabilise, or if it does it dies! New semantic meanings emerge which allow for the disassociation and the recombination of lexicogrammar and prosody affords the creation of both novel meanings which over time, and through use, may themselves emerge as stable combinations of lexicogrammatical and prosodic resources.

Language is not formed from the accretion of sound/meaning pairs. It is a stratified system with content and expression planes. The content plane, as we have shown, consists of more than one stratum, with the important addition that 'the lexicogrammar' itself consists of two independent meaning making components

– the lexicogrammar in Halliday's terms and the prosody – both of which exist in a redundancy relation with the semantics. Halliday's view of stratification resembles the earlier proposal by Hjelmslev (1963, 1975) who viewed language as consisting of meaningful elements (the content plane containing pleremes) and meaningless elements (the expression plane containing cenemes). The sign, the union of content and expression, connects form with substance which itself represents how a particular language perspectivises purport, the unformed and unanalysed potential thought and sound. Taverniers (2011) convincingly argues that Halliday's reinterpretation of Hjelmslev's model has blurred some important semiotic distinctions leading to an underspecified semantics in Halliday's model. Halliday's model, focused on realisation relations and metafunctional cycles, does not easily accommodate the triadic association of form, substance and purport. Specifically, she questions the equation of content form and content substance with lexicogrammar and semantics. Hjelmslev argued that substance and purport are only different in relation to perspective and that substance is purport formed within a particular language. This is clearly not the same as expressing the stratal differences as redundancy relations; and hence the Hallidayan stratification of content into semantics and lexicogrammar is best considered an innovation rather than a reworking of Hjelmslev's earlier proposal.

We argue by adopting a metafunctional approach, the Hallidayan approach provides a more powerful description of how people make meaning through languaging activities. Conversely, on the expression plane, the Hallidayan equation of expression form and substance with phonology ignores the association between substance and form. There is no discussion of how the biological capacity is used to form the amorphous sound wave into discrete meaningful phonological choices, as demonstrated in Chapter 3. The Hallidayan description of the use of language is in terms of instantiation. We have shown above that this downplays the semogenetic potential of the recombination of lexicogrammar and prosody. The relation between lexicogrammar and intonation is orthogonal and a reflection of two independent redundancy relations with the semantics and not a matter of the phonology realising the lexicogrammar (see also O'Grady and Bartlett 2019; and O'Grady 2020a).

To conclude, we have illustrated that only the presence of a stratified system comprising (meta)redundancy relations can explain the flexibility required for human languaging which itself is the glue that binds societal relations. Yet, the recombining of choices into novel meanings is only half the story. Language, while flexible, simultaneously forms predictable patterns. Indeed, without the metastable background of language structure and systems of contrast and equivalence, it would not be possible to recognise novel meaning and produce flexibility. Of course, as we have argued, the stability of structure is itself an illusion created by the timeframe of a human's semiotic lifespan. In a similar manner a wave strikes us as an ephemeral structure, while a rock is, by contrast, solid and permanent. Yet, as the physicist Carlo Rovelli reminds us, both structures are actually formed out of the vibrations of subatomic quanta that maintain their structure for a while (Rovelli 2016). The difference lies in our perception of 'a while'. In the next chapter we will examine predictability and assume a temporal scale equivalent to a human's semiotic lifespan.

Chapter 5

Prospection: The emergence of target states and common ground in speech

5.1   INTRODUCTION

We pointed out in Chapter 2 the obvious fact that people do not speak to produce grammatical structures but rather to convey experiential and interpersonal meaning. Text is both goal orientated and undetermined. Speakers in pursuit of a communicative goal are usually unaware of the actual wording of the message they will produce. Speech is created on the fly and is both reactive and predictive. It depends on what has been said, and on what is allowable in a particular context. It constrains what is possible in the future. In this chapter we will explore the constraints which operate in order to illustrate that, while general principles exist, the actual mechanisms of how language patterns emerge are language specific. First though we briefly set out our vision of how spoken text emerges in real time.

Here we examine how language unfolds in real time for speakers and hearers. It is important to note that we are not claiming that the mechanism we illustrate does more than describe used language; there is no claim that the mechanism we describe has any psychological reality. We simply show how the conventions of a language enable meaning to emerge across a text and how the interlocutors' expectations as to what will come next are both afforded and constrained by the rules of the particular language at any particular time and in any particular context. Accordingly, in this chapter, we will not discuss the underlying choices but rather restrict ourselves to surface forms. We do this to illustrate the importance of the concept of prospection by which we mean that an earlier element creates the expectation of a further element occurring. Earlier elements may determine the production of a later element as, for instance, the presence of a determiner in English mandates the later occurrence of a nominal element. Through use, certain elements may fuse together into formulas – in certain contexts the production of later elements is entailed by the earlier ones.

Spoken text emerges as a process of negotiated co-construction between interlocutors who share sufficient common ground; the presumed background information shared by the speaker and the hearers (Stalnaker 2002:701). Speech is experienced as a temporal sequence of words and phrases that conform to an interlocutor's expectations, based on their previous experiences of interacting with the language in particular, and of operating in the individual communicative contexts. Language use has both a synchronic and diachronic reality: it is simultaneously what is spoken in the moment and the result of historical accident. Speakers employ the linguistic resources handed down to them to achieve their communicative purposes, but at the same time their individual purposes can only be achieved by the affordances produced by the linguistic system they and their hearers have access to.

Linguists such as Hopper (1987) have produced cogent arguments rejecting traditional sentence level grammars as being unable to account for how discourse operates in real time. Hopper proposes that grammar is a real time metastable and contingent phenomenon, in which meaning is at once a system of contrasts and relations, but also a system that is deferred (cf Derrida 1973, 1982:21). By this Hopper means that linguistic structure emerges from generations of discourse interactions. But, as discourse interactions are ongoing, it is emergent and cannot ever fully emerge. It is a jumble of elements – some of which are on the way in, while others are on the way out. As individuals develop language in particular contexts in time and space, through initially interacting with caregivers and, subsequently, with other members of their community, they are in contact with only a small fraction of the semiotic potential of their language at any one time. They develop the linguistic patterns or codes which are prevalent in their communities: initially the patterns found within their families and, later, the more standardised ones found in more formalised settings such as schools (Bernstein 1971). As we will see in the following sections, the linguistic patterns and expectations that emerge are both biologically and culturally formed.

5.2   THE EMERGENCE OF ORDER

Semiosis emerges within a human being from the interaction between the two primary modes of experience: the conscious, or Innenwelt, and the material, or Umwelt (Halliday 1992). The child, like presumably all other mammals, experiences material processes as outside the soma while mental processes are experienced as occurring within the soma.[1] Halliday recounts the story of an infant whose initial

---

1   The distinction between the outer and the inner world is an illusion (Thibault 2020). We agree with Thibault that we as organisms are not distinct from the world but part of it; for instance our skin is permeable, and the air we inhale is as much inside us as outside us. Nonetheless we argue that humans do experience the world as things that happen in our bodies, and things that we observe outside the skin, and hence the distinction between Innenwelt and Umwelt is of importance and should be maintained.

sign was a very high pitched squeak which his caregivers interpreted as their son commenting on things he perceived as being of interest in the material world. The child's sign was not self-directed. As a material event it represented an ostensive stimulus that others were able to interpret in a contextually appropriate manner. The child's squeak functioned as a bridge between his own projecting consciousness and the material world. Through repeated practice in situated contexts a predictive link may emerge between proto-semiotic gestures such as the high pitched squeak and material stimuli. The materiality of the external element is, we claim, of importance. As well as being 'doomed to semiosis' we are also trapped by our biological capacities. Thus, for a difference or meaning to emerge it must be sensible, in the sense described in Chapter 4.

Our biological heritage has allowed us to move beyond our genotype and incorporate technology into what we can label an extended phenotype – showing that the boundary between us and the world is neither fixed nor determined by genes – (Dawkins 1982). The exchange of meanings between us and our technology, such as microscopes, allows us to construe differences – for example in cellular organisms that are invisible to the naked eye. We are able to construe the data from microscopes into semiotic differences which we add to the scientific common ground. This also, of course, implies that differences that are currently insensible may, in the future, become sensible; while others may remain impervious to semiotic construal and hence will never form part of our reality.

What we perceive as real is what emerges from our interaction with the world. We internalise material sensations, be they vibrating air molecules or configurations of light as meaningful semiotic elements, and incorporate them as part of our shared knowledge (Halliday and Matthiessen 1999).[2] Thibault (2020 loc:2659) notes that people do not so much adapt to their environments as modify them through their languaging practices, which consist of meaning exchanges formed out of utterances that leave traces in the world. In other words, the exchange of meanings enables people to internalise the flux they traverse, and form it into reproducible semiotic patterns which they share in order to establish common ground and shape the context we operate in (Halliday 1978).

McGregor (2019) argues that, for semiosis to emerge, the interaction between Innenwelt and Umwelt is necessary but not sufficient. Semiosis is a triadic process where a child learns to jointly interact with an external caregiver and an external

---

2   To illustrate, the period of human gestation is constrained by biology and lasts on average for 268 days with a variance of 37 days. Yet, this biological fact only became a social fact in the 20th century when it became part of the shared background. Prior to that there are reports of men, away at war or at sea, accepting paternity for babies who were born after an apparent gestation period of a year.

object, and this represents the beginnings of symbolic thought and hence language in the child. Tomasello (2008, 2019), as we noted in Chapters 2 and 3, similarly argues that it is the ability of humans (and humans alone) to recognise and copy intentional actions, which subsequently led to the emergence of linguistic communication. And, revisiting the argument in Chapter 2, if one accepts that ontogeny recapitulates phylogeny, we may be witnessing how language emerged from protolanguage in every normal child's development. Here we can see the major distinction between even proto-semiotic gestures, such as the child's squeak, and animal calls, such as the warning signs produced by vervet monkeys. Vervet meaning is fixed; a particular call entails the vervet's assumption of the presence of a particular type of predator. In other words, the vervet's system has emerged and reached senescence. No new meanings are possible. For the child, the relation between the sign and the stimuli is predictive or redundant, but not fixed. She is free to employ the sign to refer to various things that she finds interesting: its use is not confined to its original use. To illustrate, the daughter of one of the authors produced the protoword ['vaɪiː] at around age 18 months. Initially she used it only if in the co-presence of her water bottle but, subsequently, her use of the protoword expanded and she used it to signal a request for a drink in the absence of her water bottle, her perception of rain on the window and her acknowledgement that she had spilled liquid on the table.

A gesture such as the high-pitch squeak or protoword ['vaɪiː] (i) develops a relation between the perceived material stimulus and the inner organism; and (ii) integrates the infant with his/her caregiver by coordinating their actions and allowing them to attend to the same material stimulus (Thibault 2004a, 2004b). Over time, interacting languageless communicators may develop the genesis of a proto-semiotic system as has occurred in the case of the emergence of sign languages such as Nicaraguan sign language, and Al-Sayyid Bedouin sign language in Israel. After the success of the Sandinista revolution, Nicaraguan deaf children who had previously been scattered and isolated throughout the country, where they had communicated with their caregivers through idiolectal home sign, were brought to a newly formed boarding school in the capital, Managua. The new government imported teachers from overseas to teach both lip reading and finger spelling. It was soon noticed that the children communicated among themselves through a combination of gesture and their idiolectal home signs. While such communications were first frowned upon as being detrimental to the children's ability to learn language, it was soon realised that younger children who had not been isolated were systematising the pidgin-like signs used by their older counterparts into a rule governed communicative code. Linguists, depending on their theoretical position, have interpreted the emergence of Nicaraguan sign language very differently. For instance Kegl (2002), from an innatist generative view, argues that the emergence of Nicaraguan sign language proves that language is hard wired within the brain. Conversely others such as Tomasello (2008) have seen the development of Nicaraguan sign language as a learned activity resulting from the interaction of a language ready brain, external stimuli, shared attention and the human need to communicate. We, as the reader will expect, subscribe to the latter view. In the next few paragraphs we will turn to typological evidence of the type of communicative codes which have emerged. To do this we will first survey word order. We do this because in speech it is through the language specific syntactic ordering that meaningful elements emerge and through their emergence create expectancies.

Our claim is that spoken discourse comprises chains of lexical elements/structural units, which are both grammatical and appropriate to their context and the historical development of the individual language. Languages are commonly classified as having seven types of word order. Table 5.1, based on Dryer (2013), presents information on the word order of 1376 languages. It can be seen that the first 3 orders are the most frequent, comprising 83% of the entire data set – the A curve again! – and indeed 97% of the 1188 languages which Dryer classes as having a dominant word order.

Table 5.1 Word order across languages based on Dryer (2013)

Word order	Number	Example of languages
Subject Verb Object	564	English, Mandarin, Spanish, Russian, Xhosa
Subject Object Verb	488	Japanese, Korean, Basque, Hindi, Persian
Verb Subject Object	95	Gaelic, Welsh, Arabic, Berber, Tahitian
Verb Object Subject	25	Nias, Malagasy, Taglog, Kiribati, Chinook
Object Verb Subject	11	Hixkaryana, Tuvaluan, Mangarrayi
Object Subject Verb	4	Nabeb, Wik Ngathana, Kxoe
No dominant order	189	German, Greek[3], Hebrew, Hungarian, Cree

---

3   We are conscious of the fact that the word order of Greek is a matter of dispute. Some linguists class Greek as an SVO language (e.g. Tomlin 1986), while others such as Phillippaki-Warburton (1985), classify it as VSO. We accept Dryer's classification as we feel that it respects Givon (1988) who cautions against (i) pigeonholing all languages as having a rigid word order and (ii) deciding on the word order in the absence of corpus evidence. Furthermore, the short sentence *John loves Maria* can be translated into Greek as either (i) O Ιωάννης αγαπάει την Μαρία (SVO) or (ii) Την Μαρία αγαπάει ο Ιωάννης (OVS) with the subject and object marked by the nominative and accusative case markers o and την respectively. The belief that Modern Greek is an SVO language may arise as a result of Givon's claim that in languages with flexible word order the most important information is fronted – with subjects tending to outrank objects (1988: 275).

Table 5.1 makes clear that word order is not dependent on genetic relationship. English, and German[4] are part of the same sub-family but differ in word order, while having the same word order as less related or unrelated languages. Givon (1988) notes that word order across languages may be the result of cognitive constraints aimed at minimising information processing while simultaneously boosting information salience. Thus, the exact word order of an utterance in any language, while constrained by the language's characterology[5], depends on the interplay of a number of factors such as task importance and informational predictability. For instance in English the canonical word order is SVO, but utterances such as 'Outside stood a little angel' (Martinez-Caro 1993), and 'Honey, bears love to eat' (Halliday and Matthiessen 2014) are both grammatical and acceptable in context.

As we noted earlier, the production of an element prospects the production of a following element. For instance, in English the production of a determiner predicts the following production of a nominal element; the production of a nominal group predicts the following production of a verbal group and so on. In Japanese, however, the class of determiner is not present (Teruya 2004:221) and so different prospections arise. In Japanese the production of a nominal element may predict either the occurrence of a further nominal element or a verbal element. Thus, speakers engaged in meaningful discourse within their languages produce differently ordered chains which generate different prospections. In this way rather than seeing structures as being schema that are generated and then filled, we see structure as emerging in the act of production. In Chapter 6 we will argue that prospection, or the emergence of structure in the act of production, extends beyond the clause and operates at the level of text and beyond. In a follow-up we volume we will further demonstrate how the process extends to ideological formations and is central to how societies see themselves.

5.3   GRAMMATICAL CHAINS IN THREE LANGUAGES

In this chapter we will not only look at data from English but also from Greek and Japanese in order to examine prospection in discourse. We are, however, able to describe the chaining rules for English, and English alone, in some detail as there have

---

4   German is probably best described as a V2 language where the verb is in second position (Harbert 2007). In this it differs from Greek where, under appropriate discourse conditions such as contrast or emphasis, it is possible to say *Αγαπάει ο Ιωάννης την Μαρία* (VSO), *Ο Ιωάννης την Μαρία αγαπάει* (SOV).

5   By this we mean the contingent development of a language which has emerged from the historic interaction of its speakers in particular eco-social settings.

been previous monographic length treatments e.g. Brazil 1995 and O'Grady 2010. Consequently our discussions of the workings of the other languages must remain regrettably vague and somewhat speculative.

We will illustrate the workings of the chaining rules in English through an analysis of a short text. We will further illustrate the concept of prospection which we define following work such as Sinclair and Coulthard (1975) and Tadros (1985) as referring to something in the discourse which creates an expectation that something else will occur within the context in which it is spoken. In order to explore the concept of prospection in more detail we will examine the relationship between sequentially produced elements in Japanese and Greek translations of the short English text.

Prior to the start of the verbal interaction, regardless of the language in which the interlocutors operate, the communication between speaker and the hearer is in an initial state, which we define as the special set of communicative circumstances which speakers assume they are operating in before they speak. This includes their perception of what they need to tell the hearer or be told by the hearer. Each lexical item modifies the existing state of circumstances by creating a new expectation. Target state refers to the modified circumstances that arise as a result of the hearer been told what they need to be told (Brazil 1995, O'Grady 2010). Target state can be achieved by the speaker alone through the production of a telling increment or with the assistance of a second speaker as part of an asking exchange. In a telling increment tellers simultaneously initiate and achieve their purpose; the hearer may (or may not) then acknowledge the achievement. In an asking exchange speakers produce a preliminary increment but their own communicative need to achieve target state is not achieved until their hearers make an appropriate contribution by producing a telling increment which the initiators may or may not acknowledge.

In order to achieve target state in English an increment must satisfy three criteria:

1   that it represents a successful run through of a grammatical chain;
2   that it contain at least one example of a falling tone movement; and, most importantly;
3   that in the context of telling it represents an actual telling.[6]

---

6   We can imagine a situation where a speaker produced the grammatical chain *I saw John* which, in context, might or might not represent an actual telling. For instance if John is an old friend who the speaker rarely sees, an utterance saying that John was seen is newsworthy but if the meeting was already known it is not. In the latter case the chain is preliminary to the actual telling which might be something like *and he's back with Grace.*

Thus, and in line with the principle of metaredundancy, while an increment is identifiable using lexicogrammatical and prosodic criteria, it is a semantic unit which constructs a proposition by means of which speakers update the common ground they share with their hearers. We recognise that the notion of common ground is nebulous and that various scholars differ in their treatment of it. For instance, some such as Sperber and Wilson (1995) do not see any need to posit shared attention and shared intentionality. It is sufficient if based on a speaker's own 'cognitive environment' – the sum of a speaker's prior experiences with the language, interlocutors and context etc. – for a speaker to be able to produce contextually appropriate language and to interpret the dialogic response. Language, in this view, is an ostensive and inferential signal and so, in effect, all speakers sharing a linguistic situation can be said to have shared attention. They claim their solution gets around the thorny problem of the 'Mutual Knowledge Paradox', which correctly notes that: for knowledge to be shared it must be known to be shared, and that such sharing leads to an infinite regress of knowledge which cannot be processed in a finite time.

Lee (2001) notes that two not entirely satisfactory solutions have been proposed for the Mutual Knowledge Paradox. The first of which assumes an infinite regress, but has a mechanism for inferring mutual knowledge; and the second, which assumes a truncation heuristic for inferring mutual knowledge. Clarke (1992) assumes an infinite regress, but also claims that speakers are able to rely on extra linguistic evidence in inferring mutual knowledge or common ground. This includes the physical context, co-membership of a community, assumptions based upon humans' shared biological, physical and mental abilities. Together they form the ground upon which the speakers meet. Clarke further posits that humans share an induction schema for inferring mutual knowledge based upon the evidence provided by the ground. Other scholars, chiefly Bach & Harnish (1979) have argued that mutual knowledge can be established without the need for an infinite regress. They argue that three steps are all that is required, e.g. mutual knowledge is established if the speaker knows that the hearer knows that the speaker knows that the hearer knows that the speaker knows X. Others in the literature argue for a five or even six truncation cut-off point. Yet, regardless of the actual number of regressions required, it is unclear what psychological mechanism is required in the brain to enable it to infer mutual knowledge in the absence of infinite regress. Furthermore, Sperber and Wilson (1995) elegantly provide counter-examples which show that mutual knowledge cannot always be established by six levels of regression.

Lee himself argues that part of the problem relates to terminological confusion between terms such as mutual knowledge and shared belief. Like Sperber and Wilson he does not premise that successful communication is grounded in mutual knowledge. Instead he distinguishes between knowledge which, following Plato, he equates with episteme, and belief, which he equates with doxa. For Lee, mutual knowledge refers to the type of knowledge which at least two people possess with 100% certainty. By contrast, a shared belief is a belief which the speakers assume is true, and that they share with a greater or lesser degree of certainty. Evidentially, it is based on indirect evidence such as hearsay or apparent membership in a community. Shared knowledge is knowledge which has been established in the discourse history. In the previous chapter we argued that knowledge is not something to be shared between interlocutors, but rather a resource which speakers have access to and assign responsibility for. Speakers, based on their previous experiences, can predict that they both have access to the same resource or that one of them has more or less access.

Therefore, like Lee and Sperber and Wilson, we accept that communication does not need to rest upon mutual knowledge, and that speakers' assessments of the degree of knowledge they share with their interlocutors may not be entirely accurate. They may incorrectly position their hearers as having more or less access to knowledge than that which their hearers actually have. Thus, what we define as an act of telling is best understood as a projection of the speakers' assessment of updated access to knowledge required for their communicative need to be satisfied. We will return to considering the increment as a semantic unit once we have discussed the formal lexicogrammatical criteria required to identify an increment.

5.3.1   The grammatical chaining rules

The grammatical chaining rules of English are set out in Table 5.2 (p. 157). For now, our assumption is that all the made-up English examples presented below contain at least one falling tone, and that they represent an act of actual telling. Asking exchanges are specific types of tellings and are of two types: those initiated by a polar interrogative and those initiated by a Wh element. e.g.

5.1

(i) Did she catch her train?   (ii) What time is your train?
     Yes she did.   It's just after one.

In both cases, the first speaker's contribution is a preliminary increment, and the actual telling occurs in the second contribution.

Some simple examples

We will start with a simple illustrative English example. We are shown the following photograph and asked to fill in the blanks:

Figure 5.1 A black door

5.2

(i)   What is it?   It is ....
(ii) What colour is it? It is ....

For (i) the expected answer is a black door and for (ii) black. If we ask the equivalent questions in two other languages, Greek and Japanese the question and answer pairs are as follows.

5.3

Greek[7]

(i)   Τι είναι αυτό;   Είναι μια μαύρη πόρτα
      (Ti einai afto?)   Einai   mia mavri porta)
      What be it   be/3rd one black   door
(i)   Τι χρώμα είναι;   Είναι μαύρη
      (Ti chroma einai?)   (Einai mavri)
      What colour be   be/3rd   black

Japanese[8]

(i)   それ は 何 です か   それ は 黒い ドア です
      (Sore wa nan desu ka?)   (Sore wa kuroi   doa   desu)
      That   what is   That   black door is
      何 色 です か   それ は 黒い です
      (Nani iro deus   ka   (Sore wa   kuroi   desu)
      What   colour is   That   black   is

---

7   As the word πόρτα is a feminine noun the adjectives 'μια' and 'μαύρη' are inflected to agree with the gender of the noun. For instance had the answer been it is a black car the adjectives would have been ένα (ena) and μαύρο (mavro) to agree with the neutral gender for the noun car and had the answer been a red sun the adjectives would have been έναν (enan) and μαύρος (mauvros) to agree with the masculine gender of the sun.

8   I have not transliterated the particles は and か into English as they convey grammatical rather than lexical information. は is the topic marker and か an interpersonal negotiator which signals interrogative mood, (see Teruya 2004) for further details.

Even in these simple examples the transliterated pairs show that the three languages create very different expectations as to the ordering of the words. As gender, topic marking and question particles are not shared across the three languages we will not discuss them further. The expectations created are as follows. In all three languages the first speaker initiates but their purpose remains unachieved until the second speaker makes an appropriate contribution which may or may not be followed by an acknowledgment by the first speaker.

As we will see in English, speakers signal the start of an increment by producing a nominal and verbal element in either order. Once the speaker has produced an initial nominal or verbal element the speaker prospects the presence of the other. In the examples below the arrows indicate a modification of the existing state of circumstances and the small letters indicate that the element does not modify the existing state of circumstances by satisfying the previous expectation.

5.4

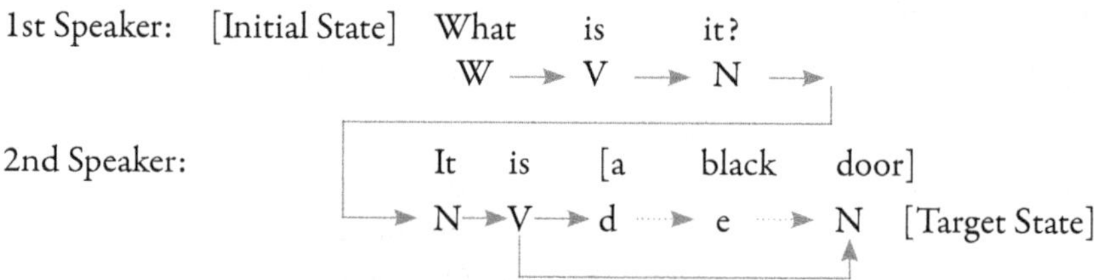

In the English example the speaker produces the W N V chain to signal his/her communicative need to know the identity of the object presented in the picture. The communicative need is satisfied by the 2nd speaker's production of the N V N chain with the second nominal element, consisting of a determiner which entails the subsequent production of a nominal ,which in this case is suspended by the intervening adjectival element: verbs do not prospect determiners they prospect nouns.

5.5

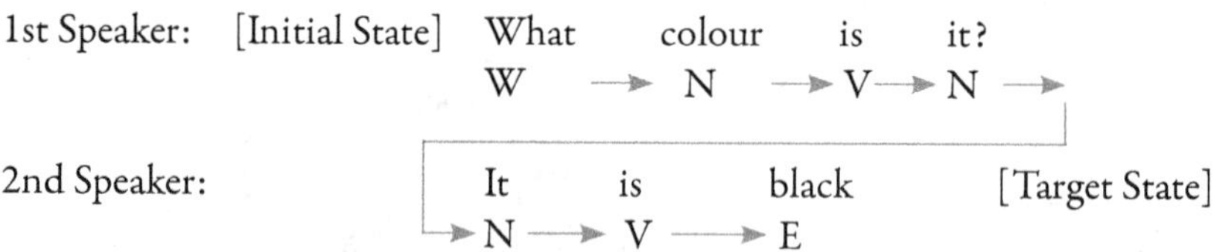

In the second example we see that in English the Open selector (W) element refers to a missing piece of information namely the colour of the door. In the paragraphs below we will sketch out the full grammatical criterion necessary for the production of legal and appropriate chains in English. But first we will compare the English asking exchanges with their Greek and Japanese equivalents.[9]

5.6

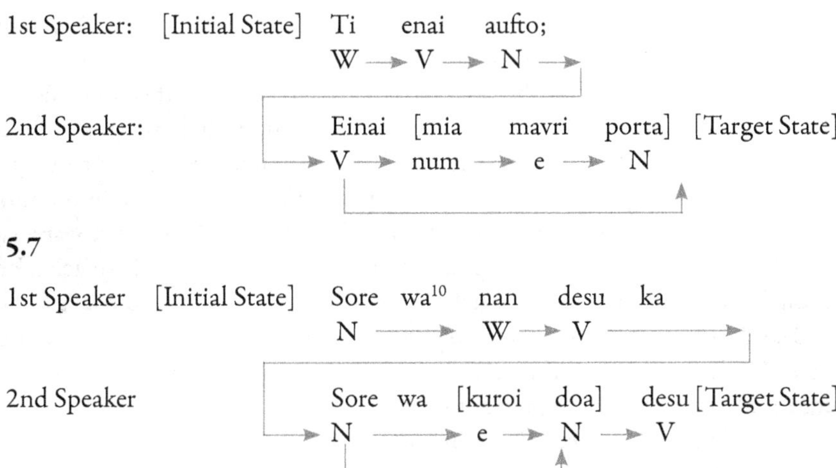

5.7

In the Greek example, as in English, the speaker produces a WVN chain in order to signal his/her communicative need to know the identity of the object represented in the photograph. But in addressing the communicative need, and in modifying the circumstances in order to tell the identity of the object, the 2nd speaker produces a V num N chain[11]. Yet, in response to the W V N chain the second Greek speaker

---

9   In the interests of readability the Greek and Japanese examples will be written using the Roman alphabet.

10   In the examples here I have not coded wa which is traditionally described as the topic marker where it contrasts with ga which is traditionally described as a subject marker. Wa is used to introduce new topics into the discourse. Ka signals interrogative mood, which because of the presence of the open selector is predictable but consider:

    Sake o nondemasu which literally expresses the proposition *alcohol (accusative) drinking* which in the context it was produced will have a recoverable subject and thus translates into English as *X is drinking alcohol*. The addition of the particle *ka* literally expresses the proposition *alcohol (accusative) drinking (interrogative)* and thus translates into English *Is X drinking alcohol*. Hence, unlike in English, Interrogative Mood is not prospected early in the clause and hearers have to wait until the end of the clause to discover the grammatical Mood. And, in this case, the presence of *ka* prospects another speaker's contribution..

11   As in the prior English example the lower case refers to the fact that the numeral and the adjective entail the presence of the following nominal element. More crucially, we are aware that coding *mia* as a numeral may be imposing an English label. However, it is well beyond the scope of this book to attempt to produce a coding which describes the Greek or Japanese chaining rules in any detail and in their own terms. We intend our coding choices as no more than a heuristic aimed at exploring the concept of prospection.

does not prospect the same expectations as the English speaker. The saying of the element *mia* not only informs us of the quantity of the object but also narrows down the semantic search space of the object by specifying that its grammatical gender will be feminine. Unlike in English only a subset of Greek nominal elements are prospected. The second speaker produces a chain commencing with a Verbal element: unlike in English there is no expectation that a declarative mood utterance will necessarily commence with a nominal element. In each case, therefore, there are different options open to the speaker as to how they will continue as well as different signals that provide clues for the hearer and hence facilitate speedier interpretation.

The unfolding Japanese chain creates very different expectations. In traditional typological descriptions Japanese is described as a Subject Object Verb language with the grammatical case and mood indicated by the presence of particles. Traditionally it is classed as a left branching language with phrase final heads (Dryer 1992). Like Greek the subject is frequently elided. However, the expectations prospected by the production of an element as circumstances are modified during the sequential unfolding of the proposition from initial state to target state differ. In the second speaker's response the chain speaker produces a N N V chain. Consider:

5.8

[Initial State]

What	colour	is	it?
W →	N →	V →	N →

It	is	black	[Target State]
N →	V →	E	

5.9

[Initial State]

Ti →	chroma →	einai? →
W	N	V

Einai	mavri[12]	[Target State]
V →	E	

5.10

[Initial State]

Nani	iro	desu	ka
W →	N →	V →	

(Sore ga)	kuroi	desu	[Target state]
N →	E →	V	

---

12   The realisation of the adjective indexes an unstated feminine object.

In the three equivalent responses three very different lexical chains are produced. In English the speaker produces an N V E chain, in Greek a V E chain and in Japanese an E V[13] chain. The Greek and Japanese chains cannot satisfy a potential communicative need in English. Hence we see that the three languages have, through time, developed contingent conventional patterns in response to the communicative needs of their speakers. This has resulted in similar communicative acts being realised by different structures which entails that (i) the equivalent communicative acts can be realised in a myriad of culturally appropriate responses, and (ii) despite the arbitrary nature of the structural chains the expectations created have created slightly different valuers e.g., gender in Greek, the overt subject in English, and the final positioning of the verb in Japanese.

Previous work (Brazil 1995:51) identified the eight simple chains which lead from initial state to target state in English. The chains are presented in Table 5.2. In the examples below, N elements can be realised by (i) noun, (ii) pronoun, (iii) determiner followed by noun, (iv) determiner followed by adjective(s) followed by noun and (v) any of the nominal elements in (i) to (iv) post modified by a Prepositional Phrase which itself is a Prep followed by any of the nominal elements in (i) to (iv).

It is immediately obvious that the chains described above are unable to explain how speakers move from initial to target state in much everyday spoken English. Thus, Brazil proposed a number of further formal features and devices. The first of which is suspension. We illustrate using an example from the text below.

Table 5.2 The chaining rules for English

	Chain	Examples
1	N V	(i) Grace smiled. (ii) She smiled. (iii) A lady smiled. (iv) A red-haired lady smiled. (v) A red-haired lady in blue jeans smiled.
2	N V N	The dog chased the cat.
3	N V N A	John ran the mile slowly. John ran the mile in a slow time.
4	N V N E	John likes tea hot.
5	N V E	The green door is open.
6	N V A	The angry protestor shouted angrily.
7	N V N E A	The young girl made Jill sad by accident.
8	N V E A	John was sad as well.

---

13   While it is possible that that the Japanese could commence with a nominal element *sore* ('that' in English), it is more likely that it would not.

5.11   Suddenly   they   saw   a   traveller
Initial State   a   N ⟶ V ⟶ d ⟶ N

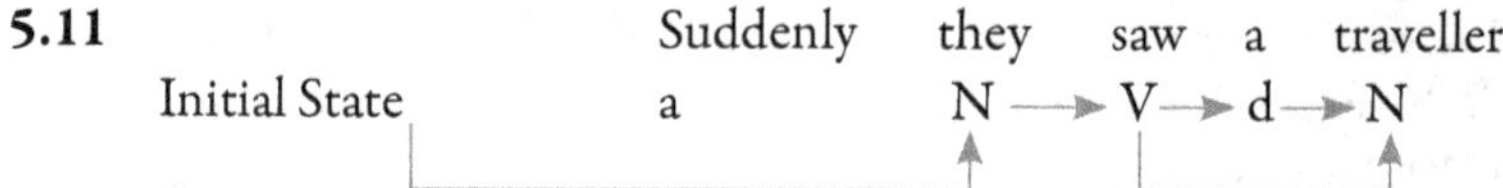

Here, the suspensive A element suddenly does not relieve the speaker of the obligation to produce a following N element.[14] While 'suddenly' clearly is of informational relevance in that it describes the manner of the verbal process it does not lead to an updating of the target state. In the text studied here, while Example 5.11 above represents a complete run through of an N V N chain, it does not satisfy the communicative need and move to target state. In the context in which it was produced the communicative need was not only to state the existence of the traveller but rather to describe the traveller's action. This brings us to our second formal device reduplication where the speaker extends the chain through the production of a second N or A element. The element to be reduplicated is noted with a + sign. In this example, the N element – a traveller in line with Brazil's rule – has zero realisation because its realisation has been prohibited as it would have been the second mention of an N element in a reduplicating pair (1995). The chain is further extended by the reduplication of the circumstantial elements. Thus:

5.12   Suddenly   they   saw   [a   traveller]   coming   down   the road
Initial State   a   N ⟶ V ⟶ d ⟶ N+ ⟶ Ø ⟶ V ⟶ a   d ⟶ N

                                                                    Target State

A further possibility where the speaker has exhausted the formal possibilities of the chain without achieving target state is that he/she may extend the chain. Brazil (1995: 57) provides the following example:

5.13   We   wanted   to search   your   car
[Initial State] ⟶ N ⟶ V ⟷ V¹ ⟶ d ⟶ N   [Target State]

Brazil argues that the production here of the non-finite VI element 'to search', while in theory completing the expectations set up by the verb 'want', resets the expectations and prospects the final N element in a manner analogous to the V element in the agnate chain 'we searched your car'. The first verbal element is coded as V and the following as VI. He states:

> It is this ability to trigger a doubling back in what we are representing as a left-to-right progression, so as to start a second run through a

---

14   In English, in declarative mood utterances, the first non suspensive element must be an N element; in Wh questions an open selector (W element); in polar questions a V element; and in Imperative mood a V element.

specified part of the rule system, that distinguishes VI from other kinds of element. (p. 59)

The following example illustrates an example of a suspension in the chain.

5.14

The wind and the Sun	were	disputing	which	was	the stronger

d N   c   d N → V ↔ V^I → N → V → d → e   ØN

The non-finite verbal element disputing triggers a doubling back of the chain and results in the prospection of the following N element. With these rules in hand we can code the English text below. However before so doing we need to discuss in more detail the notion of the increment as a semantic unit.

5.3.2 The Increment as a Semantic Unit

As we noted, following Brazil (1995), a stretch of speech such as 'I saw John' may fulfil the formal criteria of being an increment, but in the context in which it was produced it may not realise an increment. Thus, an increment must be understood as a semantic unit which expresses a proposition; simply put, speakers do not merely produce grammatical chains, they produce meaningful utterances. An increment conveys a telling and represents a thought. In Chapter 4 we detailed the view that language is a stratificational system and that the relationship between strata is probabilistic. Following Halliday and Matthiessen (2014), Hjelmslev (1961), Lemke (1995) and Chafe (2018) we argue that the semantics predicts the lexicogrammar and, indeed, itself is predicted by the lexicogrammar; and extrapolating from this we can talk about increments as grammatical structures realising semantic units in predictable ways.

In this section we will test the coding above in order to show how speakers may use the achievement of target states to assist in the management of the presumed common ground. Our original English text 'The Wind and the Sun'[15] was punctuated into sentences with each sentence representing a possible increment. We have assumed that, as our translated texts were similarly punctuated into sentences, these sentences are similarly possible increments with Initial and Target States. We will discuss later the mismatches in punctuation between the languages.

---

15   The text of 'The Wind and the Sun' is available at https://www.aesopfables.com/cgi/aesop1.cgi?4&TheWindandtheSun [Last accessed 30/05/2022]. The English text was then used as the source text for the Japanese and Greek texts. The translations were produced by native speakers of the languages who have both earned PhDs from UK universities.

As we saw in Chapter 4, a proposition, the movement from an initial to a target state, is situated in our stratified model of language on the semantic stratum. It is realised in wording by the lexicogrammar at the lower stratum. Thus, our assumption is that the three texts are equivalent thoughts on the semantic stratum, though obviously they are realised very differently by the lexicogrammars. Within the English text there are seven sentences as indicated by the presence of the full stops. We do not claim that there are seven increments in any of the spoken texts, as without consideration of intonation we cannot know. However, for now, as the seven English sentences all conform to various combinations of the chaining rules, we will treat them as if they were increments. Once we have illustrated the workings of the chaining rules we will examine a reading, where we will see how intonational choices lead to a reanalysis of the number of increments, and of our provisional conflation of sentence with increment. We will start with an analysis of the English text.

Sentence 1 is an example of an N V chain which is extended by the VI element 'disputing'. However, target state is not achieved until the nature of the dispute has been told. This Target State becomes the Initial State of sentence 2. The initial A element in sentence 2 does not release the speaker from the expectation to produce an N or V element. In fact, the speaker produces an N V N chain which introduces us to the traveller. This though does not achieve the speaker's communicative purpose and so the speaker produces a reduplicated N element which informs what the traveller was doing. Yet, despite the speaker producing a run through of a chain, no communicative purpose has been satisfied. The relevance of the traveller to the dispute is unstated. And so the speaker continues his chain and produces an N V chain, which creates the expectation that he will produce a verbal projection. His production of an N V N chain, while grammatically complete, does not fulfil his communicative purpose, which is only achieved by the overt articulation of the VI N subchain 'to decide our dispute'.

The new Target state is now the initial state for sentence 3 where the speaker works through a chain which contains a preliminary subchain which relays the condition upon which the dispute – as to which is stronger – can be judged. Target state is achieved by a chain which includes two VI elements. Sentence 4, a simple N V chain, achieves an updated target state by specifying the order in which the two protagonists will compete. Sentence 5 commences with a preliminary scene setting chain, which suspends the actual modification of the initial state through the production of an N or V element that fulfils the expectation of informing what the wind did. Target state is achieved only by articulating what the wind did. Increment 6 is prospected towards a description of the traveller's reaction to the wind's action. This is achieved through the production of an N V N A chain with the A element comprising a PN sequence. The final increment contains a complete chain which details the Sun's action. But this does not achieve target state as this can only be achieved by describing the effect of the sun's action on the traveller. This target state is achieved by a reduplicative N V N E chain which is itself extended by the production of a N V A+ A chain.

5.15   Analysis of Text [16]

(1)

The wind and the Sun were disputing which was the stronger.
d   N   c   d   N   V   V^I N+   V   d   e   ∅N

Kaze to Taiyo ga dochira ga tsuyoi ka iiarasoi o shite imashita.
Wind and sun   which   strong   struggle making had
N   c   N   N+   E   N   V   V

O aeras ke o ilios malonan   pios itan o   pio   dinatos.
  Sun and wind argue(they) who   was   more powerful
  N   c   N   V   N   V   A   E

(2)

Suddenly they saw a traveller   coming down the road,   (preliminary)
a   N   V   d   N+   ∅   V^I p   d   N
and the Sun said: 'I see a way   to decide our dispute.'
c   d   N   V   N   V   d   N   ∅   V^I d   N

Sonotoki, tabibito ga michi o yatte kuru   no ga mieta   node,
At that time traveller   road   doing come   of   appeared because
a   N   N   V   V^I p   V   c
Taiyo ga iimashita. 'Kachimake o kimeru hoho   ga arimasu.' (2 increments)
Sun   said   win/lose   decide guarantee   is there
N   V   V   V^I N   V

Ksafnika idan   ena taxidioti   na   katiforizi to dromo
Suddenly saw(they) one traveller   to   descends   road
a   V   num N   p   V   N
ke o ilios ipe: Vlepo ena   tropo na chiristoume ti[17] diafonia   mas.
and sun said   See (I) one   way to decide(us)   disagreement us
c   N   V   V   num N   p   V   N   N

---

16   We have not attempted to mark any extensions or suspensions in Japanese and Greek as we do not know enough about the internal language expectations produced by the production of a lexical element. We have, however, coded suspensions within nominal groups and have coded initial Adverbials as suspensive.

17   'Ti' is a specifier which identifies which dispute is meant.

(3)

Whichever of us can cause that traveller to take off his cloak shall be regarded as the stronger.
n   p n v v^I d n   v^I   d n ∅ V V^I V^I   a d e ∅N

Tabibito no gaito o nugaseta   ho   ga tsuyoi to shimasho.
Traveller of cloak take off/did-cause keep   strong   make-let's
N   P A   V   N   E   V

Opios bori na kani afton ton taxidioti na vgali tin kappa tou tha theorithi o pio dinatos
Anyone do to can him   traveller to take off cloak his will/considered who powerful
N   V p V N   N   p V   N   d V   N E

(4)

You begin.
N   V

Anata kara hajimete.
You   From State-imperative
N   p   V

Esy ksenikas.
You   start
N   V

(5)

So the Sun retired behind a cloud,
 c d n   v   p   d n
and the wind began to blow as hard as it could upon the traveller.
c   d N V   V^I   A E   N V   P d N

Soitte   Taiyo wa kumo   no   ushiro ni^18   kakure,
Meanwhile sun   cloud of   behind into   hiding
a   N   N   p   p   V
Kaze wa tabibito   ni   mukatte   dekiru dake tsuyoku kaze o fukimashita.
Wind   traveller into head-towards can   only strongly wind   blew
N   N   p   A   V^I   A   A   N   V

---

18   The particle 'ni' in Japanese indicates a direction or travel towards. Accordingly I have in the word for word translation translated it as either 'into' or 'in'.

Etsi o ilios kriftike piso   ap' ta   sinefa
so   sun hid   behind from clouds
c   N   V   A   p   N
kai o aeras archise   na fisa   oso   pio dinata   borouse pano ston taxidioti.
And wind started(he) to blowing as much as more powerful could(he) onto traveller
c   N   V   V   A   E   E   V   p   N

(6)
But the harder the wind blew the more closely did[19] the traveller wrap his cloak round him,
c   d   n   d   n   v   d   n   a   d N   V d N P   N
till at last the Wind had to give up in despair.
a   a   d N   V   V[I]   P N

Shikashi, Kaze ga tsuyoku   fukeba fuku   hodo,
However wind   strongly   if-blow blow   about
c   N   A   V   V[I]   A
tabibito wa gaito o shikkari karada ni   makitsukemashita.
Traveller   cloak tightly   body   into   wrapped around
N   N   A   N   p   V
Soshite tsui ni   kaze wa akiramemashita. (2 Increments)
And   just in   wind   gave up
c   A   p   N   V

Alla oso   pio dinata fisouse   o aeras toso pio   sfikta tylige
but   as much as more strongly blew(he) wind such more tightly wrapped(him)
c   A   A   A   V   N   d   A   A   V
o takidiotis tin kappa pano tou,
   traveller   cloak onto
   N   N   p
mechri pou   o aeras anagkastike telika apelpismenos na egatalipsi tin prospathia[20].
Until where wind   forced   stop   desperate   to capture the attempts
c   A   N   V   A E   p V   d   N

---

19   In increment 6 *did wrap* has been coded as a single V element in a manner analogous to
     wrapped. Sequentially the production of *did* prospects the following N element which itself
     prospects the finite verbal element,

20   'Tin prospathia' which translates into English as *the attempts* introduces a lexical item
     which was not overtly present in the original English version. But our translator added it
     because the Greek utterance would not have made sense without explicit realisation of the
     object of *give up*.

(7)

Then the Sun came out and   shone in all his glory upon the traveller,
a   d N   V   c   ∅ V   P+d e N   P   d N+
who soon found it too hot   to walk with his cloak on.
N   a   V   N E   ∅ V¹   P+   d N   P ∅N

Kondo wa Taiyo ga dete kite,   tabibito ni   atatakana hizashi o mukemashita,
Now   sun   arrive come traveller in   warm   sunlight   pointed
A   N   V   V   N   P   A   N   V
Suruto sugu ni tabibito wa atsusugite gaito wa kite irarenai   to omoimashita.
And   soon in traveller   collecting cloak   come can't/afford and thought
A   A   N   V   N V   V   V

Tote o ilios vgike kai   elampse me   oli tou ti doxa pano ston taxidioti
Then sun got out and shone   with all   his glory onto   traveller
c   N   V   c   V   p   E d N   p   N
pou eniose   oti ekane polli zesti,   gia   na kratisei pano tou tin kappa tou.
Who felt(he) that made very warm   for   to keep   onto   coat his
N   V   N   V   A   E   P   P V   P   N   d

As well as translating the short text into their native languages our Japanese and Greek translators also provided us with an audio recording of their reading of the story. Both are speakers of the standard form of their languages, centred on Tokyo and Athens respectively. Prior to discussing the transcriptions we will first contrast the intonational resources of Japanese and Greek with the intonational description of English set out in Chapter 4. This is because we cannot assume that similar forms across the three languages realise the same forms.

5.3.3   A word on Japanese and Greek intonation

In contrast with English far less work has been done on Japanese and Greek intonation, especially as regards functional meaning, and so we cannot attempt to fully describe the communicative significance of the intonational choices in these languages. A further complication is that the most complete descriptions of Japanese and Greek intonation, see Venditti (2005), Venditti et al. (2008) and Arvaniti and Baltazani (2005) respectively, are transcribed in ToBI notation, while we have couched our description in traditional British School terms. We have done so because a description which recognises the functional unity of the nuclear tones in English is needed for us to (i) identify increments, (ii) to describe the informational flow within and between increments, and (iii) to examine how competing informational and interactional needs were balanced.

The ToBI intonation system emerged from a series of interdisciplinary workshops in the 1990s between phonologists, phoneticians, speech scientists and engineers. There are two separate components: the tone component (To) and the break index component (BI) which emerged out of the works on tone of Janet Pierrehumbert e.g. Pierrehumbert (1980) and the work on chunking by the phonetician Patti Jo Price – see Silverman et al. (1992) for full details. The original ToBI system was designed for Standard American English (see Beckman et al. 2005). Its conventions have been adapted and expanded to cover a range of other languages and dialects such as British English, German, Italian, Korean etc. as well as Japanese and Greek. The original ToBI transcription comprised three tiers: a lexical tier, a tonal tier and a break index. The tonal tier consists of a string of tonal targets. Phonetically they represent turning points in the pitch curve which can be visualised by software such as Praat. The transitions between the tones are unimportant. In English and other Germanic languages the theory has been extended by showing that the tonal targets occur in rhythmically stronger syllables (Ladd 2008). In the original model the tones were transcribed as H* (high) and L* (low), peaks and troughs respectively. The speech signal is chunked into intonation phrases, which are equivalent to our tone units. These are usually signalled by the combination of a break index of 4, equivalent to a perceptible pause, and the presence of a phrase accent and boundary tones. Phrase accents and boundary tones can be H or L, which indicate the presence or absence of a rising contour. The final tone in the intonation phrase is equivalent to a tonic or nuclear syllable in the British tradition. All other tones within the intonational phrase are equivalent to pretonic prominences. The combination of final tone plus the phrase accent and the boundary tone is equivalent to the nuclear tone movement on British intonation descriptions. Table A.1 in Appendix A compares ToBI and traditional descriptions in the three languages.[21]

The ToBI notation is more delicate than the primary British School coding but we do not employ it as it is unclear whether all the differences are functionally discrete or merely variances of the same function. To illustrate what is coded as a primary tone movement of fall has five possible realisations in English, two in Japanese and four in Greek. It is clear that the intonational resources across the three languages are different and, even where two of the languages appear to employ the same contour, we cannot say whether or not the function realised is the same. It is also clear that Japanese does not appear to have as rich a tonal system as the other

---

21   The comparison between ToBI and British School notation is taken from Ladd (2008) and O'Grady (2013a). The ToBI description of Japanese is from Venditti (2005) and for Greek from Arvaniti and Baltazani (2005) The descriptions of Japanese and Greek are also based on Abe (1998) and Botinis (1998) who both adopt a narrow phonetic based transcription system. The translations into British School notation are our own and in need of empirical validation. We have not included combinations of starred tone !H-L% as these are not presented in Arvaniti and Baltazani.

two languages, though it is premature to state what this means for the functions of intonation in Japanese.

Japanese is a pitch accent language. Unlike English and Greek, pitch is a lexical property and does not operate as a speaker choice within tone groups. Some words contain pitch accents, while others do not. Venditti (2005:173) gives us the example of the verb *ueru* (plant) which does not have a lexical accent in the phrase *uerumono* (a thing to plant), but does have a falling lexical accent in the phrase *ue\rumono* (the ones who are starved). Hence, pitch accents or prominences can play no role in the assignment of information structure in Japanese. Furthermore, Jun & Kubozono (2020) point out that the position of the fixed lexical accent varies between Japanese dialects. Abe (1998:362) states that post lexically pitch prominence operates in Japanese by adding to the lexical pitch accents in one of three possible ways, which he labels (i) cumulative, (2) copulative, and (3) conflictive. He explains the terms using the example of a speaker who wishes to produce a statement. Post lexically this will result in an intonation which falls across the tone group. In the case of a cumulative accent this will result in the rising accent becoming less rising, In the case of a copulative accent the rising lexical accent will remain unchanged but be followed by a falling tone movement and realise a rise-fall or a (fall)-rise-fall. In the case of a conflictive accent the original rising lexical accent will be lost and it will be realised as a fall. Venditti et al. (2008) suggest that focus prominence in Japanese is realised through a number of prosodic features unrelated to prominence – notably increased pitch range and the insertion of an unexpected tone group boundary. Thus, a sudden jump to a higher pitch and/or a tone group boundary which is not congruent with the phrase structure signals informational focus.

Japanese has a five tone system but, as yet, little is known as to the functions of the tone other than the (rise)-fall-rise and rising tones seem to be associated with reaching out to hearers and signalling a greater insistence. It appears that a high rising tone conveys the expectation of surprise (Abe 1998:367). Falling tones signal completion: that what has been said has been said. Thus, we would expect that Japanese speakers, like their English counterparts, would signal the achievement of target state by producing a falling tone.[22]

In Greek, as in English, stressed syllables[23] serve as the site of pitch prominences. While the assignment of stress patterns in English is quite idiosyncratic, and depends on the presence or absence of a suffix, the type of suffix, word class, vowel

---

22   As Abe's description is not based on the study of how intonation functions in actual discourse, but rather on decontextualized, made-up, single sentence examples, his description of the functions of Japanese intonation is in need of empirical validation and, for now, must be treated with caution. But as it is all we have got we will employ it here.

23   In English there can be minor exceptions to this statement e.g. Bolinger (1961:83) who reports on whisky which was not <u>imported</u> but <u>deported</u>.

length and the number of the syllables, the case in Greek is in some ways simpler. The stressed syllable must occur in the final three syllables of a word. But the assignment of stress to a particular syllable is largely unpredictable and it can occur anywhere in the last three syllables. Additionally, the site of the lexically stressed syllable may vary depending on plurality e.g. mathima vs mathimata (lesson vs lessons), case e.g. o eboros vs tou eboros (a merchant nominative vs a merchant's genitive) and the aorist e.g kano vs ekana (do 1st sing present vs did 1st sing past). Like English though, pitch prominences are significant informationally and they appear to signal the pragmatic salience of lexical items. Within a tone group a tonic syllable, which represents the focal point of the tone group, is identified as the largest pitch gesture in the tone group and, again like English, the tonic accent occurs on the focal item which represents the culmination of the New. The following example adapted from Botinis (1998:301) illustrates:

5.16 | i Maria estile to gramma stin Ellada (Mary sent the letter to Greece)
                                    Focus
5.17 | i Maria estile to gramma stin Ellada |
    Focus

In the first example, the entire tone group is in focus and the utterance is a possible response to a question such as 'what happened?' In the second example, only Maria is in focus and the utterance is a possible response to a question such as 'who sent the letter to Greece?' The Greek tone system seems to share some superficial similarities with its English counterpart. The primary cut appears to be the choice between end falling and end rising tones with rising tones signalling either continuation or polar questions.[24] Falling tones signal statements and, like English, tend to realise Wh questions and imperatives. Thus, it seems probable that (i) a Greek speaker will need to signal that they have projected an act of telling or achieved target state by producing a falling tone movement and (ii) that the placement of focal accents within the speech stream will project information structure.

Now that we have sketched the form and function of intonation across the two languages we will investigate the form and the functions of our speaker's intonation choices in the unfolding of their respective readings of the short passage. We will commence by describing each reading in its own terms before finally comparing and contrasting the contextualised meanings generated by the combination of intonational and lexicogrammatical choices.

---

24   Greek, unlike Japanese, does not have question particles in polar interrogatives and, unlike English, does not use word order to signal interrogative mood.

5.18   The Spoken Text in English [25]

Sentence 1/Increment 1

  1. | the Hwind and the Sun were dis\puting |

  2. | which was the L\stronger.   [END OF FIRST TOPIC]

Sentence 2/Increment 2

  3. | H\suddenly |

  4. | they saw a traveller coming down the \road | |

Increment 3

  5. | and the H\sun said |

  6. | i H\see a way |

  7. | to decide our \dispute |

Sentence 3/ Increment 4

  8. | H/\whichever of us |

  9. | can cause that /traveller |

 10. | to take off his \cloak |

 11. | shall be regarded as the L\stronger | [END OF SECOND TOPIC]

Sentence 4/Increment 5

 12. | H \you |

 13. | be\gin |

Sentence 5/increment 6

 14. | so the H sun re\tired behind a cloud |

Increment 7

 15. | and the wind began to blow as hard as it \could |

 16. | u\/pon the traveller |

Sentence 6/Increment 8

 17. | but the harder the wind /H blew |

 18. | the more \closely did the traveller |

 19. | L\wrap his cloak round him |

Increment 9

 20. | till at /last |

 21. | the \wind |

 22. | had to give up in des L\pair | [END OF THIRD TOPIC]

Sentence 7/Increment 10

 23. | then the H\sun came out |

 24. | and \shone |

 25. | in all his \glory |

 26. | upon the L/traveller |

 27. |who Hsoon found it too \hot |

 28. | to \walk |

 29. | with his L/cloak on | [END OF FOURTH TOPIC/NARRATIVE]

---

25   In the interests of readability we have not reproduced the grammatical coding presented
    earlier.

It can be seen that the reader produced the seven sentences as 10 increments. Thus, in his[26] reading of the fable, Sentences 2, 5 and 6 were each presented as consisting of two increments. The increments contained between 1 and 7 tone groups with a mean of 2.9. There was a tendency for the reader to place initial adverbials and subject nominals into their own tone groups. See tone groups 3 and 20 for initial suspensive adverbials and tone groups 8, 12 and 21 for subjects.

The first increment comprises two tone groups/information units each of which contains a falling tone. The increment starts with a high key and is completed with a low termination signalling that, in the reader's view, the achievement of target state results in the realisation of a topic. The high key which starts increment 2 presents the information that follows as something the hearer will find unexpected; the sudden introduction of a new character, the traveller, into the narrative is not predictable from the prior co-text. The reader's choice of a falling tone to complete increment 2 renders the entire a N V d N+ $\varnothing$ V p d N chain into an increment: it is not preliminary to the telling. The proposition that the disputants saw a traveller approaching results in the achievement of a target state, but one that is signalled as part of an ongoing topic or paragraph. Increment 3 comprises 3 tone groups all with falling tone, and achievement of target state is signalled by the correspondence of the falling tone with the satisfaction of the grammatical chain. The accretion of the target state achieved by the completion of topic 1 and the target states 2 and 3 represent the initial state for increment 4. The presence of the high key in the initial tone group signals that the target state, to be achieved through the production of increment 4, is itself unpredictable. The hearer, in the reader's judgement, will not be able to predict the sun's proposed solution to ending the dispute. The low termination signals the closure of topic 2.

Topic 3 consists of five increments, and the initial state prior to its articulation is the accretion of the target states achieved by the closure of the first two topics. As in the previous two topics, the reader chooses to present the following stretch of speech as unexpected. The first increment in topic 3 contains falling tone groups and realises an N V chain. Somewhat surprisingly, the two item chain is articulated in two tone groups which functions to overly focus on the contrast between the two disputants and the prospected activity of one, and the passivity of the other. Increment 5 is realised by a single tone group with a falling tone, which completes the grammatical chain The choice of a falling tone rather than a rising tone indicates that the speaker signals an act of telling and therefore, unlike the analysis of the written sentences above it, does not represent a preliminary piece of information but an increment that achieves a target state. The speaker's decision to make the verbal element 'retired' tonic, and the focus of the tone group, indicates that

---

26   As the gender of our speakers is known we use gender appropriate pronouns,

informationally the target state was achieved by the chain 'and so the sun retired'. The following P/N elements, 'behind the clouds', while informationally given were required to satisfy the grammatical expectations created by the production of the chain. Otherwise the verb 'retired' might have been misconstrued as ceasing function rather than temporarily withdrawing.

Increment 7 comprises two tone groups with the final tone group realising a fall-rise. This choice of tone signals to the hearers that the achieved target state contains information that is knowable by, or inferable to, the hearer – after all, in the context, what else would the wind be blowing upon? This strategy has the effect of drawing in the hearers and making them active co-constructors of the narrative; wind tends after all to cause people to fasten their garments tightly. Thus the achieved target state previews the proposition that is articulated in the following tone group. Increment 8 contains three tone groups of which the first contains a rising tone which signals (i) that the incomplete grammatical chain has not achieved target state, and (ii) prospects that the information in the tone group is information that, in a sense, is potentially available to the hearers. The tonic syllable on the adverbial element 'closely' in the next tone group signals that the V N elements were informationally Given. The concluding tone group in increment 8 commences with a low key choice which signals the speaker's projection that the target state reached after the completion of the increment will elaborate on, but not add to, the existing context. The fact that the traveller responds to the wind by wrapping his cloak around himself is a foreseeable consequence of the futile nature of the wind's action.

Increment 9 consists of three tone groups with the first containing a rising tone signalling its incompleteness which coincides with the suspensive a elements. The first intermediate state is realised by the production of the N element 'the wind' which is presented in its own tone group. The effect is to signal that the speaker is going to tell us about the actions of the wind and not the traveller. The final tone group in the increment not only fulfils the grammatical expectations but also the informational ones. Target state is achieved by the production of the final adverbial element which conveys the wind's state of mind. Increment 9 closes topic 3.

The high key commencing increment 10, which is coterminous with topic 4, signals a further unexpected turn of events: the wind may have struggled to demonstrate its strength through toughness but the sun will not struggle. The increment contains 7 short tone groups of which 5 contain falling tone. The rising tone in tone group 26 coupled with the low key and the previous availability of the referent traveller in the context signals (i) incompletion, (ii) the fact that while tone group 26 moves the discourse on by supplying the prospected noun it does not move the discourse on informationally, and (iii) the speaker is reaching out to the hearer. The effect of this reaching out is to involve the hearer in actively co-constructing the remainder of the increment. A possible target state is achieved by the production of the N element in tone group (28) but the speaker needs to produce one further tone group with low rising tone and a focus on the previously mentioned referent 'cloak'. Otherwise, had the speaker not included the final P/N elements with his cloak on, the hearer would have been left with an image of the traveller suffering from sunstroke! The narrative final low rise reaches out to the hearers by signalling that the speaker projects them as being in a position of being able to predict the content of the final tone group. Had the speaker chosen a falling tone rather than a rising one he would not have presented the state of affairs as one that both speaker and hearer could lay claim to.

Figure 5.2 schematises how the reader employed lexicogrammatical, intonational and semantic resources to prospect his message and manage the hearer's expectations. As the description above illustrates, at the lexical level the production of an element prospects a further element until a grammatical chain has been articulated. At the semantic level, the achievement of a target state represents the addition of a proposition to the existing state of affairs, and the new target state represents the new initial state which both interlocutors have access to. The reader used the prosodic systems of key and termination[27] to organise the increments textually into cohesive topics. He also employed prosody to signal the projected informational status of lexical items and to signal his expectation of the hearer's access to the propositional knowledge encoded within tone groups/information units.

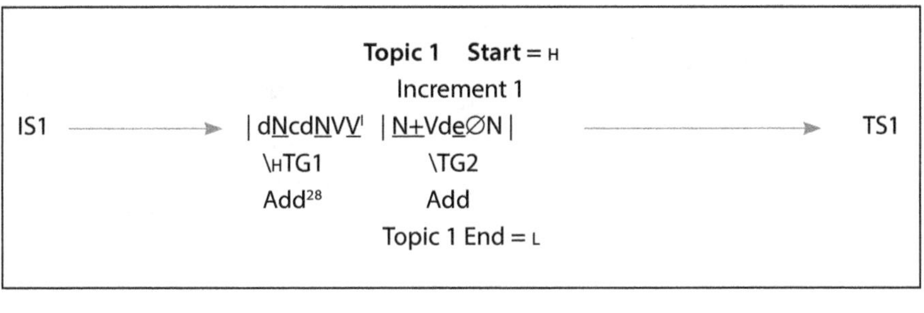

---

27   The same effect could be achieved through the use of adverbial and conjunctive elements.

28   The terms *ADD*, *REFER* and REFER/IMP indicate the speaker's assessment of who has knowledge to the propositional information contained within the tone group/information unit; with the former signalling that the speaker projects himself as having privileged access to the knowledge, while the latter projects the speaker as assuming that the hearer has equal access to the knowledge. REFER/IMP conveys the additional meaning that, as well as having equal access to the stated knowledge, the hearer additionally has equal access to a speaker produced implication.

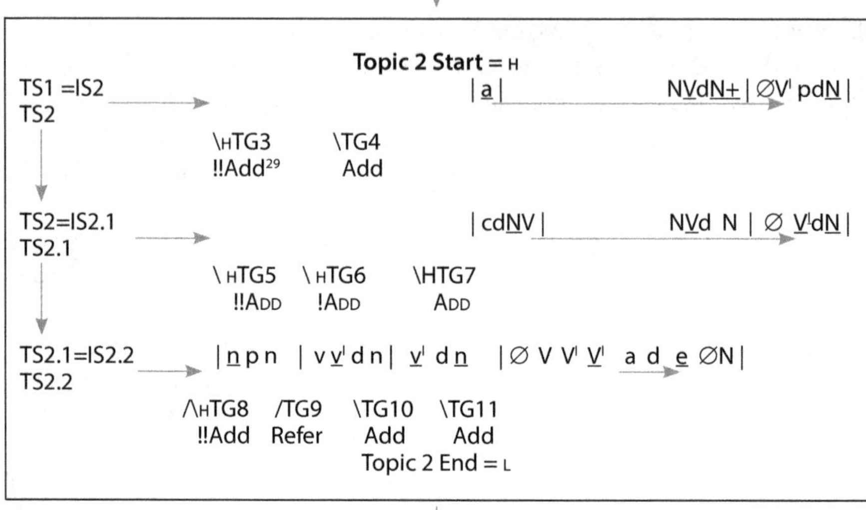

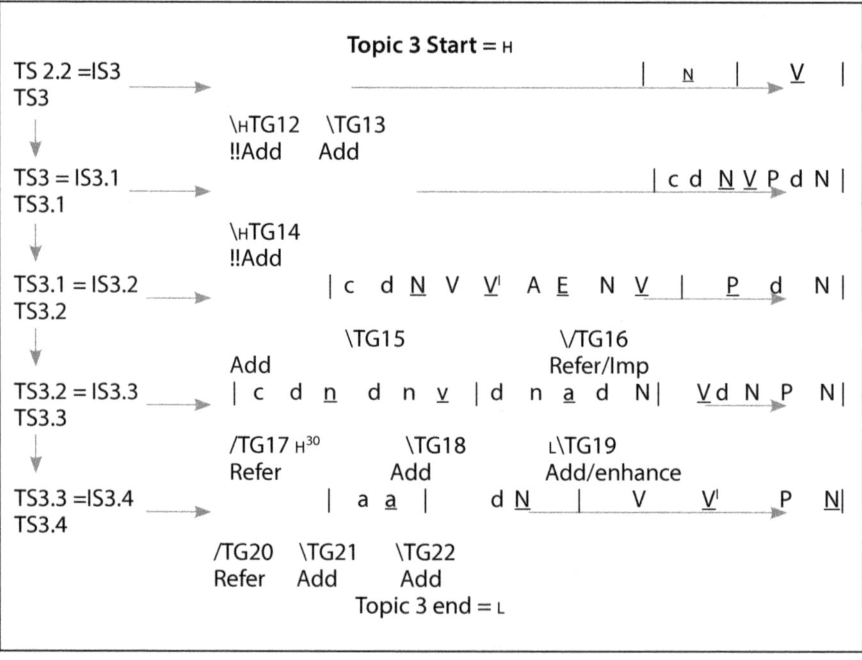

---

29   The exclamation mark ! signals the reader's anticipation that the content of the tone group/ information unit will be unpredictable. A double exclamation signals that the key has scope over the entire increment.

30   Placement of the H after the numbered TG indicates a termination choice.

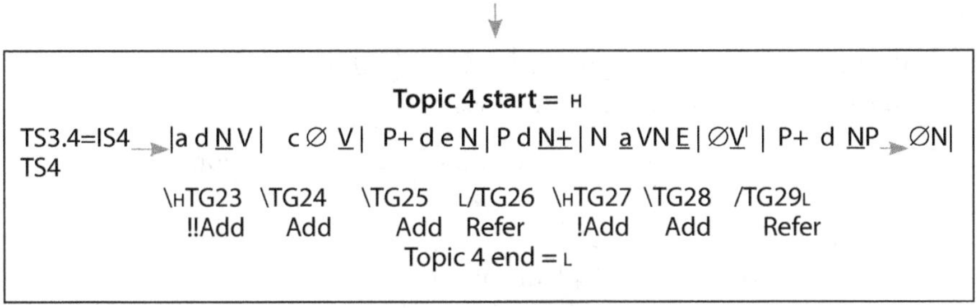

Figure 5.2 A schematic mapping of the increment structure of the Wind and the Sun (English)

Figure 5.2 shows that the multilayering of expectancies prospected by the reader in real time operates both locally and globally. Syntactic patterns emerge through use; the articulation of an element prospects a following element; in the case of English declarative mood, a nominal element prospects a verbal element, while an initial adverbial element does not remove the obligation to produce a nominal element. Spoken language, as an embodied semiotic resource, however, cannot be divorced from the physical context in which it is produced, and creates and alters the state of understanding shared by the speakers and hearers. In the text above, the shared state of understanding refers to access to knowledge but, in conversations involving actions, it may lead to physical change such as the procurement of goods.

The production of a lexical element, however, does not merely prospect a following lexical item, it simultaneously prospects the achievement of a target state: the speaker warrants that they will produce an utterance of relevance to the present communicative needs. The achievement of that target state may or may not satisfy the communicative need. If it does not, the target state – which itself is simultaneously a following initial state – prospects that more will be said. Speakers may use intonational resources to organise their message into topics; the opening of a topic prospects the hope that at some future point the topic will naturally be closed. Within and between increments tone selections are used to project which tone groups/information units convey propositional information that add to the existing state of understanding. Rising tone choices may be used to reach out and involve the hearer by asking for a notional response to an achieved target state. Within tone group/information units speakers signal their expectations of the accessibility of lexical items by choosing to make a particular lexical item prominent or not. The interaction of the linguistic resources mapped above enables the reader of the English text to produce his intended meanings.

The previous discussion of the intonation systems and chaining rules of Japanese and Greek has shown that they differ from the English systems. As such, we can say that the Japanese and Greek readers deployed different resources to convey equivalent meanings to that expressed by the English reader. Example 5.19 shows the intonation choices of the Japanese speaker.

5.19   The Intonation Transcription of the Japanese translation
1. | <u>Ka</u>ze to \<u>Tai</u>yo ga |
2. | /\Hdo<u>chi</u>ra ga tsuyoi ka |
3. | /\<u>ii</u>arasoi o shite imashita | End of Increment one

4. | Sono\ H <u>to</u>ki |
5. | tabi\<u>bi</u>to ga |
6. | L <u>mi</u>chi o <u>ya</u>tte \/H <u>ku</u>ru no ga mieta node |
7. | H <u>Tai</u>yo ga \<u>ii</u>mashita | End of Increment 2

8. | "Kachi H <u>ma</u>ke o <u>ki</u>meru \<u>ho</u>ho ga arimasu | End of increment 3

9. | Tabi H <u>bi</u>to no <u>ga</u>ito o / H <u>nu</u>gaseta |
10. | <u>ho</u> ga <u>tsu</u>yoi to \H <u>shi</u>masho | End of increment 4

11. |A<u>na</u>ta \/<u>ka</u>ra hajimete. | End of increment 5

12. |" /<u>So</u> itte |
13. | H \<u>Tai</u>yo wa |
14. | H <u>ku</u>mo no ushiro ni ka \<u>ku</u>re |
15. | \<u>Ka</u>ze wa |
16. | tabi<u>bi</u>to ni mu\<u>ka</u>tte |
17. | /<u>de</u>kiru dake |
18. | \H <u>tsu</u>yoku kaze o fukimashita | End of increment 6

19. | Shi\ H <u>ka</u>shi, |
20. | <u>Ka</u>ze ga <u>tsu</u>yoku <u>fu</u>keba fuku \<u>ho</u>do |
21. | tabi\<u>bi</u>to wa |
22. | \<u>ga</u>ito |
23. | o shik H <u>ka</u>ri ka/\<u>ra</u>da ni makitsuke<u>ma</u>shita | End of increment 7

24. | /<u>So</u>shite |
25. | H <u>tsu</u>i ni <u>ka</u>ze wa aki\<u>ra</u>memashita. | End of increment 8

26. | \ H <u>Ko</u>ndo wa |
27. | \ H <u>Tai</u>yo ga dete kite |
28. | tabi\<u>bi</u>to ni |
29. | a \H<u>ta</u>takana |

30. | hizashi o \H mukemashita |
31. |Suruto H suguni tabi\bito wa |
32. | atusugite \gaito wa |
33. | kite /\irare nai to omoimashita | End of increment 9

The first thing to note about the above transcription is that, as Japanese is a pitch accent language, no informational significance can be ascribed to the prominent syllables which we transcribed. Secondly, while we were able to transcribe high beginnings on tone groups, akin to key selections, there is not sufficient previous work done to allow us to claim any functional significance other than they may simply help to demark tone group boundaries. Thirdly, as mentioned previously, we cannot comment in detail on what chains are required to satisfy grammatical expectations. All we can say is that points in the written transcriptions, where our translators placed full stops, represent places where grammatical expectations have been satisfied. The Japanese text was organised as a chain of 9 sentences which we have equated with increments.

Each increment contains one or more tone groups/information units ranging from 1 to 8 tone groups per increment with a mean of 3.67 tone groups in an increment. The Japanese reader demonstrated a tendency to place initial adverbials and subject nominal elements within their own tone groups e.g. TGs 1, 13, 14, 15, 21 and 26 for subjects and TGs 4, 12, 19 and 24 for initial adverbials. All increments are completed by an end-falling tone, except increment 5 which contains a fall-rise, but it is not clear if this is of any functional significance.

Example 5.20 presents the Greek reader's reading of her translation. In her translation her punctuation choices produced seven sentences coterminous with their English equivalents.

5.20   The intonation transcription of the Greek translation
 1. | o aeras ke o \/ilios |
 2. | malonan pios itan o   pio   dina\tos | (End of increment 1)

 3. | ksafni L /ka |
 4. | \idan |
 5. | ena taxidioti na katiforizi to L \/dromo |
 6. | ke o ilios \ipe |
 7. | H vlepo ena tropo na chiristoume ti dia Lfon\ia mas | (End of increment 2)

 8. | Opios bori na /kani |
 9. | afton ton taxi L dioti na vgali tin L \/kappa tou |
10. | tha theori//thi |
11. | o pio di na\tos | (End of Increment 3)

12. | e H \\s̲y̲ ksenikas | (End of increment 4)

13. | /e̲tsi |
14. | o L̲ilios k̲r̲i̲f̲t̲i̲k̲e̲ piso ap' ta \\/s̲i̲nefa |
15. | kai o L/a̲e̲ras |
16. | a̲rchise na fi\\s̲a̲ |
17. | oso pio dinata bo\\/r̲o̲use |
18. | p̲ano ston taxi\\d̲i̲o̲ti | (end of increment 5)

19. | alla oso pio dinata f̲i̲s̲o̲u̲se o L /a̲e̲ras |
20. | t̲o̲so pio sfik/t̲a̲ |
21. | t̲y̲lige o taki L /d̲i̲o̲tis |
22. | tin L̲ k̲a̲p̲p̲a̲ \\p̲ano tou |
23. | m̲e̲chri pou o L /a̲e̲ras |
24. | anag̲k̲astike telik̲a̲ apelpis/m̲e̲nos |
25. | na egatal̲i̲psi tin pro\\s̲p̲athia | (end of increment 6)

26. | t̲o̲te o L /i̲lios |
27. | L v̲g̲ike kai e̲lampse me oli tou ti L /d̲o̲xa |
28. | H p̲ano ston taxi L /d̲i̲o̲ti |
29. | pou /e̲ni̲o̲se |
30. | oti ek̲a̲ne polli /z̲e̲sti |
31. | gia na krat̲i̲sei p̲ano tou tin \\k̲a̲p̲pa tou | (end of increment 7)

The reader has chunked her reading into 31 tone groups ranging from 1 to 6 tone groups within an increment with a mean of (4.4) tone groups per increment. She demonstrates a tendency, though not a strongly as the other two readers, to place suspensive initial adverbials and subjects within their own tone groups e.g., for adverbials tone groups, 3 and 13 and for subjects 1 and 16 with tone group 26 containing both a suspensive adverbial and a subject. All of the increments are completed with a final fall. As the pitch height of Greek prominent syllables seems to be absolute and not relative, Greek speakers do not appear to have the option of organising their increments into topics through the deployment of key, though it is noticeable that, of the multi tone group increments, all commence with an end-rising tone. Indeed, 3 of the 6 multi tone group only are sequences of rising tone groups completed by a falling tone group.

This may suggest that the division between falling tone and a following rising tone may signal a boundary and, therefore, that prosody indicates that both increments 5 and 6 may actually represent two increments. However, in the case of increment 5, the grammatical expectations have clearly not been satisfied as tone groups 17 and 18 contain material prospected by the verbal elements archisena fisa (blow

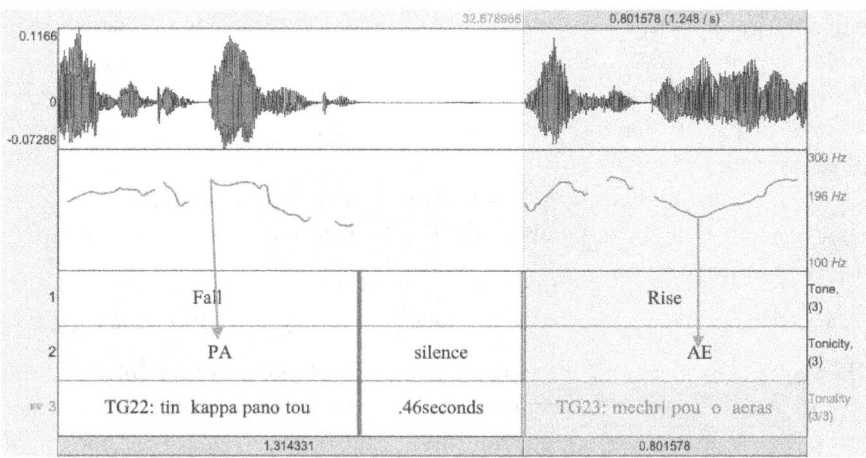

Figure 5.3 Spectrograph of Greek reading Tus 22 and 23

3rdsing start future); namely, the extent of the verbal action and its target. The absence of punctuation in the written translation also provides evidence for the absence of a boundary between tone groups 16 and 17. However, in increment 6, in her written translation, our translator placed a comma between tone groups 22 and 23 indicating that the grammatical chains pre and post comma are satisfied, which is evidence of a potential boundary. Furthermore, the speaker produced an extended pause of 0.5 second between the tone groups 22 and 23. See Figure 5.3 which visualises the Greek speaker's reading.

While it seems possible that there is an increment boundary between tone groups 22 and 23, it is also clear that production of a falling tone on its own is not always sufficient to signal an increment boundary as discussed in the case of tone groups 16 and 17. However, it may well be that the combination of falling tone followed by an extended pause is evidence for an increment boundary when grammatical criteria have been satisfied. While this argument remains in need of empirical validation, it does agree with that argument that the relationship between strata is redundant. The completed semantic units (the increments) are realised through the production of bounded lexicogrammatical meanings. The increment – a movement to a target state – is present on the semantic stratum and has a redundancy relationship with the lexicogrammatical chain and the intonation systems of tone and tonality.

While both Greek and English are pitch accent languages, which means that speakers tonicity choices are meaningful, the languages do not operate in an identical manner. Vallduví (1992) and Vallduví & Engdhal (1996) classify languages as plastic or non-plastic. By this they mean that in plastic languages such as English or German the speaker is free to place the tonic focus anywhere within the tone group. Other languages are non-plastic and have less malleable intonation and the tonic focus must appear on a fixed place within the tone group. Despite having a free order, the intonation of modern Greek is malleable: the focal accent is not restricted to final position if the final lexical items are being presented as recoverable (Georgountzou 1993:46)

Words occurring after the tonic accent are presented as recoverable as in English – see Example 5.17 above. Consider the English tone group 14 and its Greek cognate, also tone group 14.

5.21 | so the H <u>sun</u> re\<u>tired</u> behind a cloud | o L<u>i</u>lios <u>kriftike</u> piso ap' ta \/<u>sinefa</u> |

The English reader treated the elements 'behind a cloud' as recoverable from the context and made the verbal element 'retired' tonic. By contrast, the Greek reader made the nominal 'sinefa' (cloud) tonic indicating that, for her, she did not regard it as recoverable from the context. Both readers agreed that, in the following example, the focus was on the nominal element, but they produced very different strategies to achieve the same meaning.

5.22 | then the H\<u>sun</u> came out | | <u>To</u>te o L /<u>i</u>lios | L <u>vgike</u> kai <u>elampse</u> me oli tou ti L /<u>doxa</u> |

In the English tone group 23 the reader made the nominal element 'sun' tonic and thus, the remainder of the tone group is presented as being recoverable. The Greek reader similarly made the nominal 'ilios' (sun) tonic and final. The following verbal material 'vgike' (got out) appears in the following tone group. Hence, we can see that despite the arbitrary conventions of both languages resulting in different lexico-grammatical patterns and prospecting differing expectations, there seem to be some correspondences between the intonational systems of English and Greek in how intonation contributes to the marking of information structure.

Skopeteas (2016) argues that Greek clauses usually start from what is known, or is the topic, and culminate in what is new, or in focus. In her translated reading of the text, the Greek reader produced the following nominal references at the start of each increment.

5.23

Increment	First nominal reference	Greek	Note
1	The wind and the Sun	O aeras ke o ilios	Nominal Group
2	they (wind and sun)	idan	3rd person/pl past *see*
3	Any or (wind and sun)	Opios	Nominal Group (pronoun)
4	You = Wind	Esy	Nominal Group (pronoun)
5	The sun (Contrastive)	O ilios	Nominal Group
6	He = wind	Fisouse	3rd person/sing/past *blow*
7	The sun (Contrastive)	O ilios	Nominal Group

We can see that in all cases the first nominal reference was some combination of the Sun and the Wind. The traveller was not presented as topical in any of the increments. In increment 1 the references to the wind and the sun 'O aeras ke o ilios' were both accented, with the sun receiving the tonic accent: the reader presented the nominal group as containing referents which were not available from the context. This is natural as this was the beginning point of the fable. It concerns the topic of the wind and the sun. In the second increment the nominal reference is only present through the verb ending signalling person. The verb receives a tonic accent but this is to do with the action and not the actors. In the third increment the reference to either the wind and the sun is realised by the pronominal 'opios' which receives a pre-tonic accent: indicating that the choice between the wind and the sun is newsworthy. In the fourth increment the speaker reader overly includes the pronoun 'esy' ('you' singular) even though the reference is available from the verb ending '-as'. The informational significance of the pronoun is further accentuated by its receiving a pre tonic accent. The reader draws attention to the contrast between the wind who will do the action and the sun who will not. The nominal reference 'O ilios' in the next increment receives a pretonic accent again signalling the contrast between the actors. In the sixth increment, as it has been established who is doing the blowing, the nominal reference to the wind is found only in the verb ending '-se'. In increment 7, to signal a change of actor and to avoid ambiguity of reference, the reader produces the nominal reference 'O ilios'. Despite this being the third time that it has been overtly realised in the reading she makes it tonic to signal who is doing the action.

The brief gloss in the previous paragraph illustrates that while there are clearly differences in how intonational and lexicogrammatical choices interact in Greek compared with English, similar underlying principles exist. As noted above, speakers do not produce increments to satisfy grammatical chaining rules but rather to satisfy communicative needs. Accordingly, in the next section, we will briefly examine the semantics of the English text, and see that prospection on its own is incapable of explaining the valeur of the linguistic choices that form increments. Meaning does not only arise from the linear accretion of structure (see Martin 2013, and Matthiessen 2022 for further discussion). The systemic choices underlying the grammatical chains generate meaning potentials independent of structural similarity. For example, the N V N chains 'She kicked a boy' and 'She liked a boy' realise very different target states. In the next section we will briefly map out the options.

5.4   THE SEMANTICS OF THE WIND AND THE SUN

While we have demonstrated that prospection is capable of describing the structure of an English increment it is insufficient to map how meaning unfolds within an increment. For instance, the pronominal element 'she' functioning as subject prospects a following verbal element, but it is the verbal element that allows us to identify the semantic role of the subject pronominal element.

5.24   (a)   She is <u>dancing</u> (Actor)
       (b)   She <u>sees</u> the man (Senser Perceiver)
       (c)   She <u>likes</u> ballet (Senser Emoter)
       (d)   She <u>knows</u> the answer (Senser Cogniser)
       (e)   She <u>wants</u> more money (Senser Desirer)
       (f)   She <u>has</u> a house (Possessor)
       (g)   She <u>is</u> Intelligent (Carrier)
       (h)   She <u>is</u> the boss (Token)
       (i)   She <u>smiles</u> (Behaver)
       (j)   She <u>tells</u> the children to eat (Sayer)

As Example 5.24 illustrates, we can only know the participant role filled by the subject pronoun once the predicator has been articulated. While in most cases the participant role of the post-verbal element is predictable this is not always so. In the following example the material process predicator 'cross' can prospect either a Goal or a Range.

5.25   *She crossed <u>the ball</u>* (Goal),
       She crossed <u>the room</u> (Scope)

The unfolding of semantic meaning is not solely linear but is rather predicted by the semantic relations encoded in the predicator (lexical verb). In the active voice examples above, linearity signals that the subject will encode the most active participant role – be it Actor, Senser, Possessor etc., but the verbal process encoded in the predicator signals the actual participant role. To illustrate, we will look at the English text broken down into increments. We have underlined predicators and italicised subjects.

5.26
1. *The wind and the Sun* were <u>disputing</u> which was the stronger
2. Suddenly *they* <u>saw</u> a traveller coming down the road
3. and the *Sun* <u>said</u>: 'I <u>see</u> a way to decide our dispute
4. *Whichever of us can <u>cause</u> that traveller to take off his cloak* shall be <u>regarded</u> as the stronger.
5. *You* <u>begin</u>'.
6. So *the Sun* <u>retired</u> behind a cloud
7. and *the wind* began to <u>blow</u> as hard as it could upon the traveller
8. But *the harder the wind* <u>blew</u> *the more closely* <u>did</u> *the traveller* <u>wrap</u> his cloak round him,

9. till at last *the Wind* had to <u>give up</u> in despair.
10. Then *the Sun* <u>came out and shone</u> in all his glory upon the traveller *who* soon <u>found</u> it too hot to walk with his cloak on.

In the short text we can see that the most common process type is Material with only increments 1, 2 and 3 containing other process types. In increment 1 the wind and the sun are construed as behavers engaging in an active social activity with material consequences. In increment 2 the Sun and the Wind are construed as Senser Perceiver, and the first appearance of the third participant in the fable – the traveller – construes him as contained within the shared Innenwelt of the Sun and the Wind. He has no independent existence in the Umwelt. The Sun and the Wind are construed as Actors who cause change in the world. The traveller in increment 8 and 10 is construed as Actor, but the change he produces is ultimately caused by the Wind's blowing or the Sun's shining. Increments 3 to 5 represent a single verbal projection and thus function as the verbiage of the Sun's words. The Sun, and the Sun alone, is Sayer and hence he is the one who ultimately causes the actions described in increments 6 to 10.

To sum up, we can see that the meaning unfolded on two scales: one linearly between the increments where each target state was the initial state of the following increment; the other scale though was neither linear nor temporal. Instead it was formed out of the relations determined by the predicator, which governed the other participant roles be they Actor/Goal Senser/Phenomenon etc. While we have not looked at the semantics of the other two texts our prediction would be that Japanese would function rather like English with the predicator and associated particles predicting the participant in a manner similar to English. Teruya (2004) states that Japanese has four primary process types: Material, Mental, Relational and Verbal. So our expectation would be that realisation of the predicator and particles would predict the participant roles e.g.

5.27	彼女は<u>ダンスしている</u> Actor	She is dancing
5.28	彼女はその男**を**<u>見る</u> Senser	She sees the man
5.29	彼女は家**を**<u>持っています</u> Possesser	She has a house
5.30	彼女は子供たちに食べるよう**に**<u>言い</u>ます Sayer	She tells the children to eat

In each case the participant role filled by the pronoun 彼女 (kanajo) is only predicted after the realisation of the predicator underlined above and the presence of the emboldened particle. As of yet, there is no comparable functional grammar of Greek and so we are not able to comment on the participant roles in Greek. However, as in many cases the filling of the subject is only realised after the production of the predicator, it is likely that the language may be more accurately described using an ergative rather than a transitive description as in Example 5.31.

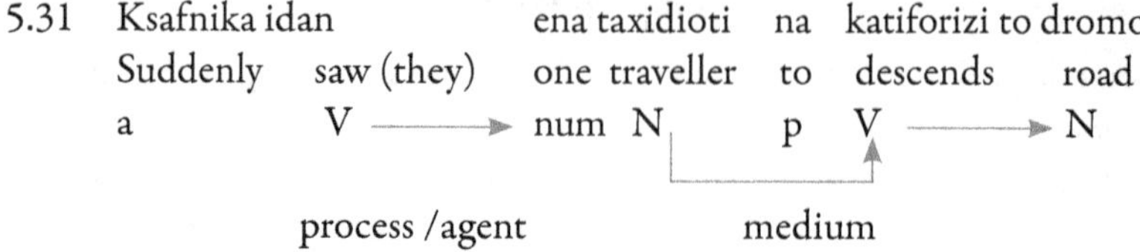

Semantically, the traveller's movement along the road is actualised in the inner cognition of the wind and the sun. While target state is realised by the production of the final nominal element 'dromo' the experiential potential radiates from the mental process, 3rd person 'see'. The traveller and his actions are encoded as part of the process, which itself is actualised in the traveller's actions. In the transitive model, the seeing is presented as being consciously directed at the traveller's movement, with the possibility that before long the gaze may switch focus; but in the ergative model the agents' seeing itself has no independent existence outside the medium of the traveller's movement – it is formed by the traveller's movement. Hence, despite the English and Greek readers both achieving target state through the production of the cognate nominals 'road' and 'dromos'[31] the propositions realised by the readers are not identical.

5.5   CONCLUSION

Our investigation of the expectations created by the production of lexical material across the three languages has revealed, not surprisingly, that each language represents a unique configuration of lexicogrammatical and intonational resources. However, we have also seen that key notions such as prospection and redundancy function across all 3 of the languages and enable the speakers to produce language appropriate to the context and suitable to achieving the speaker's communicative purpose. We schematised the options for our English reader and showed how he built up his message, increment by increment, into macro units we called topics to enable him to achieve his communicative purpose. Our descriptions of how our Japanese and Greek speakers' lexical grammatical and intonation choices moved the message towards the final target state were necessarily far vaguer. We have shown, however, that speakers of different languages use similar strategies, though ones with differing structural realisations, to achieve the same communicative purpose. And that these individual differences create different sets of relations across the grammar

---

31   'Road' and 'dromos' do not have the same value in their respective lexical systems. In Greek, 'dromos' covers the semantic domain, which in English is divided into 'street' and 'road'.

as a whole in order to achieve communicative equilibrium in relation to higher orders of meaning. This is what we refer to as the distinctive characterologies of languages (Bartlett and O'Grady 2019). This confirms the view that translating is not about choosing words but rather about how meanings realise wordings in contexts, see (Wang & Ma 2021). Such meaning choices are in redundancy relationships with the lexicogrammar and with the intonational choices. We ended the chapter by looking at the semantics of the English text and saw that linearity on its own could not explain the encoding of participant roles and that, unsurprisingly, what is encoded is language specific.

Chapter 6
Emergent creativity

The limits of my language indicate ~~the boundaries~~
the raw materials of my **future** world

With apologies to Ludwig Wittgenstein,
Tractatus Logico-Philosophicus 5.6

6.1   INTRODUCTION

Throughout this book we have stressed that person, language and society form an irreducible triad and that it is impossible to consider any one without reference to the others. In Chapter 2 we explored in some depth the embodied human capacities that make the social act of languaging possible and introduced the concept of prospection in relation to the relatively stable phonetic systems of English. In Chapter 3 we considered the structural properties of language as an external system and emphasised the metaredundant relationship between the various strata and the indeterminacy and unfinalisability that are the inevitable consequence of humans' dual propensity to follow norms and to take risks as they constantly adapt to new contexts, both natural and human-made. In Chapter 4 we revisited the concepts of strata and redundancy, and applied these to an analysis of Tony Blair's 7/7 press announcement. And, in Chapter 5, we further developed the concept of prospection, with a focus this time on the lexicogrammatical systems of three different languages, as another example of relatively stable and conventionalised systems. In this chapter we revisit the concept of prospection to consider how systems of meaning are produced, reproduced and challenged in the everyday process of languaging at different scales.

We begin by expanding on the account of language ontogeny in earlier chapters to consider language – or languaging – as a productive process in which speakers respond to a rich context, including the current social activity, the ongoing linguistic interaction and their personal semiotic histories. In order to do this, we build on the concept of prospection as this has been developed so far. In general terms, prospection captures the idea that the production of a particular element of structure anticipates the production of other elements and, more specifically, that each structure produced recalibrates the probability of what structure will follow (with up to a 100% chance for a specific structure[1]). In Chapter 2, prospection was illustrated in relation to the phonetic system in English and the idea that different syllable onsets prospect different probabilities for the vowels that follow. And, in Chapter 5, we examined how elements of lexicogrammatical structures prospect for following structures, pointing to differences in the lexicogrammatical systems of English, Greek and Japanese. In the current chapter, we interpret the key concept of prospection in terms of the production of texts as these realise the context of situation. At this level of abstraction, we are not looking at syllable structure or the completion of individual communicative acts, but at register and generic structure, as this emerges through the real-time concatenation of such communicative acts, each of which in turn creates constraints and affordances on those structures that potentially follow. Here we note that the probability of a specific act being produced is not a function of the preceding act alone, but also of the sociocultural environment in which the interaction takes place, including the centripetal forces of generic convention. These elements, taken together, produce a cognitive-emotional response from the speakers and an impulse to achieve a vaguely defined communicative target state. Speakers' contributions build towards this target state in incremental fashion, drawing on a shared reservoir of function-structures, with each completed act perturbing the ongoing situation and potentially recalibrating the elusive target state.

Speakers' cognitive-emotional responses to a situation are largely a function of their previous exposure to comparable situations and their means of formulating their responses are shaped by the conventions of those previous encounters. However, no situation is an exact replica of a previous situation, and no two speakers' semiotic histories are identical. Every instance, therefore, is the result of the tensions between centripetal and centrifugal forces. As a result, while the ongoing interaction shows a strong resemblance to previous situations of the same social type, and is hence recognisable as a similar event, there is also a degree of atypical or *non-criterial* activity.

In line with the discussion of the evolved human tendency to mix mimicry with informed risk-taking in a healthy ratio, we would predict that the distribution of features in stable examples of language use (at whatever level of abstraction) will roughly conform to an A-curve. This may well approach Kretzschmar's ideal ratio of 80:20 (with 20% of the features carrying out 80% of the work), though we are not so interested in backing up these specific predictions as with making the more general point that there will be a small number of features (the head of the curve) performing a highly disproportionate percentage of the work, and that these features will also be ranked. We consider these features *criterial*, in that they appear

---

1   Though speech disorders, lack of fluency in a language, wordplay and other factors may mean that a 100% probability is an idealisation even for 'fixed' phrases.

regularly in similar situations and are consistent means by which speakers can recognise not only what is going on in any situation, and what roles they are expected to play, but also the linguistic means by which they can perform these appropriate actions – what Bernstein (1971, 2000) labels speakers' *recognition* and *realisation rules*. Criterial features are not limited to the head of the curve, however. As with ant colonies where, in the event of attack, a small number protect the queen rather than fighting, there are features that appear in the tail of the A-curve that are not only regular but also essential for the reproduction of the system. Other aspects of the tail – those features that are not regularly repeated and which serve no immediate purpose in maintaining the system – are labelled background *noise*, inasmuch as they distract from the main activity, but not sufficiently to prevent its successful functioning. On the contrary, if these features, which are not random but overdetermined, fill unpredicted niches, then they are likely to be replicated in similar situations and may eventually become criterial features in future adaptations of the language activities in question. Similarly, criterial features in the tail of the A-curve may rise to the head as the system adapts (and features in the head fall away). *The features in the tail, therefore, represent a reservoir of resources that can be drawn on as needed, and which can thus serve to protect the system from senescence.*

In this chapter, then, we consider the productive forces that give rise to both the maintenance and the recalibration of the system, focusing on the dynamics operating at the level of text and the articulation of individual semantico-pragmatic acts within distinct contexts of situation. However, in accordance with the ideas developed in this book so far, it is important to remember that such dynamics are operating at all levels of language activity simultaneously, and that the situated speaker must attend to all these levels simultaneously as they develop their contributions in incremental fashion. After a return to theory, and a discussion of the relationship between reception and production, we turn to an analysis of a nurses' handover meeting in order to show the tensions between centripetal and centrifugal forces in action and the emergence of a recalibrated register that fills a previously neglected cultural niche.

6.2   FROM RECEPTION TO PRODUCTION IN CONTEXT

In Chapter 3 we considered Tomasello's (2003:58) three sets of processes in language acquisition, repeated below:

1   Prerequisite processes: segmenting speech; conceptualising referents;
2   Foundational processes: joint attention; intention reading; cultural learning;
3   Facilitative processes: lexical contrast; linguistic context.

While these are expressed in terms of reception rather than production, the existence of such receptive capacities suggests the parallel existence of the converse properties in the production of language by mature speakers (or there would be no such phenomena for infants to perceive). This, therefore, suggests an ontogenetic progression from receptive to productive processes, or what Tomasello (2003:25*ff*) labels *role-reversal imitation*. Thus, an infant's ability to segment in reception presumes the converse ability in adults to *sequence* in production, while the ability to contrast in reception presumes for adult speakers the converse ability to *select* in production. And just as the receptive processes rely on joint attention sharing and context to enable them, so social interaction and shared attention within context will stimulate production. In these terms, language acquisition is a form of cultural learning, the reproduction of recognisable behaviours and symbols in 'familiar' contexts, rather than the output of a universal grammar (though universal neurological capacities are clearly involved). This occurs, in acquisition, when an infant matches their intention with productive behaviours previously recognised in an adult and reproduces the symbolic means by which this was achieved. Tomasello (2003:307) thus rejects the Chomskyan idea that 'children are...putting together creative utterances with meaningful words and meaningless rules' and adopts instead a usage-based view, in which:

> ...what they are doing is constructing utterances out of already mastered pieces of language of various shapes, sizes and degrees of internal structure and abstraction – in ways appropriate to the exigencies of the current usage event. To engage in this process of symbolic integration, in which the child fits together into a coherent whole such things as item-based constructions and a novel item to go in the slot, the child must be focused on both form and function.

In these terms, item-based constructions of various lengths are the templates that the children have picked up and committed to habit on the basis of past interactions[2], and which are brought to the surface of the mind by their present situation, while the novel items are those elements which, although only newly encountered or encountered previously only in different situations, now form the point of contrast between the recycled template and the details of the current situation (for the empirical evidence underpinning this point of view, see Tomasello 2003:307*ff*.). Language acquisition (as both reception and production) is not, in these terms, the emergence in speech of underlying cognitive principles, but the ability to compare and contrast, to recycle and adapt, and the internalisation and sedimentation of practice as a mental template for future action (*cf.* Vygotsky 1978).

---

2   *Cf.* Bourdieu (1990) on the concepts of *practice* and *habitus* in relation to social activity in general.

We would go further in saying that acquisition of language practices, of form–function pairings in context, continues through the speaker's life as they not only expand their overall repertoire, but also as they learn to match the form and function of their productive practices to the specifics of the context in which this interaction takes place. This is expressed by Bernstein (1971, 2000) in terms of the socially acquired and internalised *recognition rules* by which we understand not just individual utterances, but how these articulate to define what is happening in situated interactions, and the range of behaviour that is appropriate within these interactions; and the socially acquired and internalised *realisation rules* by which we know the appropriate linguistic means of realising these behaviours within the context recognised. Recognition rules and realisation rules thus connect us to the idea of metaredundancy and the advanced cognitive ability to associate different contexts with different associations of linguistic form and function.

What Bernstein expresses in sociological terms finds a parallel in the biolinguistics framework of Pennisi and Falzone's (2016:85) description of this combination of receptive and productive processes as *performing procedures*, consisting of:

- a set of analogic operators that compare, in the absence of contextual identities, similarities with other contextual conditions memorised in specific libraries (analogic libraries);
- a set of exploratory operators capable of recognising contextual clues that analyse contextual factors of any nature whatsoever;
- a set of pragmatic operators that predict the effects of any actions on the context:
    - (i)   this set can predict generic actions that can be attempted or actions that can be explored;
    - (ii)   generic actions constitute a library of organised solutions already tried and which have had a certain degree of success;
    - (iii) specific actions arise from changes in general ones obtained by comparing generic actions of different types or trying actions never used before that could be suitable for unknown contexts;
- a set of operators or performative agents running cyclically (iii) until they find a safe but stabilised solution (approximately coming close to the purpose as much as possible, which will allow the enrichment of the library of generic actions and allows the prosecution of the activity and the one relative to the events produced).

The operations described by Pennisi and Falzone here correlate with the concept of prospection at the level of utterances, with production seen as the sequencing of selected templates of various sizes, with each choice perturbing the ongoing context and hence recalibrating the range of potential choices for subsequent productions.

We have previously described prospection as the tension between immanence and emergence. This captures the idea that, at each point in production, recognisable higher-order structures begin to emerge and future structures become immanent, such that the prospects for what follow are disturbed but not determined.

Complete utterances and larger linguistic acts are rarely formulated in full before production but emerge on an incremental basis in the process of production itself, with the formulation of each new unit prospecting but not determining the units that follow on the basis of the affective and communicative context as this is over-determined by past interactions including the latest increment itself. Thus, while speakers produce linguistic acts in anticipation of imprecisely imagined futures, the route taken to attain this future is recalibrated after each act as speakers constantly respond to and evaluate their ongoing production, the relationship between the present situation and their learnt expectations (*cf.* Eagleman 2015:56, 57, 93; Feldman Barrett 2017), and the potential effect of future choices (Huebner and Dennett 2009:149; Dennett 2017:353). Cyclical prospection results in more than the concatenation of individual communicative acts in a temporally extended text, however, as the various semantic elements made available by that temporal extension articulate to create meaning at a higher order of abstraction, the context of situation (Taverniers 2019, 2021).

In these terms, speakers not only attend to the grammatical and communicative adequacy of individual utterances, but also, and simultaneously, to the effect that these utterances will have upon the ongoing situation as a whole and, at a further remove and with varying degrees of awareness, to the longer-term histories and relations within which the situation itself is embedded (see Bartlett 2008 for an illustration of these ideas). Drawing on Bakhtin's work on chronotopes, Blommaert (2005:130–131) coins the term *layered simultaneity* to capture this idea – that the present context is not simply synchronous with the ongoing interaction but is rather a space in which 'multiple timescales and multiple contexts coalesce around [the] instance of interaction' (Bartlett 2017:388; see also Blommaert 2005:130–131) and in which the various speakers attend to multiple scales of interaction simultaneously (Corballis 2017:78; Collin, Milivojevic and Doeller 2015).

This is not just a linguistic response, but an embodied cognitive-affective response, or what Thibault (2021:86) calls 'thought-meaning complexes'. Following Wilkins and Wakefield (1995), in Pennisi and Falzone (2016:268; *cf.* Eagleman 2015:53; Maturana and Varela 1980:55; Feldman Barrett 2017:167) verbal, contextual and longer-term information are 'integrated into a single-modal representation' via the POT junction (the Parietal, Occipital and Temporal lobes, including Broca's and Wernicke's areas), while reflection across timescales is a function of the hippocampus (Corballis 2017:78). Lemke (2015:25) develops this relationship between language production and the embodied mind in some detail:

Somatic states, or conditions of the organism-in-interaction, are as much produced by the affective aspects of languaging and symbolic visualizations, etc. as they are the sources of them. We do not just use language and other semiotic meaning-making resources to interpret and evaluate somatically-based feelings, we also, by using semiotic resources and imaginative capacities generally, evoke feelings in ourselves and others through the affective connotations of our symbolic productions, and these in turn stimulate associated somatic states. It is very important to understand this circularity or reciprocity between meaning-and-feeling and the conditions felt and meant. Making meaning changes how we feel and how we are, both physiologically and in terms of how we are interacting with the world. Semiotic artifacts or works (texts, images, video, etc.) evoke meanings and feelings through the process of our interaction with them, which is at the same time both a material interaction and a semiotic and "aesthetic" (i.e. feeling-making) one. As we interpret a text, we are producing not only meanings but feelings, nor is it possible not to, because the same material processes that make one make the other as well. This is especially clear if we consider that a different interpretation of the meaning will be accompanied by a different feeling.

Complicating things further, we must also note that any situation will bring together a number of speakers, all with differing semiotic histories and attendant language practices operating across simultaneous layers. At any point, therefore, the recognition rules and realisation rules in play amongst the collective will be more than a simple matter of Pavlovian stimulus and response. Given the complex and multi-layered nature of context, along with the individual semiotic histories of the speakers involved, we should rather talk of the potential for response at any point as being *overdetermined*:

> First used scientifically by Freud, overdetermination refers to a non-reductionist account of human experience and [posits] that the constitution of each thing is given by the totality of cause and effects that give it instantiation. In Freud, that includes things not remembered, elements of the sub-conscious that act without being recognised. To understand something we cannot just look at the most visible and obvious causes, and overdetermination is a counter to these totalities of simple determination. Representation is problematised by the presence of non-visible or not articulated sentiments [which] must be included in the cognition of various aspects of social life, especially subjectivity.

> More generally overdetermination refers to multiple coexistent and complexly integrated structures, non-transparent modes in which certain types of activity express themselves. It is a counter to the idea of single determination of a whole and in its structuralist use is a counter to functionalist ideas of static harmonious wholes. Thus overdetermination is used to refer to multiple causality – or for instance in Freud a hysterical symptom or in Althusser a revolutionary situation – or just the social itself.
>
> http://www.generation-online.org/c/coverdetermination.htm
> (accessed 10/12/18)

This is in no way to suggest that production in context is entirely unpredictable, as copresent speakers are likely to have a shared level of understanding of the situation and their respective roles within it as well as the shared norms as to how to carry out these roles. Or, in the terms of Scollon and Scollon's *nexus* theory (2004; summarised in Blommaert 2018b [2013]:75), each instant is both a nexus of individual histories and a nexus of evolving discourses in which 'each act of communication is at once exceptional and typical... [and] while it derives its communicability from sharedness and recognisability of patterns...uniqueness always has a pedigree.' This is to say that, although recognisable situation types emerge from the articulation of individual utterances, these will be subject to both centrifugal and centripetal forces as different codes come into contact; as speakers attend to immediate needs that deflect from the emergent trajectory of the register; and as speakers choose between imitation and innovation, between normative and marked behaviour.

As suggested in Chapter 3, bringing together Rendell's and Kretzschmar's work, the mix of normativity and innovation in a healthy system will approximate to an A-curve distribution. It is worth repeating, however, that while the head of the A-curve comprises a small number of criterial features that allow the genre to function, and to be recognised, as a specific kind of activity, the features in the tail are a more mixed bag. Some of the form–function features in this 'tail' of the A-curve may be fleeting responses to immediate and unique contextual conditions, and these will be different in each running of the situation. Other minority form–function pairings, however, may carry out important generic functions despite their relative scarcity – acting perhaps as regular counters to the excesses of the criterial features. Features of this sort will recur again and again in the tail of the A-curve and can be considered criterial, if marginal, features. Both of these elements are available for increased uptake, potentially relegating other dominant features to the tail as a prelude to their eventual disappearance (though these too may remain stable or even rise back up the curve).

All of the features in the tail are motivated in some way, overdetermined by unique combinations of contextual features, and may prove to be *serviceable* in future situations. That is, if they fill a functional niche that was not necessarily anticipated by the collective, and that may not even correspond to the precise communicative function foreseen by the speaker, they may be replicated in similar situations in the future. In other words, the novel behaviour may be interpreted as functional by other participants (or the speaker themself) and incorporated as a new feature in the larger system of utterances that define the ongoing social situation. In this case, it is not only the novel element that derives a new communicative valeur, but the system as a whole. This idea is expressed in the language of neurological biolinguistics by Pennisi and Falzone (2016:191; cf. Corbetta and Schulman 2002) when they say that overdetermination of inputs leads to unexpected behaviours and that these 'unexpected cases "oblige" the central structure [of co-participants] by reincorporating them within our knowledge, in new and broader coordination and control systems.'

Taverniers (2018) refers to those articulations of meaning that linger on in semiotic systems as 'higher order grouping of strategies that "work" in context,' while in the terms of Laclau and Mouffe's Discourse Theory (1985:110; see also Chouliaraki and Fairclough 1999), this is a process by which disconnected *elements* become articulatory *moments* in wider networks of significance.

In Chapter 3 we considered meanings at the semantic stratum as articulations of meanings at the lexicogrammatical stratum. In this chapter we focus on the *context of situation* as the articulation of meanings at the semantic stratum as these extend over a text. It is important to clarify here that by *context of situation* we are referring only to the situation as it is construed by the language or other semiotic acts; we are not referring to those features that constrain or enable such construals. We are by no means ignoring such features, but would suggest that these are of a higher order of abstraction (see Bartlett 2017 on scalar supervenience).

6.3   ANALYSIS OF NURSING HANDOVERS

We concluded the previous section by claiming that the structure of texts emerges from the ongoing prospection and production of smaller function-structures and that the semantics of these structures, as they accumulate across a text, articulate to construe the ongoing activity as a recognisable social activity (at the contextual stratum). In this section we will look at three nursing handover sessions in order to illustrate these points and, in so doing, we will also suggest how distinctive and specialised systems of meaning emerge over time at localised scales of interaction as once peripheral activities respond to functional needs and hence move up the A-curve.

The nursing handovers we analyse were recorded for a collaborative project between the Centre for Language and Communication Research at Cardiff University and a local health board (Lloyd et al. 2021; Ylänne et al. 2021; Bartlett et al. 2020). Nursing handover sessions occur at 7am and 7pm, in between the nurses' 12-hour shifts, and involve the outgoing nurse in charge (ONIC) passing on key numbers and information to the incoming team in what is called the SPI (Safer Patient Initiative). On the ward where the research team worked, this involved a dozen or more nursing staff coming together in a cramped room for periods of up to 30 minutes. The central task in this period was the SPI itself, but the incoming staff were often gathered for 10 or 20 minutes waiting for the ONIC to be available. This time was spent chatting about different matters, including professional issues. At the end of the SPI, the incoming nursing team left the room and met with their counterparts on the ward for individual debriefs. These three aspects of the overall handover, while clearly separated, are not entirely discrete, and there is a significant flow of registers between them, as explored in Bartlett et al. (2020). For the purposes of the present chapter, however, we will just focus on the SPI itself as the formal means of handing over key information.

A lot has been written about handovers and similar practices, and the emphasis is usually on the need for the concise and accurate transfer of key information with as few deviations or distractions as possible. In other words, recommended practice is that the criterial features of the register should be maximised and that there should be as little background noise as possible. In our own data, however, we observed many occasions where the SPI departed from its standard format, sometimes for quite lengthy digressions. Given that we had been asked to work with the nursing staff on this particular ward, a team that was noted for both its efficiency and attention to patient and staff welfare, we were interested in exploring the form and function of the apparent digressions. Our main findings were that the nursing team in question used this space not only to pass on the key information required – a process with the potential to depersonalise the patients on the ward – but also to build solidarity with the patients in their care and to strengthen their group identity as a team. The digressions observed, therefore, filled a functional niche, one that was not foreseen by the those who seek to prescribe the linguistic format of these meetings, but which emerged spontaneously within the nursing team as a community of practice (Wenger 1998). Moreover, in the interactions we observed, the ONIC involved was always able to manage the digressions in terms of making them relevant, limiting their duration, and getting the talk back on track in terms of the goals and format of the SPI (Lloyd et al. 2021).

Over the course of our research, between February and May 2016, we recorded a total of twelve handover sessions. Here we will focus on three of them: Text 6.1, which exhibits the highly streamlined features generally advocated for the SPI with very few digressions; Text 6.2, which demonstrates a greater degree of digression without straying too far from the conventional format; and Text 6.3, which demonstrates significant – yet serviceable – digressions from the norms observed in Text 6.1. The analysis and discussion will be related to the key concepts set out at the beginning of this book as they operate at different scales: the formation of a register as an articulation of features at the semantic stratum (as these are realised by the articulation of features at the lexicogrammatical stratum); the metaredundant relation between these levels of meaning; the A-curve distribution of features at both levels; the systematisation of the distinctions realised; the prospection of meanings at several contextual scales simultaneously; and the potential for non-standard features to rise up the A-curve.

Text 6.1 is taken from a longer recording of the 7pm handover of May 12th 2016. As noted above, the SPI follows on from the informal talk of the incoming nursing team, and we have taken ONIC's "okay" in line 1 as a signal that the SPI itself is about to begin. Or, in the terms we have been developing throughout the book, we can say that ONIC's utterance *prospects* those registerial features typical of the SPI. Similarly, we consider that that ONIC's "thank-you" of line 7n overtly signals the end of the SPI and so prospects a change in both activity and registerial style.

Given the nature of the SPI, the text has been marked up to capture units of information, with each of these considered in terms of its speech function as a statement, question etc. We will use the term *act* to refer to each such unit. In these terms, the utterance "At risk of falling: A3, A4 and A6" counts as three acts (each of which is a statement): that A3 (referring to the patient in A bay, bed 3) is at risk of falling; that A4 is at risk of falling; and that A6 is at risk of falling. Whether these units of information are realised as full and separate clauses or by other means is a second aspect of the analysis. When we come to look at ratios in terms of the A-curve, therefore, the analysis focuses on the units of information and how these are realised and not on the relative length of the different contributions (though that would be an area worth researching in terms of the disruptiveness of digressions).

A quick overview of Text 6.1 shows that it exhibits the virtues of brevity, clarity and accuracy that many call for in handover meeting. We will therefore take it as a point of comparison with other, less constrained examples in order to compare the styles and functions of each. A more definitive statement about the distribution of the semantic and lexicogrammatical features typical of handovers in general would require the detailed analysis of a much larger corpus. Nevertheless, the relationships demonstrated between the three texts here will serve to illustrate the means by which non-criterial features can be introduced into text, with the potential to become criterial features in a recalibration of the register as the nature of the handover adapts to changing circumstances.

Text 6.1   May 12th 7pm Handover (see Appendix B for transcription conventions)

	1a	Okay (7) ((door shutting)) okay
ONIC	1b	we've had-
NURSE 1	2	Oh what's that (.) that by there
ONIC	3a	No cardiac arrests today (.) urm (.)
	3b	everybody's for resus
NURSE 1	4	[sounds surprised]: Oh
ONIC	5a	We've had no falls (1)
	5b	at risk of falling (.) A3 (.)
	5c	A4
	5d	and A6 (3)
	5e	B2 (.)
	5f	3 (.)
	5g	and 4 (2)
	5h	C2 (.)
	5i	3 (.)
	5j	4 (.)
	5k	5 and
	5l	6 (1)
	5m	D1 (.)
	5n	D4
	5o	and D6
	5p	trolleys 1 (.)
	5q	trolley 2 (.)
	5r	trolley 8 (.) and
	5s	trolley 11 (2)
	5t	there's no POVA's (.)
	5u	no sections urm
	5v	no self-discharge
	5w	no absconds (.)
	5x	no drug errors
	5y	or clinical incidents (1)
	5z	there are a few patients giving cause for concern (.) urm (1)
	5aa	no one in A
	5bb	B
	5cc	or C (.)
	5dd	D bay bed 4 urm (.) [FNLNM]
	5ee	just to make you aware that he's just on CIWA-Ar (1)
	5ff	and D6 (1) [FNLNM] ur:m (.)

	5gg	just to make you aware that he's due for dialysis in the morning (.)
	5hh	urm (1) Kelly's emailed (.) the (.) dialysis transport
	5ii	so that should be fine (1) ur:m (1)
	5jj	trolley 3 [FNLNF]
	5kk	she's a lady that's come from (3) ur:rm (2)
	5ll	she's come from home query sepsis (1)
	5mm	trolley 7 (.) [FNLNM]
	5nn	this is a chap that's just arrived (.) urm about 10 15 minutes ago
	5oo	he's a gentleman from YYF (.) (?) (?) (MI) (.)
	5pp	his troponins (.) like 4- 500 (1)
	5qq	an:d trolley 8 is [FNLNM] (.)
	5rr	and he's a gentleman with new fast AF (.) and CCF (.)
	5ss	he's had peroxin (1) urm
	5tt	there are no new (.) patients with pressure ulcers (.)
	5uu	CT check (.) (still being) done (1)
	5vv	there are no C- COPD patients on bundles (.)
	5ww	no trans- blood transfusions (.)
	5xx	infection
	5yy	or isolations
	5zz	there's just a gentleman in B3 (.) a (FSLNM) (1)
	5aaa	and he's on IV anti-biotics (.)
	5bbb	and he's had a couple of like episodes of diarrhoea (.) ur:m
	5ccc	samples been sent (.) ur:m but (.)
	5ddd	Isabelle said that it's not offensive
?NURSE	6	Hm
ONIC	7a	She thinks it is secondary to his (1) anti-biotics (1) urm (.)
	7b	there are no (.) patients on the unit needing palliative (.) urm (.) resus
	7c	trolleys (.) being checked by yourselves tonight (.)
	7d	hand hygiene audit's not been done (.) urm
	7e	boards are updated (.)
	7f	there aren't any staffing issues (1)
	7g	there's no one returning tomorrow that I'm aware of (.)
	7h	there's (.) been 37 admissions today (.)
	7i	there's still three patients to come in (.)
	7j	and there's roughly 50 patients on the unit at the moment (.)
	7k	5 patients (.) deemed at risk (.)
	7l	5 have had appropriate treatment (.)
	7m	and one of those is diagnosed (.) urm query sepsis (1)
	7n	Thank you
		((shuffling and moving))

Our point of departure in analysing the text is to consider the overall semantics of the text in terms of the interpersonal, experiential and textual features it exhibits. We start with a quick eyeballing of the text before providing more detailed analysis in terms of the key concepts we have been developing throughout the book.

In terms of interpersonal meanings, it can be seen that the text is overwhelmingly the passing on of unhedged information about impersonalised third parties; the talk shows few signs of interruptions; the transfer of information is almost exclusively from the ONIC to the incoming team; and there are a few markers of solidarity. In terms of textuality, the information presented appears very much in list form with few structural cohesive ties, and there is a highly restricted anchoring in space and an almost complete absence of temporal relations. In terms of experiential meanings, the text deals almost exclusively with medical and organisational issues on the ward, falling into three distinct sub-fields: a presentation of patient information according to predetermined medical categories (1b–7b); embedded within this phase, more detailed background information for 'patients giving cause for concern' (5z–5ss); and, finally, a summary of organisational issues (7c–7n).

6.3.1   Articulation, strata and redundancy

We next consider Text 6.1 in terms of the redundancies of meaning between different features of the text and the articulation of elements at one level of meaning to realise meanings at a higher level of abstraction. Starting with redundancy at the lexicogrammatical stratum, we will focus on the highly distinctive construction of the majority of what we can classify as statements (the passing on of information).

In lines 5b to 5s, in particular, we see that statements are made up entirely of a category label followed by a nominal group in the form of a locative description (bay and bed number). This gives us the minimal structure Category^Locative, with the category realised on a fall-rise tone and the locatives in each category realised through the standard listing intonation of a series of mostly level tones and a final falling tone (Tench 1997). Notice that, in this extended structure, there is neither mood, indexing negotiability, nor modality, indexing uncertainty, and that there is thus a degree of redundancy between these two (non-)elements in that both index in their own way the idea that the information being passed on is definitive. This is also indexed through the use of the listing intonation, with the final falling tone signalling completion (see Chapter 3). Lines 5t to 5cc mark a minor variant in this structure in that, whenever there are no category members to relate to the category label, an existential structure is employed with all the null categories following it in the same listing-stye exhibited in the previous construction. We thus see lexicogrammatical and intonational forms with redundancies in meaning articulating to realise a specific semantico-pragmatic act in what would be a highly marked manner within many contexts of situation, but which is one of the criterial features of the nursing handover, as well as in other contexts, such as the shipping forecast, where minimal information, clearly and uniformly transmitted, is optimal.

In terms of *redundancy* between interpersonal features at the semantic stratum, we can say that the overwhelming preponderance of statements, the lack of hedging and the one-way flow of information all index the authority of the speaker (ONIC). Alongside this marking of power differences, the occasional use of nurses' first names and the highly formulaic and impersonal reference to patients all overlap in indexing the distinction between the nurses as a team and the patients in their care. It is the articulation of the meanings created by these redundancies that define the overall tenor of the text, in which ONIC is at once part of the team yet set above the other nurses in terms of authority and expertise. In terms of experiential meanings, there is a clear redundancy in meaning in the way the many technical terms index the subject matter as belonging to the field of nursing, and there are similar redundancies in meanings relating to the spatial arrangements of the ward and the daily activities of the nursing team. Taken together, these meanings serve to create the specific field of the handover meeting. In terms of the textual meanings, the formulaic utterances, the lack of specification and the paucity of cohesive ties share the underlying features of brevity and focus, while the highly restricted use of temporal and spatial references both serve to focus information on the ongoing activity on the ward. The articulation of these textual features indexes the accuracy, efficiency and timeliness that mark out the nursing handover as a specific social activity. And the articulation of the specific interpersonal, experiential meanings described creates something that is not just the sum of its individual parts, but a distinctive and recognisable register in its entirety and its own right.

This brings us to the concept of metaredundancy and a more detailed analysis of the structures and their numbers from Text 6.1.

6.3.2   Criteriality and metaredundancy

In this section we consider the relationship between the different strata in more detail in order to illustrate the principle of metaredundancy and to test the hypothesis that different features will show an A-curve distribution across extended stretches of language. When analysing the context of situation, the features we are concerned with are, primarily, the different semantico-pragmatic acts that construe the situation as a distinctive social activity. Following the principle of metaredundancy, however, we will also be looking at the lexicogrammatical structures by which these acts are realised. From here we discuss the relationship between the head and the tail of the A-curve and between criterial features and noise.

Table 6.1 Acts per stage in Text 6.1 [3]

Semantic category	Number	%
Presenting numbers	35	46%
Providing background	25	33%
Organisational information	11	14%
Opening and closing	2	3%
Other	3	4%
Total acts	**76**	**100%**

Starting with the semantic stratum, we repeat the observation above that the text is overwhelmingly the passing on of medical information from the ONIC to the rest of the nursing team. Of the 76 acts in the text, 71 fall within this category, with the exceptions being the use of 'okay' (1a) and 'thank-you' (7n) to open and close the SPI; the off-topic question in 2; and the back-channels at (4) and (6). We also said that the text could be divided into three key stages on the basis of the experiential meanings involved. These were: a presentation of patient numbers according to predetermined medical categories (1b–7b); embedded within this stage, a more detailed provision of background details for 'patients giving cause for concern', occurring across two stretches (5z–5ss; 5aaa–7a); and a summary of organisational issues (7c–7m). Table 6.1 presents the number of acts in each of these stages and their relative percentages.

These figures provide a relatively good A-curve, with some features clearly dominant and others less so. While the two top categories perform 79% of the work, however, these figures do not appear to conform to Kretzschmar's 80/20 distribution in that there is not a large number of variants in the tail. However, over a larger corpus we could meaningfully subdivide the category 'other' into a broad range of distinct functions without altering the fact that the two top categories still carry out roughly 80% of the work. We will see evidence of this as we look at the figures in more detail. A further point to note is that, in terms of relative numbers, Organisational Information and Opening and Closing are elements of the tail. Here we clearly have a case where the two categories are not so much background noise as fulfilling vital if less frequent functions, as with the 20% of ants that protect the queen in times of attack.

We can drop a stratum now to consider a couple of the distinctive lexicogrammatical features of Text 6.1. Starting with nominal reference, we see that a number of different strategies are used, many of which include the location on the ward of the patient being referred to. These are presented in Table 6.2, along with their total numbers and relative frequencies. The category 'Location alone' refers to examples

---

3   Owing to rounding up of individual percentages these do not always add up to exactly 100%.

Table 6.2 Referring strategies in Text 6.1

Structure	Number	%
Location alone	18	36%
Pronoun	12	24%
'patient'	7	14%
Location^FNLN	6	12%
First name	2	4%
Other	5	10%
Total references	**50**	**100%**

such as 5b, where the patient is simply identified by their ward and bed number. The category Location^FNLN refers to examples such as 5dd, where both the location and the patient's first and last names are given, in that order.

Again we see a small number of forms carrying out the vast majority of the work, with the less frequent term 'patient' clearly a criterial feature of the 'tail 'and the category 'other' potentially containing numerous categories.

Alongside the use of location to refer to patients, the most striking feature of the text is probably the use of the minimal category^member constructions, such as 'at risk of falling: A3', to realise statements[4]. These constructions are further distinguished in that a single category can be followed by a large number of members (18, for example, in 5b–5s). Of the 71 statements in the text, 23 are realised this way, with a further 11 realised by negative existential clauses with a list of members following. There are 4 further statements that ellipt the finite element. The remaining 33 statements have the 'canonical' mood structure of subject plus finite, but 11 of these are marked in that the subject of the full declarative is coreferential with the participant in an immediately preceding moodless construction. This is exemplified below, where the member in 5dd is one of a long list following the category in 5z):

5z   There are a few patients giving cause for concern (.) urm

5dd   D bay bed 4 (.) [FNLNM]

5ee   just to make you aware that he's just on CIWA-Ar

5dd and 5ee are each analysed as statements here, with 5dd categorising the patient as 'giving cause for concern' and 5ee elaborating on what the cause for concern is.

---

4   It is an interesting observation here that the distinction in transitivity between identifying and other clause types is bleached. For example, we cannot say for certain whether 5dd is an elliptical form of 'D bay bed 4 (Ac) is giving cause for concern', or 'D bay bed 4 (Tk) is a member of the category "giving cause for concern" (Val)'. This is a nice example of the very language dynamics we have been talking about in play.

Table 6.3 Lexicogrammatical realisation of statements in Text 6.1

Structure	Number	%	Sub-category	Number	%	Second level sub-category	Number	%
No full mood	38	54%	category ^member	34	48%	Basic	23	32%
						After negative existential	11	15%
			No finite	4	6%			
Full declarative	33	46%	single	22	30%			
			combined	11	15%			
Total statements	**71**	**100%**						

5dd is therefore analysed as a moodless category^member construction, while 5ee is analysed as a 'combined' structure in which 5dd functions as a preposed theme (as well as a statement in its own right). Using these lexicogrammatical distinctions in the form of statements gives us the following distribution in Table 6.3.

According to these figures, non-canonical forms account for 70% of all statements in the text and so give it its distinctive profile as a specific register. In accordance with the concept of metaredundancy, this suggests that there is a distinctive lexicogrammatical profile within the specific context of the nursing handover. We should emphasise here that Halliday's approach to register differs from most others in that, while some analyses focus on the distribution of semantic features and others at the distribution of lexicogrammatical features, Halliday's definition (echoing Bernstein's combination of recognition rules and realisation rules) is that the context of situation is realised through the semantics as realised through the lexicogrammar. In other words, a register is not defined solely in terms of the semantic categories that are articulated within it, but also by the lexicogrammatical means by which *these semantic features* are realised. The numbers in Table 6.3, however, are to all intents and purposes based on a jump from the lexicogrammatical stratum to the contextual stratum, with only a very broad semantic category of 'statement' intervening. To rectify this, we can return to the observation, above, that Text 6.1 divides into three main stages (ignoring the peripheral opening and closing), each with their own communicative function. If we now analyse the lexicogrammatical characteristics of these individually, a more interesting picture emerges.

We start with stage 1 'presenting numbers of patients in key categories', embedding stage 2 (providing the background details of patients) (1b–7b). As nearly all references to patients occur in this stage, the figures here don't differ much from the figures from the whole text. In relation to clause structure, however, we see

Table 6.4 Lexicogrammatical realisation of statements in Text 6.1 Stage 1 (embedding Stage 2): presenting numbers of patients in key categories

Structure	Number	%	Sub-category	Number	%	Second level sub-category	Number	%
No full mood	36	60%	category ^member	34	57%	Basic	23	38%
						After negative existential	11	18%
			No finite	2	3%			
Full declarative	24	40%	single	13	22%			
			combined	11	18%			
Total statements	**60**	**100%**						

Table 6.5 Referring strategies in Text 6.1 Stage 1 (embedding Stage 2): presenting numbers of patients in key categories

Structure	Number	%
Location alone	18	38%
Pronoun	12	26%
'patient'	4	9%
Location^FNLN	6	13%
First name	2	4%
Other	5	11%
Total references	**47**	**100%**

here that non-canonical forms now account for 78% of all realisations, with the category^member structure hugely predominant at 57%. And if we take away those acts realising the semantics of 'explaining the background', which we have analysed as realising a separate stage embedded within the presenting numbers stage, we are left with an even more striking profile for the realisation of statements, as shown in Tables 6.6 and 6.7.

In Table 6.6 we see that non-canonical sentences drop marginally from 78% to 77% of all realisations, while the structure category^member (in its two variants) now accounts for 74% of all realisations. In Table 6.7 we see an increased predominance of referring expressions for patients or staff using locations alone or in combination (79%), and an almost complete disappearance of the use of pronouns. As well as the references to patients and staff, there are also eight references to problems or medical conditions after negative existentials.

Table 6.6 Lexicogrammatical realisation of statements in Text 6.1 Stage 1 alone: presenting numbers of patients in key categories

Structure	Number	%	Sub-category	Number	%	Second level sub-category	Number	%
No full mood	27	77%	category ^member	26	74%	Basic	18	51%
						After negative existential	8	23%
			No finite	1	3%			
Full declarative	8	23%	single	8	23%			
			combined	0	0%			
Total statements	**35**	**100%**						

Table 6.7 Referring strategies in Text 6.1 Stage 1 alone: presenting numbers of patients in key categories

Structure	Number	%
Location alone	18	75%
Pronoun	1	4%
'patient'	3	12%
Location^FNLN	1	4%
First name	0	0%
Other	1	4%
Total references	**24**	**100%**

We next turn to Stage 2, 'providing the background details of patients' (5z–5ss; 5aaa–7a), now separated from the presenting numbers stage. The profile of Stage 2 is shown in Tables 6.8 and 6.9.

The most striking feature here is that 11 of the 25 statements in this stage (44%) are realised by the combined declarative structure, whereby a patient introduced via a category^member structure serves as a preposed theme for a full declarative structure. This would account for the overwhelming reliance on pronouns to refer to patients in the clauses providing background information (both uses of first name here refer to nurses) and for the total disappearance of reference by location, either alone or in combination. However, looking in more detail at the text, we see that each example of background information relates to patients giving cause for concern, and that each of these was referred to, in the presentation of numbers stage, by the Location^FNLN structure rather than the location alone and, in one case, by a full declarative clause (5zz, which we will return to later). We can say, therefore, that

Table 6.8 Lexicogrammatical realisation of statements in Text 6.1 Stage 2: providing the background details of patients (5z–5ss; 5aaa–7a)

Structure	Number	%	Sub-category	Number	%	Second level sub-category	Number	%
No full mood	9	36%	category^ member	8	32%	Basic	5	20%
						After negative existential	3	12%
			No finite	1	4%			
Full declarative	16	64%	single	5	20%			
			combined	11	44%			
Total statements	**25**	**100%**						

Table 6.9 Referring strategies in Text 6.1 Stage 2: providing the background details of patients (5z–5ss; 5aaa–7a)

Structure	Number	%
Location alone	0	0%
Pronoun	11	50%
'patient'	1	4%
Location^FNLN	5	21%
First name	2	9%
Other	4	17%
Total references	**23**	**100%**

the production of the Location^FNLN structure in the presentation of numbers stage prospects the production of a stretch of background information realised by full declaratives and personal pronouns, features which are almost entirely absent in other sections of the text. Adding to this the fact that the four examples of 'other' from this section are 'lady', 'chap' and 'gentleman' (twice), we see a pattern whereby those cases giving cause for concern are introduced and discussed in more personable terms than other patients.

We now turn to Stage 3, 'summarising key organisational information about the ward' (7c–7m), which has the profile shown in Tables 6.10 and 6.11.

We see here that the predominant features of stage three are the use of full and uncombined declaratives and references to 'patients' (in full or ellipted form), marking it as distinct from either of the two previous stages.

Looking at Text 6.1 as a whole, and (provisionally) taking it as a textbook example, we can state that the register of handover meetings is realised by the articulation

Table 6.10 Lexicogrammatical realisation of statements in Text 6.1 Stage 3, summarising key organisational information about the ward

Structure	Number	%	Sub-category	Number	%
No full mood	2	18%	category^member	0	0%
			No finite	2	18%
Full declarative	9	81%	single	9	81%
			combined	0	0%
Total statements	**11**	**100%**			

Table 6.11 Referring strategies in Text 6.1 Stage 3, summarising key organisational information about the ward

Structure	Number	%	Sub-category	Number	%
Location alone	0	0%			
Pronoun	0	0%			
patient	5	100%	'patient'	3	60%
			Number with 'patient' understood	2	40%
Location^FNLN	0	0%			
First name	0	0%			
Other	0	0%			
Total references	**5**	**100%**			

of three distinct stages, each with their own characteristic properties. Within the presenting cases stage, the semantic category of statement dominates the acts performed, and these are realised predominantly by the lexicogrammatical structure category^member. The act of referring to patients is overwhelmingly realised by the structures location (for general cases) and location^FNLN (for cases giving cause for concern). The production of this latter category prospects the activity type "providing the background details of patients", with its associated structures.

Within the stage "providing background details", the semantic category of statement dominates the acts performed and these are realised predominantly by the combined declarative structure, with the subject of the clause referring back to the patient identified in the location^FNLN clause that prospected the provision of background information. The semantic act of referring to patients is overwhelmingly realised by pronouns and 'patients' with terms of respect also included.

Within the stage 'organisational matters', the semantic category of statement dominates the acts performed and these are generally realised by the lexicogrammatical

Table 6.12 Statement type and lexicogrammatical realisation in Text 6.1

Function Structure	Number	%	Sub-category	Number	%	Second level sub-category	Number	%
Statement	71	93%	Category ^member structure when presenting numbers	34	45%	*With referent as loc*	21	28%
						With referent as loc^FNLN	5	7%
						**With referent as problem or procedures*	8	11%
						Other	0	0%
			Combined declarative when providing background information	11	14%	*With referent as pronoun*	9	12%
						Other	2	3%
			Full declarative when reporting organisational matters	9	12%	*With referent as (ellipted form of) patient*	5	7%
						Other	4	5%
			Other	17	22%			
Other	5	7%						
Total acts	**76**	**100%**						

structure full declarative. The semantic act of referring to patients is entirely realised by the word 'patient' or by a numeral with the term 'patient' ellipted. Table 6.12 brings all this information together.

We can see from this table that three very specific combinations of semantic field and lexicogrammatical structure (that is, the register as realised by the semantics as realised by the lexicogrammar) account for 71% of all acts (and 76% of all statements). Narrowing this registerial specificity still further by including specific forms of reference in the categories, we find that five very specific function-structures (in italics) account for 65% of all acts (and 68% of all statements). These analyses, therefore, present strong support for the metaredundancy principle and the claim that register is not just a matter of semantics but of the semantics as realised by the lexicogrammar.

6.3.3   A-curve, tail and serviceable noise

The various figures presented above have all shown that a few tightly defined categories account for the majority of acts in Text 6.1, both at a global level and, more markedly, when we divide the text up into stages according to semantic content of the information transmitted. There is good evidence then to combine the metaredundancy principle with the distributional pattern of the A-curve. Although the ideal 80:20 A-curve distribution predicted by Kretzschmar only appeared in a few instances, it is, as we have said, highly probable that a larger data set allowing for greater distinction in items in the 'tail' of the curve would lead to a further approximation towards this ratio. However, the precise ratio is not central to the aims of this book. What we have suggested is that there will be an A-curve distribution, which is characteristic of the language at all strata, and that the head of the curve will comprise criterial features (i.e. features by which the language form can be recognised), while the tail will comprise a mix of regular functional features (such as the opening and closing in 1a and 7n), which may therefore be considered minor criterial features, along with the background noise that comes about through the overdetermination of motivating factors and the centrifugal forces that are always present. Lines 2, 4 and 6 are minor examples of this noise. Lines 5zz–7a, however, potentially point to a more interesting example. These lines do not quite conform to any of the five principal function-structures identified in Table 6.12. For example, while 5zz identifies a further patient 'giving cause for concern' and uses the Location^FNLN form of reference that is typically used to introduce patients in this category, there are differences in that: (i) there is a further reference to the patient through the use of the respectful term 'gentleman'; (ii) the patient is first introduced in 5zz by means of a full declarative form, not category^member structure of elsewhere; (iii) 5zz also includes the interpersonal marker 'just'; and (iv) three of the background clauses following (5aaa, 5bbb and 5ddd) are introduced by coordinating conjunctions, so diminishing the list-like properties of information, including background information, in other parts. The reference to one of the nurses as 'Isabelle' within the background information (5ddd) is also distinctive, as this represents one of only two such cases in the whole text. These six lines, therefore, while they share features with other examples of cause for concern, go further in singling out this particular patient for attention and empathy. We can, therefore, consider these six acts taken together as: (i) elements of the tail; (ii) overdetermined by both centripetal and centrifugal forces (conforming to generic expectations while manifesting professional empathy); yet (iii) only marginally digressive from the activity in hand (*cf.* line 2). As such, this section represents a good candidate for serviceable noise – an idea we will develop when we look at the two texts following.

6.3.4   Distinction and systematicity, and realisation

In this section we discuss the extent to which the semantic and lexicogrammatical features discussed above have become systematised according to distinctions relevant in the local context (see also Bartlett 2004). While we present the lexicogrammatical and semantic features in separate systems networks, the analysis above has shown there is a consistency in the relations between the two strata. Taken individually, therefore, the relations captured in these diagrams demonstrate the capacity for distinction and the tendency to systematisation discussed in the opening sections of his chapter. Taken together, they demonstrate the principle of metaredundancy and the concept of realisation between strata. On the basis of the analysis so far, we have suggested that the SPI, in its canonical or textbook format, falls into three distinct activities, or stages of the overall genre, with the systemic relations set out in Figure 6.1. At the lexicogrammatical level, the systems in Figures 6.2 and 6.3 relate to the emergent clause structure and reference strategies respectively.

As discussed above, the three systems are not to be seen as independent in practice. Rather, there are default realisations between the two strata which are not arbitrary but a function of the redundancies at each stratum and the articulatory relations between strata. Thus, for example, we discussed above how the semantic category of 'causes for concern' is prospected by a FNLN reference and is realised by a full declarative structure with pronominal and respectful references, all of which serve to personalise the patient and their condition.

The analyses have shown that these emergent systemic distinctions account for the majority of features in the text and that the correlation between semantic and lexicogrammatical distinctions is significant. In terms of Barbieri's (1985:169–170) and Maturana and Varela's (1980:93–94) claim that emergent elements must not only make sense in terms of their own make-up but must also be functional in the system operating at the next level up, we can say that, in their own terms, the

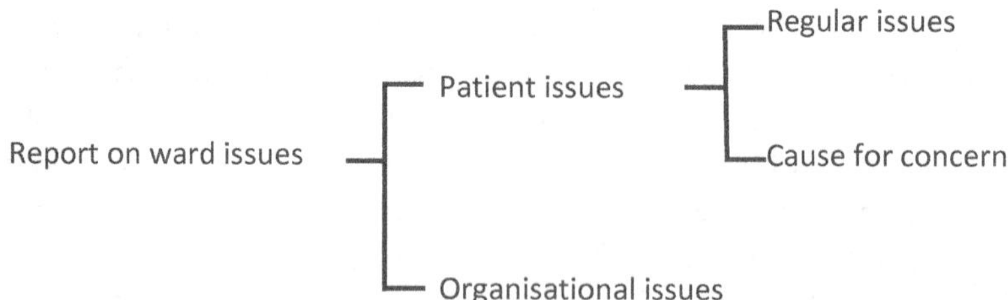

Figure 6.1 System network for activities (stages) within standard SPI

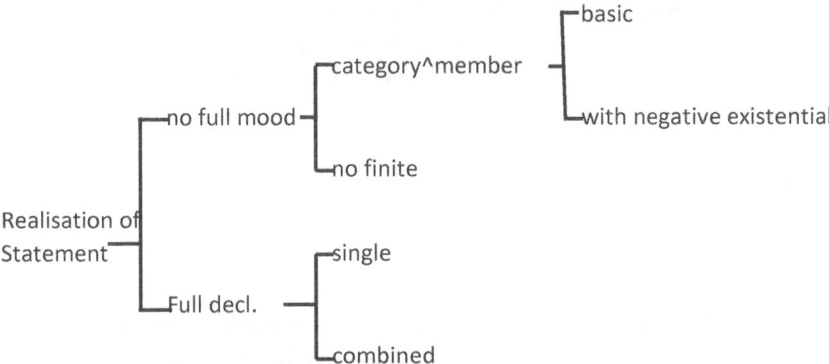

Figure 6.2 System network for realisation of statement within standard SPI

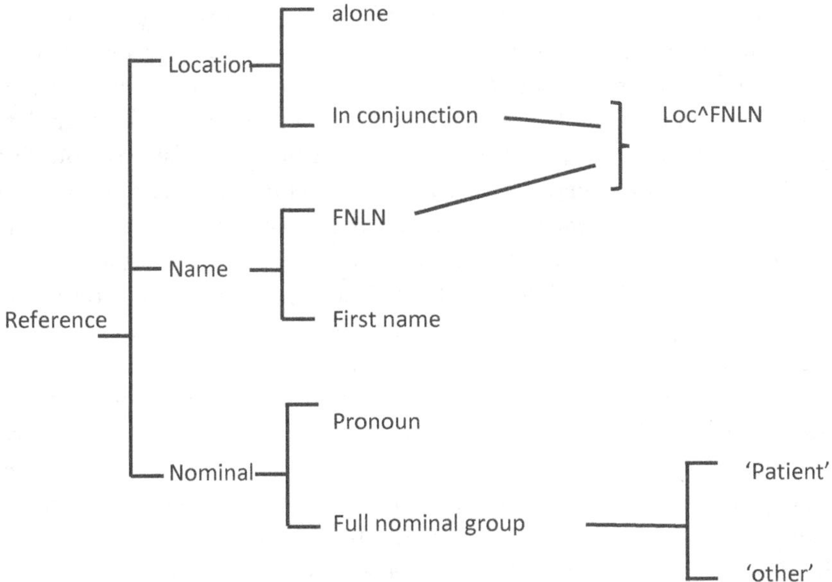

Figure 6.3 System network for reference within standard SPI

category^member structure is effective in relaying minimal information quickly and precisely; the structural addition of FNLN serves to personalise patients; and the further structural addition of full clauses is effective in providing necessary background information in more detail. Each of the structures is functional in terms of its own components, therefore. What Figures 6.1 to 6.3 show us is that the full structures themselves enter into systemic contrasts (Figures 6.2 and 6.3) and that these systems operate effectively at the next level up, as represented in the semantic system in Figure 6.1. In other words, Barbieri and Maturana and Varela's dictum turns out to be the metaredundancy principle in another guise.

We suggested above that the systems in Figs 6.1 to 6.3 represent the nursing handover register in its canonical or 'most stable' form. In the analysis of Texts 6.2 and 6.3 below, we will look at the extent to which the systems can accommodate those examples of serviceable noise that accelerate up the A-scale.

6.3.5   Prospection

Moving away from the structural properties of language systems at different levels of abstraction, we can briefly consider prospection at different levels as the process that enable these systems to emerge in use.

As suggested above, we can say that ONIC's 'okay' in turn 1 presumes the Target State of completing the SPI and thereby prospects the generic structure of Presenting Numbers^[background information for causes for concern]^Organisational issues. The first stage of the handover can therefore be considered as an intermediate TS while ONIC's formulaic phrase 'we've had' prospects a series of acts each presenting patient numbers until this intermediate TS is completed. In terms of the lexicogrammar, there are a small number of options in a metaredundant relation with this part of the handover: an (ellipted) existential structures or 'we've had' prospecting the structure *no* followed by a nominal group; or a bare category label prospecting a string of locative forms identifying members of the relevant category.

The completion of the presentation of straightforward cases prospects the movement to 'patients giving cause for concern', and the explicit announcement of this shift prospects a series of location^FNLN identifying structures, each of which in turn prospects one or more full clauses realising the embedded stage of 'providing background information'. Once the provision of background for causes for concern is complete, the presenting numbers stage in which it is embedded is also complete. The completion of this stage as an element in the generic structure of the handover prospects the organisational issues stage as the following element. In this stage, each act presenting an organisational issue represents a step towards the realisation of this stage as another intermediate TS. In terms of the lexicogrammar, there are a small number of structures available for realising the individual acts. An act may start with reference to a routine activity, which prospects a passive verb phrase signalling level of completion and an optional *by* phrase signalling who is responsible for completion. Alternatively, acts in this stage may begin with a *there is/are* structure prospecting a nominal group made up of a numeral, a *patient* referent, and a qualifier stating the patients' status, conditions or needs. The completion of the third stage as a further TS prospects a closing sequence (here simply 'thank you'), and this completes the SPI as the global TS.

We can see here the simultaneous operation of prospection at different scales, with ONIC attending to the global organisation of the handover, to the intermediate goals of each stage, and to the appropriate lexicogrammatical patterning of each increment along the way. Through this incremental process, with each completed act prospecting a range of possibilities, the generic structure of the nursing handover as an event emerges and the TS is eventually achieved.

We have been analysing Text 6.1 on the assumption that the manner of prospection and the production of acts largely followed the centripetal forces of the SPI as a regulated activity. In the analysis of Texts 6.2 and 6.3 we consider how overdetermination and centrifugal forces can perturb this structure, with serviceable elements of the tail rising up the A-curve.

Text 6.2 May 11th 7pm Handover

ONIC	1	Okay (.) evening everybody (2)
Multi		((Laughing))
ONIC	2a	we've had no cardiac arrests within the last 12 hours (.)
	2b	Not For Resus (.) D5 [FNLNM] (1)
	2c	D6 [FNLNM] (.)
	2d	C5 [FNLNF] (.)
	2e	No falls (.)
	2f	at risk of falls (.) A bay bed 3
	2g	and 4 (.)
	2h	B bay bed 3
	2i	and 4 (.)
	2j	C bay (.) 1
	2k	3
	2l	and 5 (.)
	2m	and all of D bay (1) ((clears throat))
	2n	trolleys 1
	2o	2
	2p	3
	2q	and 5 (2.5)
	2r	7
	2s	and 13 (1)
	2t	urm gentleman on trolley 3 [FNLNM] (.) he's had a POVA (.) initiated (.) urm (.) against his lo:dger (.)
	2u	his lodger lives with him
	2v	(.) a:nd takes care of his finances
Nurse?	3	ah yeh
ONIC	4	Ur::m (.) he's (1) he's an alcoholic on CIWA-Ar

Nurse?	5	Who the
Nurse?	6	[The patient or the
ONIC	7a	[The patient (.) urm (.)
	7b	and (.) he was very unkempt this gentleman (.) urm
	7c	so A and E have initiated (.) a POVA (.) just to look at his ho::me (.) u:m (.) circumstances basically (.) and see (.) you know what else needs to get involved (.)
	7d	no drug errors
	7e	clinical incidents
	7f	patients giving cause for concern (.) trolley 7 [FNLNM] (.)
	7g	he's on a naloxone infusion
Nurse ?	8	Trolley 7
ONIC	9a	Trolley 7 (.)
	9b	he's on half hourly urm (.) obs and GCS (.)
	9c	GCS is 10 at the moment (3)
	9d	Trolley 12 [FNLNF]
	9e	she's being treated for (.) cholangitis
	9f	and (.) she's on IV anti-biotics there (2)
	9g	A5 (.) [FNLNF] (.) urm
	9h	she's been spiking temps throughout the day
	9i	and she's being treated for urosepsis (1)
	9j	D1 [FNLNM]
	9k	he's scoring 7 on the NEWS (.)
	9l	being treated for lower respiratory tract infection (.)
	9m	he is on IV anti-biotics
	9n	and he's been reviewed by the medics frequently (.) throughout the day (2)
	9o	D4 (.) [FNLNM] (1)
	9p	this gentleman is sectioned
Nurse?	10	oh yeh
ONIC	11a	He's (.) in [NAME] Hospital (.) u:rm
	11b	we have got an RMN there with him 24 hours (1)
	11c	they're providing that for him (.)
	11d	he:'s had a Doppler today
	11e	he's come in with urm left leg swelling
	11f	he's had a Doppler (.)
	11g	but hasn't been reviewed
	11h	so once it's been reviewed
	11i	and treatment plan (.)
	11j	he'll be going back (.)
	11k	trolley 3 [FNLNM]

	11l	he's the gentleman (.) that I was telling you about the POVA (.)
	11m	He's on a CIWA-Ar (.)
	11n	he gets quite agitated
	11o	and he's <u>ve</u>ry anxious there (1)
	11p	patients with pressure ulcers (.) D4 [FNLNM]
	11q	he's got a grade 2 to the sacrum (.)
	11r	C5 [FNLNF] (.)
	11s	she's got a grade 2 to the sacrum (.)
	11t	and trolley 1 [FNLNF]
	11u	She's got a grade 2 to the sacrum (.)
	11v	no patients on COPD bundles
	11w	no blood transfusion (.)
	11x	infection isolation (.) trolley 4 [FNLNM] (.)
	11y	he's in the cubicle there
	11z	because he's neut- neutrapenic sepsis
	11aa	and we had the: (.) cubicle available (2)
	11bb	D1 [FNLNM]
	11cc	he's had one episode of diarrhoea this afternoon
	11dd	sample has been sent
	11ee	but he is on IV anti-biotics (1)
	11ff	pressure ulcer audit done (.) urm (.)
	11gg	a- asked the staff to update the boards (.)
	11hh	no staffing issues (.)
	11ii	we've had 20 admissions (.)
	11jj	49 patients on the ward (.)
	11kk	we've got 5 expected 3 by ambulance (.)
	11ll	s- six patients at risk (.)
	11mm	all had appropriate response (.)
	11nn	and one had a diagnosed sepsis (1)
	11oo	and that's your whole lot
Nurse ?	12	Thank you (1)
ONIC	13	Thank yo::u
		((shuffling))

At first glance, Text 6.2 appears very similar to Text 6.1 in many respects, and we can quickly go over the most significant features before looking at how it deviates from this pattern. In overall numerical terms, the passing on of information from ONIC to the incoming team represents 85 of 96 acts, with 1, 3, 5, 6, 7a, 8, 9a, 10, 11oo, 12 and 13 representing the very minor deviations from this. We can, however, break the text down into the same three subcategories as Text 6.1: Presenting

Table 6.13 Acts per stage in Text 6.2

Semantic category	Number	%
Presenting numbers	34	35%
Providing background	42	44%
Organisational information	9	9%
Opening and closing	4	4%
Other	7	7%
Total acts	**96**	**100%**

numbers (2a–11ee); Providing background (2t–11ee); and Organisational information (11ff–11nn),

The three top categories here represent 88% of the entire text, compared with 93% in Text 6.1, so showing a similar distribution. However, in Text 6.2 the majority of acts are presenting background information, with the percentage rising from 33% in Text 6.1 to 44% in Text 6.2, while the percentages for acts presenting numbers has fallen to 35% from 46%.

As suggested in the analysis of Text 6.1, however, it is not these raw figures that are of importance so much as the means by which these semantic components are realised by the lexicogrammar and the overall percentage of the distinctive sematic-lexicogrammatical pairings identified. The figures for Text 6.2 are shown in Table 6.14.

We see here that the three complex function-structures that dominated in Text 6.1 are also dominant in Text 6.2, accounting for 72% of all acts here and 71% for Text 6.1[5]. With reference forms added, five very specific function-structures (in italics) account for 66% of all acts (compared with 67% for Text 6.2). So we see that, in the case of these two texts at least, while the ratio of the different semantic categories varies between them (Tables 6.1 and 6.13), the percentage of distinctive function-structures remains stable at around 67%, or two thirds of all acts.

It would be tempting to say that the variation in ratios of the three stages on the SPI simply correlates with variations in the material context (i.e. the number of patients giving cause for concern) and hence the different lengths of the stages. There are, however, three stretches of Text 6.2 that present a slightly richer picture. First of all, lines 9o–11j, which follow the expected combined declarative structure, present an 11-line background description of the patient identified in 9o as a cause for concern. The longest stretch of background information in Text 6.1 was, in contrast, only five lines long (5ee–5ii). The reason for the greater ratio of background

---

5   The full declarative with referent as (ellipted form of) patient is marginal in Text 6.2 but not in Text 6.1 and is therefore included in the comparative analyses.

Table 6.14 Statement type and lexicogrammatical realisation in Text 6.2

Function Structure	Number	%	Sub-category	Number	%	Second level sub-category	Number	%
Statement	85	89%	Category ^member structure when presenting numbers	33	34%	*With referent as loc*	*14*	*15%*
						With referent as loc^FNLN	*14*	*15%*
						**With referent as problem or procedures*	*5*	*5%*
						Other	0	0%
			Combined declarative when providing background information	33	34%	*With referent as pronoun*	*27*	*28%*
						Other	6	6%
			Full declarative when reporting organisational matters	4	4%	*With referent as (ellipted form of) patient*	*3*	*3%*
						Other	1	1%
			Other	15	16%			
Other	11	11%						
Total acts	**96**	**100%**						

information in this text, then, is not solely connected to the number of patients giving cause for concern, but also by the amount of detail that is provided for each one.

We can take this idea further if we look at lines 2t to 7c. Here the six lines (plus interruptions) of background information precede the announcement of causes for concern (in 7f) and do not follow either the category^member structure of the presentation of patient numbers or the combined declarative structure of causes for concern. Rather, this stretch uses the same anomalous structure as 5zz–7a in Text 1, which was identified as a means of showing increased empathy with the patient.

However, lines 2t–7c in Text 6.2 have the added anomaly of appearing outside the cause for concern stage of the overall text. ONIC does, however, return to this patient in causes for concern (11k–11o), where the expected combined declarative structure is used.

Given its combination of atypical length, structure, placement and later reprise, the background information in 2t to 7c resembles more of a digression than the other instances we have seen in either Text 6.1 or Text 6.2. None of the features taken individually would be particularly striking. Rather, it is the articulation of these features that marks this stretch of text as novel. Moreover, the information in 2t–7c strays quite a distance from the core medical issues typical of the background information elsewhere in providing highly personalised and empathetic information about the gentleman's personal appearance and his domestic arrangement. We can suggest therefore that the superficially unremarkable structure of 5zz–7a in Text 6.1 represents an instance of serviceable noise in that its structure and its semantic content are coopted and expanded in Text 6.2 when the nurses in the handover (and specifically ONIC) provide more and richer background information about individual patients.

Despite the expansion of possibilities in Text 6.2, however, it would be fair to say that it largely resembles Text 6.1. This is not the case in Text 6.3, following, where the potential for personalisation and empathy that appeared very much in the tail of the previous texts, has not only expanded significantly, but also involves extensive dialogue between ONIC and other nurses as well as overlapping talk, omitted here for ease of reading (but see Lloyd et al. 2021). The text is divided into turns rather than acts here for the same reason.

In text 6.3 we once again see a serious case referenced (in turn 1) before the causes for concern are announced (in Turn 3), and again this is prospected by a combination of location and personal name as in Texts 6.1 and 6.2. In this case, however, it is only the first name that is used. This is very possibly as the patient is, in ONIC's terms, a 'young girl', so that this naming strategy both reflects and motivates compassion. This shift in reporting style prospects the possibility (delayed until causes for concern are officially announced) for less regulated structure of talk, in the form of interruptions and dialogue, and less institutional content, with the typical features of the pre-SPI chat permeating into the SPI (see Bartlett et al. 2020). This style of talk continues until turn 32, when ONIC recategorises the young girl as an official cause for concern and so prospects a return to the standard SPI format.

We therefore see, across the three texts, causes for concern being presented in a continuum of styles: from a very structured manner and with focused content, through examples with different structures or less focused content, and onto the extreme case in Text 6.3. We can analyse this in terms of a less-common criterial feature (background information) introducing serviceable noise into the tail (Text 1, lines

Text 6.3 3rd February 7pm

1	ONIC	over on MAU then you've got trolley 6 (.) 7 (1) and 9 (.) and then we've got 3 4 and 5 (.) and 11 12 and 13 (.) no absconds or self-discharges as yet but urm (.) a young girl in A1 [FN] (.) urm (2) she just- seems to spend more time off the ward than she's (.)
2	?	Hmm
3	ONIC	on (1) urm (1) no drug errors or clinical incidents (.) cause for concern
4	Nurse 1	she's urm (.) pinched] as well hasn't she
5	ONIC	Uh
6	Nurse 1	she's pinched
7	ONIC	yeh but what it is is (.) urm with her (.) she's a] young girl= she's the (?)°
8	Nurse 1	she's° pinched° yeh
9	ONIC	that I--. I thought it was that she'd- she'd been urm acq]uiring things off patients=
10	*	that she was the (?)]
11	ONIC	on the ward
12	?	£acquiring£
13	ONIC	but it wasn't-
14	?	Okay
15	ONIC	she was going out<u>side</u> (.) into shops (.)
16	Nurse 1	o::h
17	?	oh- yeh she can't go to D4 can she
18	ONIC	[selling them to the patients upstairs]
19	Nurse 1	gosh (.)[that's--]. r[eally] like [entrepreneurial] really] (.) [goh]
20	ONIC?	she's got the order (?)] ((laughing))
21	ONIC?	£the order£ ((laughing))
22	ONIC?	she got--. I got to be hones- s- say--. in all fairness [(.) she's got- (.)]
23	Nurse 1	she's got a lovely watch
24		((laughing))
25	ONIC	she's got a--. she's urm (1) got a sort of like a lot of underlying problems-
26	Nurse 1	-has she-
27	ONIC	yeh:h (.)I think I overheard her talking to one of the patients and her mum died about four five years ago
28	Nurse 1	Aww
29	?	Aww
30	ONIC	I think she's a young girl who needs to be (.) taken by the scruff of the neck and guided you know
31	Nurse 1	Yeh, yeh (2)
32	ONIC	but that's where the vi—I – they've only given me 3 cause for concerns out of (.) there's quite a few patients on the ward (.) but they've only (.) given me like 3 cause for concerns at the moment (.) gentleman in (.) A bay [FN urm LNM] is it (.)

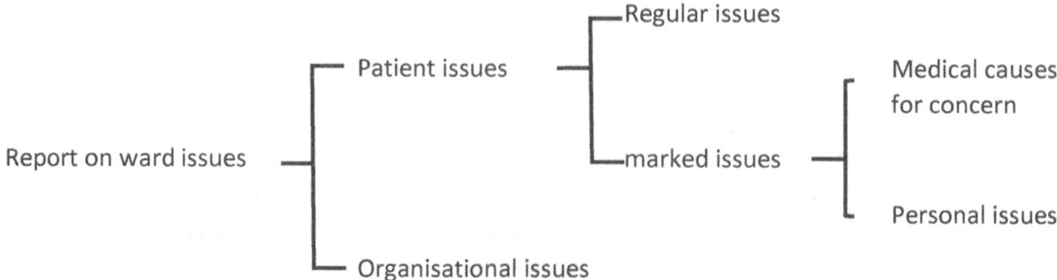

Figure 6.4 Expanded system network for activities (stages) in Text 6.4

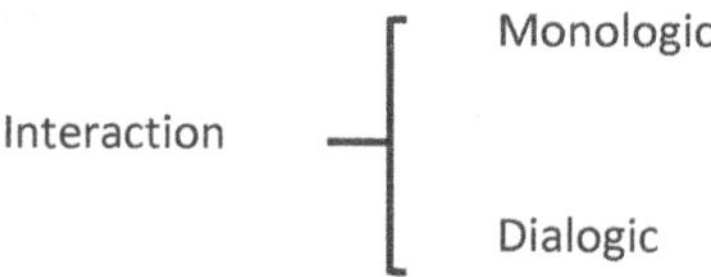

Figure 6.5 interaction type in Text 6.4

5zz–7a), with this noise evaluated positively as filling a functional niche (increasing personalisation and compassion) and so being further taken up and expanded, with successive expansions perturbing the register until it comprises a different set of systemic contrasts and, in essence, a distinct register. Figures 6.4 to 6.7 represent expanded systems for the nursing handover as these have emerged from the situated practice of the team we were working with.

Here we see the addition of a new system, monologic vs dialogic interaction (Figure 6.5). We also see that the category of 'presenting patient issues' has expanded from a contrast between regular issues (realised by the basic category^member structure) and causes for concern (realised by the combined declarative structure with FNLN), as in Figure 6.1, to a contrast between regular issues and marked issues (with marked issues signalled by the inclusion of personal names), as in Figure 6.4. This revised category now distinguishes between the medical causes for concern in the basic SPI format (realised as in the previous system) and patients with personal issues (which are distinguished in that they don't follow the usual combined declarative structure, appear out of sequence in the handover as a whole, and prospect dialogic interaction). And lastly, the use of FN alone has been extended to refer to a patient, though it is possible this will be limited to younger patients (Figure 6.7).

Note, however, that changes to the system are not accounted for solely in terms of additions and extensions. With the introduction of the new systems and subsystems and the extension of FN as a form of reference, the valeur of preexisting items in these systems is also altered, in that new points of distinction have been introduced. This will effect the potential for these items to be articulated and the meanings that emerge from such articulations in future instances of the handover.

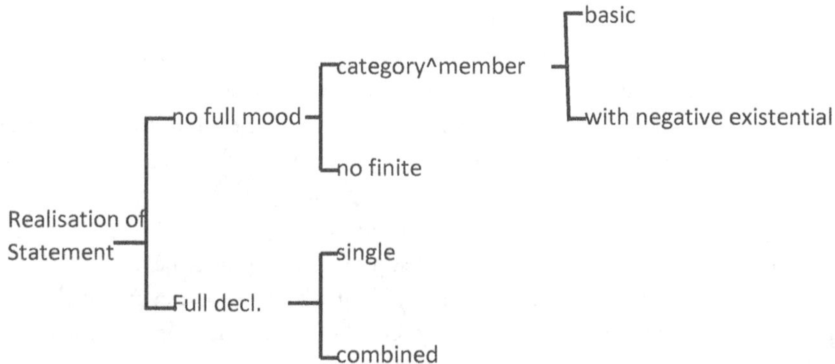

Figure 6.6. System network for realisation of statement within Text 6.3

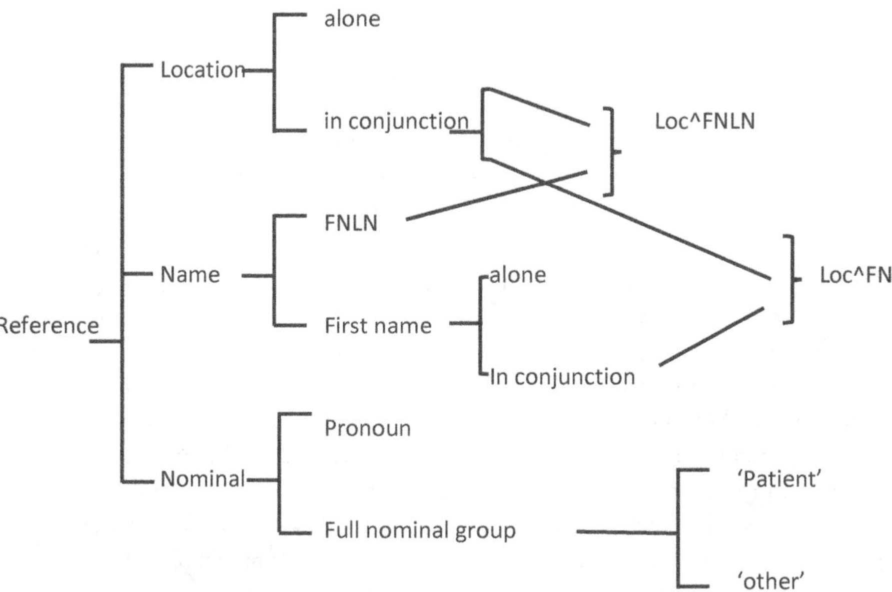

Figure 6.7 System network for reference in Text 6.3

It is also important to point out that the new features introduced have emerged organically, taking advantage of redundancies in the previous system in order to create novel articulations. The personal issues category, for example, draws on the more personal structures of FNLN reference and the full declarative, as used for causes for concern in Texts 6.1 and 6,2, and adds to this the informal and conversational features of the pre-SPI chat. Nothing arises *ex nihilo*, therefore, but (as insisted on by Maturana et al. 2016:651–652) is built by recombining the molecules of previous structures. And, following both Maturana and Varela (1980) and Barbieri (1985), we see that the new structures arising are able to function within the (recalibrated) higher level system as a whole, as evidenced by the smooth running of the handovers in Texts 6.1, 6.2 and 6.3 (see Lloyd et al. 2021 for further discussion).

Returning to our discussion in Chapter 3, we can further state that, while the systems represented above may be systems of pure values, they are motivated by the material and emotional needs of the nursing team as they operate in the real world and strive to combine the efficient transfer of meaning with compassion for their patients and care for themselves as a team. Extending the scale of context beyond the handover meeting to the hospital as an institution and beyond, it should be pointed out that the meetings we recorded were taking place against the combined backdrop of the mid-Staffordshire crisis, in which lack of compassion in hospital care was being seen as the cause of patient neglect and even deaths, and a growing concern for the welfare of hospital staff (see Lloyd *et al.* 2021 for a fuller discussion).

However, the centrifugal forces operating in Texts 6.2 and 6.3 may continue to such an extent that either the register bursts apart or we have a new register successfully responding to new demands. The question arises, therefore, whether those prescribing concise and clearly communicated information are right and minor incursions into the register lead in time to examples such as Text 6.3 as a non-functional aberration, or whether Text 6.3 represents the recalibration necessary to save a once functional register from senescence, adapting to changed needs by balancing the efficient transfer of core information with compassion for the patients and the nurses' care for themselves. Is the smooth functioning of the recalibrated handover in itself enough to positively evaluate these newly-emerged systems, given that they must, in turn, function within the wider system of meanings that constitute the operations of the hospital as an institution, and the material needs to which it must respond (primarily, the saving of patients' lives)? Given that an institutional lack of compassion was cited as the root of the Mid-Staffordshire crisis, it seems that ways need to be found to reintroduce compassion into the system. But, as one reviewer of Lloyd et al. (2021) asked, are there not other areas of nursing practice where compassion can be fostered, leaving the handover free for the concise and accurate transfer of key medical information? We are left, then, with the question of whether departure from the basic SPI format is a positive or a negative development – or, at least, the extent to which digressions should be permitted and the scope of these. This is the ongoing battle between centripetal and centrifugal forces, between karaoke imitation and risk-taking, between the twin risks of senescence and maladaptation, and the operating of systems within systems within systems.

6.4   CONCLUSION

The argument we have been developing in this book can be summarised as follows:

Elements of meaning at one level of abstraction, or *stratum*, can be *articulated* to form an element of meaning at a higher level of meaning, as when a declarative structure and a rising tone at the lexicogrammatical stratum between them create a 'check' at the semantic stratum, or when a punctual verb and continuous aspect articulate to express iterativity. This is a recursive process that leads to ever-higher levels of abstraction, from phonology to lexicogrammar to semantics to the context of situation (and beyond, though higher levels of abstraction have not been covered in the present volume). Language, and other semiotic systems, are thus stratally organised. There is a relationship of *metaredundancy* between these strata in that, for example, context is not realised simply by the semantics, but by the semantics as realised by the lexicogrammar. The concept of metaredundancy also predicts that there will not be a one-to-one realisation between individual terms across strata but rather a realisational relationship between areas of language, such that semantic areas are realised by lexicogrammatical areas. However, there is a level of metastability, in that a small number of realisational forms will account for the vast majority of realisational tokens. This skewed distribution, which has the general shape of an *A-curve*, occurs at different scales and for different registers and codes, though within such variants the elements that do the majority of the work will be different. The large number of alternative realisations that do the minority of the work, are referred to as the tail. These can either be criterial but minor features (such as openings and closings) or they can be the instance-specific results of an overdetermined context, in which case they can be considered as *noise*, in that they are not criterial in recognising and defining the higher order system in which they operate. Given the nature of overdetermination, however, such noise is always *motivated* and is therefore potentially *serviceable*. Serviceable noise is defined as novel or non-criterial articulations that occupy a *functional niche*, which may or may not have existed previously, and which will be positively evaluated and potentially *reproduced* in *equivalentially similar* situations (or contexts that share features at a particular degree of delicacy). In real time, such a process occurs through *prospection*, which means that the production of one structural element opens up the prospects for the range and type of element(s) that will potentially follow, and in this way larger structures at all scales are said to be constantly *emergent* and never synchronically stable. Within a *usage-based theory of acquisition* this means that the syntactic emergence of real-time production is the underpinning of paradigmatic emergence in the system. And given that functional niches correspond to local needs, such emergence occurs at a localised level, or *scale*, though these may be of vastly different spatial and temporal dimensions. This has been illustrated in this chapter not only in terms of the distinct systems of meaning active in the context of the handover generally speaking, but also at the more localised and unstable scale of the particular nursing team as a community of practice.

Canagarajah and De Costa (2016:2; see also Bartlett and Montesano Montessori 2021) claim that that such scalar analysis

> ...offers the possibility of going beyond the dominance of structuralist paradigms (which reduce social life to master narratives, unidirectional cause/effect analysis, static relationships, and deterministic macro-level structures) and adopt rhizomatic models (e.g. Deleuze and Guattari 1987) to consider the constant reconstitution of scales, generation of new scalar relationships, fluid connections between scales and other social and material constructs, unpredictable cause/effect relationships, and changing configurations of social processes and practices.

From our perspective, this does not mean so much an abandonment of structuralism as its reimagining in scalar, indeterminate and unfinalisable terms. In other words, while people as languaging and socialising persons will continue to explore and exploit the contrasts between the structures they encounter, the concept of a static, stable and universal language system is an illusion – an imaginary we adhere to (as speakers and linguists) in order to make life easier to understand and navigate. A more synchronically diverse and diachronically unstable perspective can be based on theoretical work into complex adaptive systems, defined in terms of the following basic operating principles (Kretzschmar 2015:11):

> (1) continuing dynamic activity in the system, (2) the random[6] interaction of large numbers of components, (3) exchange of information and feedback, (4) reinforcement of behaviours, (5) emergence of stable patterns without central control.

Within linguistics, complex systems theory has become an important factor in usage-based theories of language. Inflecting the above operations within a specifically linguistic framework, Ellis and Larsen-Freeman (2009a:2) state that language as complex adaptive system involves:

> (a) The system consists of multiple agents (the speakers in the speech community) interacting with one another. (b) The system is adaptive; that is, speakers' behaviour is based on their past interactions, and current and past interactions feed forward into future behaviour. (c) A speakers' behaviour is the consequence of competing factors ranging from perceptual mechanics to social motivation. (d) The structures of

---

6   We take issue with the idea that any interactions are truly random at a later point.

language emerge from interrelated patterns of experience, social interaction and cognitive processes.

From these basic formulations, the Graces provide an account of language development in the individual (ontogenesis) and its relation to collective language systems
(phylogenesis), which we interpret in a scalar rather than a monolithic way (and see
Matthiessen 2009 for an SFL perspective):

> An idiolect is emergent from an individual's language use through social
> interactions with other individuals in the communal language, where-
> as a communal language is emergent as the result of the interaction of
> the idiolects. Distinction and connection between these two levels is a
> common feature of CAS [Complex adaptive Systems]. Patterns at the
> collective level (such as bird flocks, fish schools, or economies) cannot
> be attributed to global coordination among individuals; the global pat-
> tern is emergent, resulting from long-term local interactions between
> individuals.

> Beckner et al. 2009:15

As we have stated it, each instance of communal language use is a realisation of the
semiotic context in which it is embedded and to which it contributes. However,
each novel instance appears as a mutation of previously encountered interactions
rather than a strict replication. Our linguistic behaviour is the product of embodied recognition rules and realisation rules evoked by the material-semiotic context.
Familiar contexts, therefore, produce familiar recognisable behaviour, but with the
complication that the myriad cognitive and affective features that comprise the immediate context, including the semiotic histories of the diverse participants, can
never be reproduced (just as you can never step in the same river twice). Repeated
instances of language activities are therefore not only approximations to previous
encounters, but ever-shifting approximations, with each new instance a mutation
of the blueprint that the context brings with it – what Gregory (1995) calls *generic
expectations and discoursal surprises*. Given the human proclivity to replication over
risk-taking, however, such surprises are only likely to be imitated if they are seen to
fill functional niches and many non-criterial forms will either disappear or remain
in the tail of the A-curve as background noise.

Linguistic adaptations of complex systems theory, such as that of the Graces,
have, however, remained focused on novelty at a single stratum, and generally that
of the lexicogrammar. In the current book we have extended this idea to consider
how existing sources at each stratum can articulate to create novelty at the next stratum up. Such a process does, however, entail washback and a reorganisation of the
system at the lower levels.

When a novel articulation at a particular stratum is imitated and taken up, it creates a complex sequence of *feedback loops* at different strata. These occur through four interconnected processes:

1   A novel articulation realises a new meaningful element at a higher stratum of meaning.
2   Following Saussurean systems logic, the introduction of each new element into the higher-order system will necessarily lead to a recalibration of the meanings within that system.
3   The meanings of the lower-order elements are themselves recalibrated within the lower-order stratum as a washback effect of their novel associations with higher-order meanings (cf. Halliday 1984 on 'the ineffability of grammatical categories').
4   These new meanings at the different strata are now available for further combinations and so the process repeats itself cyclically *ad infinitum* – which is to say that the system is always emergent but never arriving or finalised.

These are the 'recursive applications' alluded to but not illustrated in Pennisi and Falzone (2016:29). As a set, they lead not just to a reconfiguration of probabilities in an existing system, but to *an expansion of the meaning potential within the overall language system* both interstratally, through the creation of higher-order strata of meanings, and intrastratally, through the generation of new systems of meanings within each stratum.

Returning to the irreducible triad of person, language and society, our claim is that the language system is external to – but in mutual prehension with – the social system and the person, and that the production and development of linguistic forms by individuals is an *embodied* response to cognitive and emotional stimuli (see also Bourdieu 1990). We have further suggested that these responses articulate cyclically to create ever higher orders of meaning and that, in this way, linguistic and cultural evolution can be explained in entirely *materialist* terms, without recourse to concepts such as a mind–body duality or free will. In doing so we echo Pennisi and Falzone's (2016:252) central idea from evolutionary biolinguistics that the lack of a teleological principle does not mean we are dealing with a chaotically functioning cognitive system but that 'the rules of cognitive behaviour follow rational criteria of a local nature, that are derived from experiences that are organised and progressively ordered through performative experimentation.'

The language dynamic is thus both a materialist theory and a social theory. In contrast with purely stochastic models, in which A-curves naturally arise and self-perpetuate as a result of multiple interactions of random variables according to purely mathematical principles, we claim that social norms and expectations are both the product of linguistic behaviour and the guardians of future behaviour (cf. West

2017:346). These social norms and expectations, therefore, are systems of meaning at still higher levels of abstraction, a topic we will prospect but not realise for now.

Systems of interconnecting systems at different strata are not random or chaotic, but they are hugely complex, and it is this complexity that opens up the indeterminacy captured formally in the principle of metaredundancy. Alongside metaredundancy, we have drawn on the concepts of *systematicity, redundancy, stratality, criteriality* and *serviceable noise* and the processes of *distinction, articulation* and *prospection* in order to develop a theory of language dynamics, not simply in terms of synchronic variation and diachronic changes in structure, but in order to account for the increase in the meaning potential of language as a social biosemiotic system. To this end, we began the current chapter by overwriting a well-known aphorism from Wittgenstein with the view proposed throughout this book, that language does not so much indicate the boundaries of our world as provide the raw materials of our future worlds. We conclude by restating that the dynamics behind language come not from universal order, but from the interplay of indeterminacy and unforeseen functionality – as captured in another quote, this time from Leonard Cohen's 'Anthem':

> *Forget your perfect offering*
> *There's a crack, a crack in everything*
> *That's how the light gets in.*

Chapter 7

Outline of a socio-biosemiotic theory of language dynamics

We said at the beginning of Chapter 1 that the aim of this book was to identify a small set of processes and attendant properties that recur repeatedly within and across different orders of linguistic organisation and which demonstrate 'a continuity from the living of life on the one hand right down to the morpheme on the other' (Hasan 1984:57).

The recurrent processes we have discussed and illustrated throughout the book are *distinction*, *articulation* and *prospection*, and the attendant properties are *systematicity*, *redundancy*, *stratality*, *metaredundancy*, *criteriality* and *serviceable noise*.

In discussing, illustrating and, crucially, *interconnecting* these processes and properties we have presented a model of language as an external system, but one which forms part of an irreducible triad with the person and society. In doing so, we have outlined a functional theory of language that seeks to embrace, in the words of Butler (2009a, 2009b in Wray 2014:20) 'cognitive, sociocultural, discoursal, acquisitional, typological and diachronic explanations of language, besides accommodating observational evidence from corpora, experiments and intuition.'

However, as we have stressed from the outset, while we claim that the processes and properties above are essential for understanding the dynamics of language and that they recur at various spatiotemporal scales, we do not suggest that they comprise absolute rules or linguistic universals, nor that the list is comprehensive.

These processes and properties have been discussed and developed in detail in the preceding chapters. The following series of statements reviews the key concepts from these discussions and capture the essence of our socio-biosemiotic approach to the language dynamic in concise form.

Every linguistic act is an embodied response to an overdetermined affective context and is produced in anticipation of imprecisely imagined futures across multiple spatiotemporal scales.

That is to say, a speaker produces individual utterances in response to the immediate needs of the present communicative situation as this is embedded in multiple interlocking histories of interaction and in relation to their perceived interpersonal positioning within the interaction as a whole as this relates to a 'layered simultaneity' of social, institutional and cultural expectations and possibilities.

These different spatiotemporal scales are construed through linguistic formations at different levels of abstraction (or strata). A speaker must, therefore, simultaneously attend to the lexicogrammatical form of their current utterance; the function of this utterance as a semantico-pragmatic act and its interaction with other such acts in the construction of a communicative event; and the functioning of the communicative event as a whole in relation to other such events and the discursive formations which they comprise within the various social, institutional and cultural contexts in which they operate.

So, for example, a speaker must attend to formulating a declarative utterance with a first person subject and a modal verb in order to perform an offer as part of their ongoing communicative, affective and identity work within the generic constraints of a business meeting as this is embedded within a specific institution functioning in relation to other such institutions within the broader cultural context.

Complete utterances and larger linguistic acts are rarely formulated in full before production, but emerge on an incremental basis in the process of production itself, with the formulation of each new unit *prospecting* but not determining the units that follow on the basis of the affective and communicative context as this is overdetermined by past interactions, including the latest increment itself. Thus, while speakers produce linguistic acts in anticipation of imprecisely imagined futures, the route taken to attain this future is remapped after each incremental act as speakers constantly respond to and evaluate their ongoing production.

So, for example, we may begin to describe a film we saw the previous evening. We are aware of our feelings about the film and have a general sense of what we want to say, but in no way have we planned out precisely what we will say. Rather, we produce an initial utterance which sets us on the path to this general sense of what we want to say and then build on this utterance step-by-step, reflecting on where we are and where we want to go at each new point up until we feel we have more or less achieved what we set out to do or some modified version of this. This process also occurs at lower levels of language. As I start to write this sentence, for example, I know the message I want to get across, but I have not formulated in advance the complete idea nor decided on the lexicogrammatical structures I will employ to achieve my goals – I proceed one function-structure at a time, with each new function-structure both constraining and opening up new possibilities, until I feel I have expressed a relevant idea through a complete lexicogrammatical sentence. If my overall target has been reached, I may stop and hand the floor to my interlocutors; otherwise, I set out again.

Each increment both narrows down the path to the imprecisely imagined future while opening up new paths and alternative futures. Given that linguistic action is overdetermined, the paths taken and the futures imagined are neither free nor fixed. This relates to all levels simultaneously and prospection is constrained across multiple spatiotemporal scales in different ways.

So, for example, the phonetic systems of individual languages allow only allow certain sounds to follow after others; the canonical structures of grammatical units delimit the options available once an item has been uttered; and the sequencing of utterances in social situations adhere to the expectations of the relevant genre.

When, across countless acts of prospection, meaningful elements are regularly produced together, either simultaneously or in sequence, they become associated by convention as an element of meaning at a higher level of abstraction. This is a cyclical operation, which we call articulation, and the articulation of language features at different scales of abstraction correlates with the operation of these features across ever larger spatiotemporal scales.

So, for example, when an interrogative structure in the lexicogrammar is produced with rising tone, the resultant articulation is conventionally recognised as the semantico-pragmatic act of asking a question; when one speaker in an interaction articulates an abundance of questions, directives and evaluations, we conventionally recognise this as a power imbalance between speakers, while the articulation of offers, questions, request and statements, along with the appropriate politeness strategies and subject matter, are conventionally recognised as a service encounter, and specific articulations of service encounters, business meetings and office chat are conventionally recognised as an institution. And, in turn, the articulation of institutions within specific spatiotemporal bounds is conventionally recognised as a social system.

The elements at one level of abstraction articulate to form a distinguishable element operating at the next level of abstraction. By a distinguishable element, we mean that an element must be structurally different from those around it; that this difference in structure must be sensible to a perceiver; that this sensible difference should be functionally meaningful to an interpreter; and that this functional difference might carry an evaluative load for a socialised individual.

So, for example, horse and house are two different lexemes which are phonologically distinguishable; the concepts of horse and house are relevant social categories; and the concept of house potentially carries a different evaluation to the ideationally similar concept of a home. At higher level of abstraction, the semantico-pragmatic acts of bare directive and a polite directive are realised through distinct lexicogrammatical means and carry different evaluative loads, and so on.

At each level of abstraction, an element derives its meaning from its place in the system of meaningful elements at that level, each of which derives its meaning as a function of the sum of its uses at the next highest level.

So, for example, the lexicogrammatical system of English, includes elements such as declarative and interrogative structures, which are defined in opposition to each other, while these two structures between them comprise the indicative options, which are defined in opposition to imperative structures. At a higher level of abstraction, we have the semantico-pragmatic functions of language, with elements such as questions, statements and offers defined in relation to each other. The meaning of the declarative structure is a function of all the semantico-pragmatic uses to which it can be put, and this meaning is in systemic contrast to other structures such as interrogatives, which are likewise derived from the sum of semantico-pragmatic uses to which they are put. At increasingly higher levels of abstraction, we have systems of activity types (or genres), institutions, and entire social systems, each defined in relation to each other and as functions of their uses at the next highest level.

The meaning of the articulated form, as an individual element at the higher level of abstraction, is motivated by (but not reducible to) the combined meanings of the individual elements from the lower level that comprise it, but it is ultimately a function of the place of the newly articulated form within the system of relations at the more abstract level, as a function of the sum of its uses at the next again level of abstraction.

So, for example, while the meaning of an offer is motivated by the individual meaning of 'I', 'shall' and the declarative, its meaning at the semantico-pragmatic level is more than the sum of these parts and derives from its relationship to other semantico-pragmatic acts such as a command, a promise or a request (each of which derives its meaning as a function of the sum of their uses in context). Similarly, while the function of a business meeting in a specific institution is motivated by the semantico-pragmatic activities that comprise it, its meaning as an activity is defined by its place within the system of other activities that take place within that institution (each of which derives its meaning as a function of the sum of their uses within the institutional context).

Just as the meaning of the articulated form is more than the sum of its parts, so the full meaning of the articulated elements, as they operate at the level below, is not exhausted in the articulation. There is, therefore, a superfluity of meaning that is supressed but not eliminated by the conventional association of the different elements in the articulation. This superfluity of meaning is ever present as a latent potential.

To give a well-known example, the articulation of an interrogative, a second person pronoun and a modal verb is conventionally associated with a polite request; however, this articulation can be subverted by drawing on the supressed meanings of the component parts. This is the case when children reply 'Yes, I can' to the conventionalised request 'Can you pass me the salt?'

As the function of the articulation within the higher order system is motivated but not determined by the functions of the individual articulated elements, it follows that there is no unique articulation of elements that can serve to fulfil that function within the higher-order system. This allows for there to be more than one such articulation of lower-order elements fulfilling the higher-order function at any one time.

So, for example, a statement at the semantico-pragmatic level can be realised by a number of forms, such as: Tom went to the shops; Hebrides – gale force 8; *and* Saw a good film last night. *Similarly, the idea of iterativity at the semantico-pragmatic level can be expressed through the articulation of a punctual process and a continuous grammatical structure, as in* He was banging his head against the wall, *or by the use of adverbial phrases, as in* He banged his head repeatedly. *This is particularly noticeable cross-linguistically, where superficially similar languages create broadly comparable distinctions at the semantico-pragmatic level through the articulation of distinct lexicogrammatical elements. At a higher level, a social power imbalance within a specific situation may be displayed by means of direct commands and highly subjective language on one occasion but by direct questions and repeated interruptions on another occasion.*

There is not, therefore, a one-to-one correspondence between meaningful elements at one level of abstraction and the articulation of elements from the lower level. There are, however, dominant conventions within specific sub-domains of activity, within social groups and according to demographics of age, class and gender, as well as across the totality of such domains (with these last referred to as canonical forms). A socialised speaker will be able to distinguish the context on the evidence of the conventional associations in play and, conversely, they will be able to distinguish those associations that are likely to be in play on the basis of the context. Within a specific context, conventional associations are redundant, in that the presence of one element predicts the presence of the other. When different redundancy relations hold for different contexts, this is an example of metaredundancy, as the different associations between elements are predicted by the contexts, and vice versa.

So, for example, in the shipping forecast, the semantico-pragmatic act of a statement predicts the use of a simple topic and comment structure, while the topic-comment structure predicts the semantico-pragmatic act of a statement. The two structures are therefore redundant in relation to each other. Moreover, the redundancy between topic-comment structures and statements predicts the context of a shipping forecast, while the context of a shipping forecast predicts the redundancy relationship between the topic-comment structure and statement. This is a metaredundant relationship.

The potential meaning in any given situation is not linear and stable but over-determined by a number of competing features. This allows for the appearance of novel articulations, the recycling of old articulations and the take-up of the potential that was latent in the superfluity of meaning of articulated elements at various levels. Metaredundant relationships are not absolute, therefore, and a number of non-conventionalised forms will comprise a minority of those produced in any situation. A given situation is thus recognised and defined according to the *predominant* features in play. These features are therefore criterial to the distinction of that situation as a socially recognised type. The existence of non-criterial features does not prevent the socialised speaker from recognising and defining the social situation but serve, rather, as background (and potentially serviceable) noise.

So, for example, informal questions will occasionally appear in formal conversation, but this will still be distinguishable as formal conversation; gossip may occasionally occur in business meetings, but these will still be distinguishable as business meetings; and authoritarian systems may exhibit occasional libertarian tendencies, but these will still be distinguishable as authoritarian systems. An A-curve distribution of criterial to non-criterial features is the most functional in allowing for the recognition and operation of the linguistic activity in question while also allowing a reservoir of non-criterial features which can be drawn on in response to new contexts, thereby reducing the risk of senescence in the system.

The non-criterial elements that comprise the background noise at any given time are serviceable. By this we mean that elements from the background noise may, over time, become criterial features. This occurs when a non-criterial element is interpreted as fulfilling a useful function with respect to the material and social context in which it is produced; if its meaning can be integrated into the overall system of meanings at that level of abstraction (with a corresponding perturbation of the functions of the other elements in the system); and if the overall system functions more effectively with respect to the material and social context in which it operates as a result of this perturbation.

So, for example, marked articulations, such as a declarative structure with rising intonation, will become increasingly conventionalised if they fulfil a useful function in themselves, on the one hand, and can be integrated as meaningful oppositions within the existing system of semantico-pragmatic acts. At a higher level, a speaker may instinctively draw on expressions of power or solidarity relevant to one section of their audience while discussing fields relevant to a different section of the audience, resulting in a novel articulation and the ad hoc appearance of a new institutional role within the previously existing system of role relations within that institutional space. If this ad hoc role is perceived to fulfil a previously non-existent function within the institution in a relevant and previously absent way, the novel articulation realising the new institutional role will be replicated. The appearance of this new institutional role will alter the function of the other roles in play and the relations between them, and if this enhances the overall performance of the institution within its social and material context, the new role will become ever more firmly embedded in the system of role relations within that institution.

Novel articulations represent new elements at the higher-level of meaning and the introduction of a new element into a system of contrastive values must necessarily lead to a recalibration of the other elements within that system. The recalibration of the higher-level system of meanings entails, in turn, a recalibration of meanings at the lower level, as these derive their meaning, in part, as a function of the sum of their uses at the higher level of abstraction. These new meanings at each level are now available for further combinations, and the process repeats itself cyclically *ad infinitum* – which is to say that language, as an autopoietic system, is always emergent but never arriving, never finalised.

Returning to the irreducible triad of language, persona and society, we conclude that persons and societies are similarly autopoetic, indeterminate and unfinalisable systems. We should not, therefore, talk of individual languages as fixed and bounded ways of speaking, but as recognisable manifestations in time and space of ongoing and unfinalisable processes of languaging. Nor should we talk of an individual person's identity, but of an ongoing and unfinalisable process of identification (or subjectification) within a shifting but recognisable body. And so, too, we should not think of social groups as fixed and bounded units, but as the recognisable manifestations of ongoing and unfinalisable processes of socialisation. Finally, we should not talk of contexts in which languages, persons and society converge in time and space, but of a continuous and unfinalisable process of contextualisation, as each person interacts to maintain their essential unity in relation to an indeterminate society and through the indeterminate resources of language. Context is thus an immensely overdetermined space. We are therefore back where we started.

Every linguistic act is an embodied response to an overdetermined affective context and is produced in anticipation of imprecisely imagined futures across multiple spatiotemporal scales.

Appendix A

Table A.1 ToBI and nuclear tone compared in English, Japanese and Greek

English ToBI	Japanese ToBi[1]	Greek ToBI	Tone movement	
			Primary	Secondary
H*L–L%[2]		H*L–L%	**Fall**	
H*+LL–L%		H*+LL–L%		
	H* L%			
	H*+L L%			
		!H*L–L%		From Mid
L*L–L%		L*l–L%		Low
H+L*L–L%				Low (high Head)
L+H*L–L%				
	H* H%		**Rise**	
L*+HH–H%				
		H*!H–H%		Stylized rise (calling contour)
L*H–H%				Low
L*L–H%				
		L*+H H–H*		To mid
		L*+H H–!H*		
		L*+H !H–H*		
		L*+H !H–!H%		
		!H*L–!H%		
		!H*!H–!H%		
		!L*!H–!H%		
		!H*H–H%		
H*H–H%		H*H–H%		High
H+L*H–H%				
L+H*H–H%		L+H* H–H%		

(*Continued*)

1   Unlike the other two languages Japanese does not have intermediate phrases.

2   This notation could be used to transcribe what traditional British School intonation classes as high and mid falls.

Table A.1 (*Continued*)

English ToBI	Japanese ToBi[3]	Greek ToBI	Tone movement Primary	Tone movement Secondary
H+L*L–H%			**Fall–Rise**	
H*L–H%		H*L–H%		
		!H*L–!H%		
L*+HL–H%				
H*+LH–H%				
H*+LL–H%				
	H*+L H*			
L+H*L–H%		L+H*L–H%		High
		!H* L–H%		From mid
L*H–H%		L*H–H%	**Rise–Fall**	
L+H*L–L%		L+H*L–L%		
L*+HL–L%		L*+H L–L%		
	H* HL%			
		L*+H L–!H%		To mid
		L*+H !H–!H%		
		L+H*H–!H%		
		L+H*!H–!H%		
	H+L HL*		**Fall–Rise–Fall**	
L*H–L%			**Level**	Low
H+L*H–L%				Low (high head)
L*+HH–L%		L*+H H–L%		Low calling contour
		L*+H !H–H%		
H*H–L%		H*H–L%		High
		!H*H–L*		Mid
L+H*H–L%		L+H*H–L%		High (low head)
H*+LH–L%				Calling contour
		L+H*!H–H*		Calling contour stylized
		L+H*!H–!H%		Stylized level–rise
		H*!H–!H%		Stylized Level calling contour
		!H*!H–H%		Stylized Level calling contour

3   Unlike the other two languages Japanese does not have intermediate phrases.

Appendix B

TRANSCRIPTION CONVENTIONS

<u>ve</u>ry	stressed syllable
(.)	pause of less than half a second
(1)	pause in seconds
wo::	elongation of previous sound
wo--	abruptly ended, cut off sound
(( ))	contextual information
...	lines of transcript omitted
£	smiley voice
°yes°	talk noticeably quieter
FN	first name
LN	last name
F	female
M	male

All names are pseudonyms

References

Abe, Isamu. 1998. "Intonation in Japanese." In *Intonation Systems: A Survey of Twenty Languages*, edited by D. Hirst & A. Di Cristo, 360–375. Cambridge: CUP.

Abram, David. 1996. *The Spell of the Sensuous: Perception and Language in a More than Human World*. New York and Toronto: Vintage.

Amengual, M. 2019. "Type of early bilingualism and its effect on the acoustic realization of allophonic variants: Early sequential and simultaneous bilinguals." *International Journal Of Bilingualism* 23, no. 5 (November): 954–970. https://doi.org/10.1177/1367006917741364

Andersen, Thomas H. 2017. "Interpersonal meaning and the clause." In *The Routledge Handbook of Systemic Functional Linguistics*, edited by Tom Bartlett & Gerard O'Grady, 115–130. Abingdon, Oxon: Routledge.

Arbib, Michael A. 2005. "From monkey-like action recognition to human language: An evolutionary framework for neurolinguistics." *Behavioral and Brain Sciences* 28: 105–167. https://doi.org/10.1017/s0140525x05000038

Arbib, Michael. A, 2012. *How the Brain Got Language: The Mirror System Hypothesis*. Oxford: OUP.

Arvaniti, Amaila & Mary Baltazani. 2005. "Intonation analysis and the Prosodic Annotation of Greek Spoken Corpora." In *Prosodic Typology: The Phonology of Intonation and Phrasing*, edited by S. Ah-Jun, 84–117. Oxford: OUP.

Arvaniti, Amaila, and Janet Fletcher. 2020. "The Autosegmental-Metrical Theory of Intonation." In *The Oxford Handbook of Language Prosody*, edited by Carlos Gussenhoven and Aoju Chen, 78–95. Oxford: OUP.

Atkin, Albert. 2010. "Peirce's theory of signs." *Stanford Encyclopedia of Philosophy*. https://plato.stanford.edu/entries/peirce-semiotics/. Accessed March 21, 2022.

Austin, John. 1961. *How To Do Things With Words*. Oxford: OUP.

Azzouni, Jody. 2013. *Semantic Perception: How the Illusion of a Common Language Arises and Persists*. Oxford: OUP.

Bach, Kent, and Robert M. Harnish. 1979. *Linguistic Communication and Speech Acts*. Cambridge: MA: MIT Press.

Bakhtin, M. M. 1981. *The Dialogic Imagination: Four Essays*. Ed. Michael Holquist. Trans. Caryl Emerson and Michael Holquist. Austin and London: University of Texas Press.

Bakhtin, M. M. 1984. *Problems of Dostoevsky's Poetics*. Ed. and trans. Caryl Emerson. Minneapolis: University of Minnesota Press.

Barbieri, Marcello. 1985. *The Semantic Theory of Evolution*. London and New York: Routledge.

Barbieri, Marcello. 2015. *Code Biology: A New Science of Life*. Cham, Heidelberg, New York, Dordrecht and London: Springer.

Barbieri, Marcello. 2019. "Code Biology, Peircean Biosemiotics, and Rosen's Relational Biology." *Biological Theory* 14: 21–29. https://doi.org/10.1007/s13752-018-0312-z

Barth-Weingarten, Dagmar. 2018. *Intonation Units Revisited: Cesuras in talk-in-interaction.* Amsterdam: John Benjamins.

Bartlett, Tom. 2004. "Mapping Distinction." In *Systemic Functional Linguistics and Critical Discourse Analysis: Studies in Social Change*, edited by Lynne Young and Claire Harrison, 68–84. London and New York: Continuum.

Bartlett, Tom. 2005. "The Communities Strike Back: Genres of the Third Space." *Journal of Language and Intercultural Communication* 5, no. 1: 134–158. https://doi.org/10.1080/14708470408668869

Bartlett, Tom. 2008. "Wheels within Wheels or Triangles within Triangles: Time and Context in Positioning Theory." In *Global Conflict Resolution through Positioning Analysis*, edited by Fathali M. Moghaddam, Rom Harré and Naomi Lee, 169–188. New York: Springer.

Bartlett, Tom. 2012. *Hybrid Voices and Collaborative Change: Contextualising Positive Discourse Analysis.* London and New York: Routledge.

Bartlett, Tom. 2013. "'I'll manage the context': Context, environment and the potential for institutional change." In *Systemic Functional Linguistics: Exploring Choice*, edited by Lise Fontaine, Tom Bartlett and Gerard O'Grady, 342–364. Cambridge: Cambridge University Press.

Bartlett, Tom. 2014. *Analysing Power in Language.* London and New York: Routledge.

Bartlett, Tom. 2015. Multiscalar modelling of context: Some questions raised by the category of Mode. In *Essays in Honour of Ruqaiya Hasan: Society in Language, Language in Society*, edited by Wendy Bowcher and Jennifer Yameng Liang, 166–183. London and New York: Palgrave.

Bartlett, Tom. 2017. "Context in Systemic Functional Linguistics: Towards scalar supervenience?" In *The Routledge Handbook of Systemic Functional Linguistics*, edited by Tom Bartlett and Gerard O'Grady, 375–390. London: Routledge.

Bartlett, Tom. 2018a. "Rethinking (context of) culture in Systemic Functional Linguistics." In *Perspectives from Systemic Functional Linguistics*, edited by Akila Baklouti and Lise Fontaine, 26–46. New York and London: Routledge.

Bartlett, Tom. 2018b. "Positive Discourse Analysis." In *The Routledge Handbook of Critical Discourse Analysis*, edited by John Richardson and John Flowerdew, 133–148. London and New York: Routledge.

Bartlett, Tom. 2019. "Approaches to Discourse." In *The Cambridge Handbook of Systemic Functional Linguistics*, edited by G. Thompson, W. Bowcher, L. Fontaine and D. Schönthal, 285–310. Cambridge: Cambridge University Press.

Bartlett, Tom. 2020. "Time, the deer, is in the wood: Chronotopic identities, trajectories of texts and community self-management." *Applied Linguistics Review* 12, No. 3: 463–491. https://doi.org/10.1515/applirev-2019-0134

Bartlett, Tom. 2021a. "Interpersonal grammar of Scottish Gaelic." In *Interpersonal Grammar: Systemic Functional Linguistic Theory and Description*, edited by J. R. Martin, B. Quiroz and G. Figueredo, 257–284. Cambridge: Cambridge University Press.

Bartlett, Tom. 2021b. "No Gods and Precious Few Heroes: Towards a materialist account of linguistic dynamics." Lingua 261, no. 1 (October). https://doi.org/10.1016/j.lingua.2020.102953

Bartlett, Tom. Forthcoming. Atopicality as the unmarked logical structure in Scottish Gaelic.

Bartlett, Tom and Elizabeth J. Erling. 2007. "Local Voices in Global English: The Authenticity and Legitimation of Non-Standard Ways of Speaking." In *Proceedings of the 33rd International Systemic Functional Congress*, edited by Leila Barbara and Tony Berber Sardinha, 88–116. PUCSP, São Paulo, Brazil. Online publication available at http://www.pucsp.br/isfc. ISBN 85-283-0342-X.

Bartlett, Tom, and Nicolina Montesano Montessori. 2021. "Towards *webs of equivalence* and the *political nomad* in agonistic debate: Contributions from CDA and scales theory." *Journal of Language and Politics* 20, no.1: 129–144. https://doi.org/10.1075/jlp.20046.bar

Bartlett, Tom and Gerard O'Grady. 2019. "Language characterology and textual dynamics: A crosslinguistic exploration in English and Scottish Gaelic." *Acta Linguistica Hafniensia* 51, No. 2: 124–159. https://doi.org/10.1080/03740463.2019.1650607

Bartlett, Tom and Gerard O'Grady. 2017. "Reading SFL." In *The Routledge Handbook of Systemic Functional Linguistics*, edited by Tom Bartlett and Gerard O'Grady, 1–8. London and New York: Routledge.

Bartlett, Tom and Gerard O'Grady, eds. 2017. *The Routledge Handbook of Systemic Functional Linguistics.* London and New York: Routledge.

Bartlett, Tom, Virpi Ylänne, Tereza Spilioti, Michelle Aldridge-Waddon, Harriet Lloyd. 2020. "Nursing handovers as unbounded and scalar events." *Applied Linguistics Review* 12, no. 3 (February): 401–418. https://doi.org/10.1515/applirev-2019-0135

Bateman, John, and Paola Evangelisti Allori, eds. 2014. *Evolution in Genre: Emergence, Variation, Multimodality. Linguistic Insights: Studies in Language and Communication 192.* Berne, Berlin, Brussels, Frankfurt, New York, Oxford and Vienna: Peter Lang.

Bateson, G. 1972. *Steps to an Ecology of Mind.* New York: Ballantine

Beckmann, Mary E., Julia Hirschberg and Stefanie Shattuck-Huffnagel. 2005. "The original ToBi system and the evolution of the ToBI framework." In *Prosodic Typology: The Phonology of Intonation and Phrasing*, edited by S. Ah-Jun, 9–54. Oxford: OUP.

Beckner, Clay, Richard Blythe, Joan Bybee, Morten H. Christiansen, William Croft, Nick C. Ellis, John Holland, Jinyun Ke, Diane Larsen-Freeman and Tom Schoenemann. 2009. "Language is a complex adaptive system: position paper." *Language Learning* 59, no. s1 (December): 1–26. https://doi.org/10.1111/j.1467-9922.2009.00533.x

Beer, Stafford, 1980. "Preface." In *Autopoiesis and Cognition: The Realization of the Living*, edited by Humberto R. Maturana and Francisco J. Varela, 63–73. Dordecht, Boston and London: D. Reidel.

Belsey, C. 2002. *Poststructuralism: A Very Short Introduction.* Oxford: Oxford University Press.

Bekoff, Marc. 1995. "Play signals as punctuation: The structure of social play in canids." *Behaviour* 132, nos. 5–6: 419–429. https://doi.org/10.1163/156853995x00649

Benson, J., and W. S. Greaves. 2005. *Functional Dimensions of Ape–Human Discourse.* London: Equinox.

Berent, Iris. 2013. *The Phonological Mind.* Cambridge: Cambridge University Press.

Bergman, Max. 2009. *Peirce's Philosophy of Communication*. London and New York: Continuum.

Bermúdez de Castro, J. M., J. L. Arsuaga, E. Carbonell, A. Rosas, I. Martínez, M. Mosquera. (1997). "A Hominid from the Lower Pleistocene of Atapuerca, Spain: Possible Ancestor to Neandertals and Modern Humans." *Science* 276, No. 5317: 1392–1395. https://doi.org/10.1126/science.276.5317.1392

Bernstein, B. 1971. *Class, Codes and Control Vol. 1: Theoretical Studies towards a Sociology of Language*. London: Routledge and Kegan Paul.

Bernstein, B. 2000 (Revised Edition [1996]). *Pedagogy, Symbolic Control and Identity: Theory, Research, Critique*. Lanham, Boulder, New York and Oxford: Rowman and Littlefield.

Berry, Margaret. 1981a. "Systemic linguistics and discourse analysis: a multi-layered approach to exchange structure." In *Studies in Discourse Analysis*, edited by Malcolm Coulthard & Martin Montgomery, 120–145. London: Routledge and Kegan Paul.

Berry, Margaret. 1981b. "Towards layers of exchange structure for directive exchanges." *Network* 2: 23–32.

Berry, Margaret. 1995. "Thematic options and success in writing." In *Thematic Development in English Texts*, edited by M. Ghadessy, 55–84. London: Pinter.

Berry, Margaret. 2013. "Towards a study of the differences between formal written English and informal spoken English." In *Systemic Functional Linguistics: Exploring Choice*, edited by Lise Fontaine, Tom Bartlett and Gerard O'Grady, 365–383. Cambridge: Cambridge University Press.

Berry, Margaret. 2016. "Dynamism in exchange structure." *English Text Construction* 9, no. 1 (January): 33–55. https://doi.org/10.1075/etc.9.1.03ber

Berwick R., A. D. Friederici, N. Chomsky, and J. J. Bolhuis. 2013. "Evolution, brain, and the nature of language." *Trends in Cognitive Sciences* 17, No. 2: 89–98. https://doi.org/10.1016/j.tics.2012.12.002

Biber, Douglas, and Edward Finegan. 1989. "Styles of stance in English: Lexical and grammatical marking of evidentiality and affect." *Text* 9, no. 1: 93–124. https://doi.org/10.1515/text.1.1989.9.1.93

Bickerton, Derek. 2002. "Foraging Versus Social Intelligence in the Evolution of Protolanguage." In *The Transition to Language*, edited by A. Wray, 207–225. Oxford: Oxford University Press.

Blackmore, Susan. 1999. *The Meme Machine*. Oxford: OUP.

Blair, Tony. 2010. *A Journey*. London: Hutchinson

Blommaert, Jan. 2005. *Discourse: An Introduction*. Cambridge: Cambridge University Press.

Blommaert, 2015. "Chronotopes, scales, and complexity in the study of language in society." *Annual Review of Anthropology* 44 (October): 105–116. https://doi.org/10.1146/annurev-anthro-102214-014035

Blommaert, Jan. 2018a. *Dialogues with Ethnography: Notes on Classics, and How I Read them*. Bristol and Blue Ridge Summit: Multilingual Matters.

Blommaert, Jan. 2018b [2013]. "Historical bodies and historical space." In Blommaert 2018a.

Boeckx, C. 2015. *Elementary Syntactic Structures: Prospects of a Feature-Free Syntax*. Cambridge: Cambridge University Press,

De Boer, Bart. 2001. *The Origins of Vowel Systems*. Oxford: Oxford University Press.

Boersma, Paul and David Weenink. 2021. *Pratt doing phonetics by computer.* Version 6.1.38. https://www.fon.hum.uva.nl/praat/

Bolhuis J. J., I. Tattersall, N. Chomsky and R. C. Berwick. 2014. "How Could Language Have Evolved?" *PLoS Biol* 12, 8: e1001934. https://doi.org/10.1371/journal.pbio.1001934

Bolinger, Dwight L. 1961. "Contrastive accent and Contrastive stress." *Language* 37, no. 1: 83–96. https://doi.org/10.2307/411252

Boroditsky, L. 2001. "Does language shape thought? English and Mandarin speakers' conceptions of time." *Cognitive Psychology* 43, no. 1 (August): 1–22. https://doi.org/10.1006/cogp.2001.0748

Botinis, Antonis. 1998. "Intonation in Greek." In *Intonation Systems: A Survey of Twenty Languages*, edited by D. Hirst and A. Di Cristo, 288– 310. Cambridge: CUP.

Bourdieu, Pierre. 1990. *The Logic of Practice.* Cambridge: Polity Press.

Boutonnet, Bastian, Panos Athanasopoulos and Guillaume Thierry. 2012. "Unconscious effects of grammatical gender during object categorisation." *Brain Research* 1479: 72–79. https://doi.org/10.1016/j.brainres.2012.08.044

Bowcher, Wendy, and Jennifer Yameng Liang, eds. 2015. *Essays in Honour of Ruqaiya Hasan: Society in Language, Language in Society.* London and New York: Palgrave.

Brazil, David. 1995. *A Grammar of Speech.* Oxford: Oxford University Press.

Brazil, David. 1997. *The Communicative Value of Intonation in English.* 2nd ed. Cambridge: CUP.

Brock, J. E. 1981. "The origin and structure of Peirce's logic of vagueness." In , edited byA. Lange-Seidl, 133–138. Berlin: Walter de Gruyter.

Burman, J. T. 2013. 'Updating the Baldwin Effect: The biological levels behind Piaget's new theory.' *New Ideas in Psychology* 31, 3: 363–373. https://doi.org/10.1016/j.newideapsych.2012.07.003

Butler, Christopher S. 2003. *Structure and Function: A Guide to Three Major Structural-Functional Theories. Part 1: Approaches to the Simplex Clause. Part 2: From Clause to Discourse and Beyond.* Amsterdam: John Benjamins.

Butler, Christopher S. 2009a. "Criteria of adequacy in functional linguistics." *Folia Linguistica* 43, 1: 1–66. https://doi.org/10.1515/FLIN.2009.001

Butler, Christopher S. 2009b. "The Lexical Constructional Model: genesis, strengths and challenges." In *Deconstructing constructions*, edited by C. S. Butler and J. Martín Arista, 117–151. Amsterdam: John Benjamins. https://doi.org/10.1075/slcs.107

Bybee, Joan. L. 1999. "Usage Based Phonology." In *Functionalism and Formalism in Linguistics: Volume I: General papers*, edited by Michael Darnell, Edith A. Moravcsik, Michael Noonan, Frederick J. Newmeyer and Kathleen Wheatley, 211–242. Amsterdam: John Benjamins.

Bybee, Joan L. 2002. "Word frequency and context of use in the lexical diffusion of phonetically conditioned sound change." *Language Variation and Change* 14, 3 (October): 261–290. https://doi.org/10.1017/s0954394502143018

Cafferel, Alice, J. R. Martin, and C. M. I. M. Matthiessen. 2004. *Language Typology: A functional perspective.* Amsterdam: John Benjamins.

Calvin, William, and Derek Bickerton. 2001. *Lingua ex Machina: Reconciling Chomsky and Darwin with the Human Brain.* Cambridge MA: MIT Press.

Canagarajah, Suresh, and Peter I. De Costa. 2016. "Introduction: Scales analysis, and its use and prospects in educational linguistics." *Linguistics and Education* 34: 1–10. https://doi.org/10.1016/j.linged.2015.09.001

Caplan, D. 2006. "Why is Broca's area involved in syntax?" *Cortex; A Journal Devoted to the Study of the Nervous System and Behavior* 42, 4: 469–71. https://doi.org/10.1016/s0010-9452(08)70379-4

Carpentier, Nico. 2017. "Discourse-Theoretical Analysis." In *The Routledge Handbook of Critical Discourse Studies*, edited by John Flowerdew and John Richardson, 272–284. London and New York: Routledge.

Carroll, Sean B. 2011. *Endless Forms Most Beautiful*. London: Quercus.

Carré, René, and Samir Chennoukh. 1995. "Vowel-consonant-vowel modeling by superposition of consonant closure on vowel-to-vowel gestures." *Journal of Phonetics* 23, nos. 1–2 (January–April): 231–241. https://doi.org/10.1016/s0095-4470(95)80045-x

Chafe, Wallace L. 1994. *Discourse, Consciousness, and Time: The Flow and Displacement of Conscious Experience in Speaking and Writing*. Chicago: The University of Chicago Press.

Chafe, Wallace L. 2018. *Thought-based Linguistics: How languages turn thoughts into sounds*. Cambridge: CUP.

Cheney, Dorothy L., and Robert M. Seyfarth. 1980. 'Vocal recognition in Free Ranging Vervet Monkeys.' *Animal Behaviour* 28, 2: 362–67. https://doi.org/10.1016/s0003-3472(80)80044-3

Cheney, Dorothy L., and Robert M. Seyfarth. 1996. 'Function and Intention in the Calls of Non-Human primates.' *Proceedings of the British Academy*, 88: 59–76.

Chomsky, Noam. 1957. *Syntactic Structures*. The Hague: Mouton.

Chomsky, Noam. 1965. *Aspects of the Theory of Syntax*. Cambridge MA: MIT Press.

Chomsky, Noam. 1981. *Lectures on Government and Binding*. Dordrecht: Foris

Chomsky, Noam. 1995. *The Minimalist Programme*. Cambridge MA: MIT Press.

Chomsky, Noam. 2005. "Three factors in language design." *Linguistic Inquiry* 36: 1–22. https://doi.org/10.1162/0024389052993655

Chomsky, Noam, and Morris Halle. 1968. *The Sound Pattern of English*. Cambridge Mass: MIT press.

Chomsky, Noam, and Robert C. Berwick. 2016. *Why Only Us: Language and Evolution*. Cambridge MA: M.I.T press.

Chouliaraki, Lilie, and Norman Fairclough. 1999. *Discourse in Late Modernity*. Edinburgh: Edinburgh University Press.

Christiansen, Morten H., and Kirby Simon. 2003. *Language Evolution*. Oxford: OUP.

Clarke, Herbert. C. 1992. *Arenas of Language Use*. Chicago: The University of Chicago Press.

Clements, G. G., and E. V. Hume. 1995. "Internal organization of speech sounds." In *The Handbook of Phonological Theory*, edited by J. A. Goldsmith, 245–306. Oxford: Blackwell.

Cole R. A. 1973. "Listening for mispronunciations: A measure of what we hear during speech." *Perception & Psychophysics* 13 (February): 153–156. https://doi.org/10.3758/bf03207252

Collin, Silvy H. P., Branka Milivojevic, and Christian F. Doeller. 2015. "Memory hierarchies map onto the hippocampal long axis in humans." *Nature Neuroscience* 18 (October): 1562–1564. https://doi.org/10.1038/nn.4138

Corballis, Michael. 2003. "From hand to mouth: the gestural origins of language." In *Language Evolution*, edited by M. H. Christiansen and S. Kirby, 201–218. Oxford: Oxford University Press.

Corballis, Michael. 2017. *The Truth about Language: What It Is and Where It Came From*. Chicago: University of Chicago Press.

Corbetta, Maurizio, and Gordon L. Shulman. 2002. "Control of goal-directed and stimulus-driven attention in the brain." *Nature Reviews Neuroscience* 3 (March): 201–215. https://doi.org/10.1038/nrn755

Coyne, Jerry A. 2009. *Why Evolution is True*. Oxford: OUP.

Croft, William. 2001. *Radical Construction Grammar: Syntactic Theory in Typological Perspective*. Oxford: Oxford University Press.

Crothers, John. 1978. "Typology and universals of vowel systems." In *.: Phonology*, edited by Joseph H. Greenberg, Charles A. Ferguson and Edith A. Moravcsik, 93–152. Stanford: Stanford University Press.

Cruttenden, Alan. 1997. *Intonation*. 2nd ed. Cambridge: CUP.

Crystal, David. 1969. *Prosodic Systems and Intonation in English*. Cambridge: Cambridge University Press.

Damasio, Antonio 2018. *The Strange Order of Things*. New York: Pantheon.

Daneš, František. 1972. "Order of elements and sentence intonation." In *Intonation*, edited by D. Bolinger, 216–232. Harmondsworth: Penguin.

Daneš, František. 1974. "Functional Sentence Perspective and the organisation of text." In *Papers on Functional Sentence Perspective*, edited by F. Daneš, 106–128. Prague: Academia Press.

Davies, Paul. 2019. *The Demon in the Machine*. London: Penguin.

Dawkins, Richard. 1982. *The Extended Phenotype*. Oxford: OUP.

Dawkins, Richard. 2004. *The Ancestor's Tale: A pilgrimage to the dawn of life*. London: Weidenfield & Nicolson.

Dediu, D., and D. R. Ladd. 2007. 'Linguistic tone is related to the population frequency of the adaptive haplogroups of two brain size genes, ASPM and Microcephalin.' *PNAS* 104, No. 26, 10944–10949. https://doi.org/10.1073/pnas.0610848104

Deleuze, Gilles, and Félix Guattari. 1987 (trans. B. Massumi) [1980]. *A Thousand Plateaus*. London, New York, Oxford, New Delhi and Sydney: Bloomsbury.

Dennett, Daniel. 2003. 'The Baldwin Effect: a Crane, not a Skyhook.' In *Evolution and Learning: The Baldwin Effect Reconsidered*, edited by Bruce H. Weber and David J. Depew, 69–79. Cambridge, MA: MIT Press.

Dennett, Daniel C. 2017. *From Bacteria to Bach and Back: The Evolution of Minds*. Penguin Books.

Derrida, Jacques. 1973. *Speech and Phenomena and other Essays on Husserl's Theory of Signs*, trans. David B. Allison. Evanston: Northwestern University Press.

Derrida, Jacques. 1982. "Interview with Julia Kristeva." In *Positions*, edited by J. Derrida and H. Ronse. Chicago: The University of Chicago Press.

Deutscher, G. 2005. *The Unfolding of Language*. London: Heinemann.

De Waal, Frans. 2016. *Are We Smart Enough to Know How Smart Animals Are?* London:Granta.

Donald, Merlin. 2001. *A Mind So Rare: The Evolution of Human Consciousness.* New York: Norton.

Dryer, Matthew. S. 1992. "The Greenbergian word order correlations." *Language* 68, no. 1 (March): 81–138.

Dryer, Matthew S. 2013. "Order of Subject, Object and Verb." In *The World Atlas of Language Structures Online*, edited by Matthew S. Dryer and Martin Haspelmath. Leipzig: Max Planck Institute for Evolutionary Anthropology. http://wals.info/chapter/81. Accessed May 19, 2021.

Dunbar, Robin. 1996. *Grooming, Gossip and the Evolution of Language.* London: Faber and Faber.

Dunbar, Robin. 2003. "The social brain hypothesis and its implications for social intelligence." *Annals of Human Biology* 36, no. 5: 562–572. https://doi.org/10.1080/03014460902960289

Dunbar, Robin. 2014. *Human Evolution: a pelican introduction.* London: Pelican

Durkheim E. 2002. [1925]. *Moral Education.* Minneola, NY: Dover Publications.

Eagleman, David. 2011. *Incognito.* Edinburgh: Canongate

Eagleman, David. 2015. *The Brain: The Story of You.* Edinburgh: Canongate.

Eagleman, David 2020. *Livewired.* Edinburgh: Canongate

Eberhard, David M., Gary F. Simons, and Charles D. Fennig, eds. 2020. *Ethnologue: Languages of the World.* Twenty-third edition. Dallas: SIL International. Online version: https://www.ethnologue.

Edelman, Gerald. 2004. *Wider than the sky: A Revolutionary View of Consciousness.* London: Penguin.

Edwardes, Martin, 2010. *The Origins of Grammar. An Anthropological Perspective.* New York and London: Continuum.

Ellis, Nick C., and Diane Larsen-Freeman, eds. 2009. *Language as a Complex Adaptive System.* Malden MA and Oxford UK: Wiley-Blackwell.

Esser, Jürgen. 1988. *Comparing Reading and Speaking Intonation.* Amsterdam: Rodopi.

Everett, Daniel. 2012. *Language: The Cultural Tool.* London: Profile Books.

Everett, Daniel. 2017. *How Language Began.* London: Profile Books.

Fawcett, Robin P. 2001. *A Theory of Syntax for Systemic Functional Linguistics.* Amsterdam: John Benjamins.

Feldman Barrett, Lisa. 2017. *How Emotions are Made: The Secret Life of the Brain.* New York: Houghton Mifflin Harcourt.

Firbas, Jan. 1987. "On the Delimination of the Theme in Functional Sentence Perspective." In *Functionalism in Linguistics*, edited by R. Dirven and V. Fried, 137–156. Amsterdam: John Benjamins.

Firbas, Jan, 1992. *Functional Sentence Perspective in Written and Spoken English.* Cambridge: Cambridge University Press.

Firth, John. R. 1948. "Sounds and Prosodies." *Transactions of the Philological Society* 47, no. 1 (November): 127–152. https://doi.org/10.1111/j.1467-968X.1948.tb00556.x

Fitch, W. Tecumseh, Mark D. Hauser and Noam Chomsky. 2005. "The evolution of the language faculty: Clarifications and implications." *Cognition* 97, no.2 (September): 179–210. https://doi.org/10.1016/j.cognition.2005.02.005

Fodor, Jerry, A. 1975. *The Language of Thought.* Cambridge MA: Harvard University Press.

Fontaine, Lise, Tom Bartlett and Gerard O'Grady, eds. 2013. *Systemic Functional Linguistics: Exploring Choice.* Cambridge: Cambridge University Press.

Foolen, Ad. 2002. "Review of Language Form and Language Function." *Functions of Language* 9, no. 1: 87–103. https://doi.org/10.1075/fol.9.1.06foo

Forey, Gail, and Geoff Thompson. 2008. *Text Type and Structure: Essays in honour of Flo Davies.* London: Equinox.

Foucault, M. 1982. "The subject and power." *Critical Inquiry* 8, no. 4 (Summer): 777–795. https://doi.org/10.1086/448181

Friederici, Angela, D. 2002. "Towards a neural basis of auditory sentence processing." *TRENDS in Cognitive Sciences* 6, no.2 (February): 78–84. https://doi.org/10.1016/s1364-6613(00)01839-8

Fries, Peter. 1995. "Themes, methods of development and texts." In *On Subject and Theme: A discourse functional perspective*, edited by Ruqiaya Hasan and Peter Fries, 317–359. Amsterdam: Benjamins.

García, Adolfo M., William J. Sullivan, and Sarah Tsiang. 2017. *An Introduction to Relational Network Theory. History, Principles and Descriptive Applications*. Sheffield: Equinox.

Georgountzou, Anastasia. 1993. "A comparison of the intonation of modern Greek and English with special reference to Greek learners of English." Unpublished PhD Dissertation: The University of London. https://discovery.ucl.ac.uk/id/eprint/1546136/

Gibbs, Raymond W. 2005. *Embodiment and Cognitive Science.* Cambridge: CUP.

Gibson, James. 1979. *The Ecological Approach to Visual Perception.* Boston: Houghton Mifflin.

Givon, Tom. 1988. "The pragmatics of word order." In *Studies in Syntactic Typology*, edited by E. Moravcsik, E. J. Wirth and M Hammond, 243–285. Amsterdam: John Benjamins.

Gómez-Gonzàles, Maria. 2001. *The Theme–Topic Interface: Evidence from English.* Amsterdam: John Benjamins.

Gould, Stephen Jay. 1983. *Hen's Teeth and Horse's Toes.* London: Penguin.

Gould, Stephen Jay, and R. Lewontin. 1979. "The spandrels of San Marco and the Panglossian paradigm: a critique of the adaptationist programme." *Proceedings of the Royal Society B,* Vol 205, Issue 1161: 581–598. https://doi.org/10.1098/rspb.1979.0086

Greaves, William S. 2007. "Intonation in Systemic Functional Linguistics." In *Continuing Discourse on Language: A Functional Perspective*, Vol. 2, edited by R. Hasan, C. M. I. M. Matthiessen and J. J. Webster, 979–1025. London: Equinox.

Greenberg, Joseph. 1963. "Some Universals of Grammar with Particular Reference to the Order of Meaningful Elements." In *Universals of Language*, edited by Joseph Greenberg, 73–113. Cambridge, MA: MIT Press.

Gregory, Michael. 1995. "Generic expectancies and discoursal surprises: John Donne's *The Good Morrow.*" In *Discourse in Society: Systemic Functional Perspectives*, edited by P. Fries and M. Gregory 67–84. Norwood, NJ: Ablex.

Gussenhoven, Carlos. 2004. *The Phonology of Tone and Intonation.* Cambridge: CUP.

Gwilliams, Laura, Tai Linzen, David Poppel, and Alec Marantz. 2018. "In spoken word recognition, the future predicts the past." *Journal of Neuroscience* 38, no. 35 (August): 7585–7599. https://doi.org/10.1523/jneurosci.0065-18.2018

Hagoort, Peter. 2005. "On Broca, brain and binding: A new framework." *Trends in Cognitive Sciences* 9, no. 9 (September): 416–423. https://doi.org/10.1016/j.tics.2005.07.004

Hagoort, Peter, Lea Hald, Marcel Bastiaansen, and Karl M. Petersson. 2004. "Integration of word meaning and world knowledge in language comprehension." *Science* 304, no. 5669 (April): 438–441. https://doi.org/10.1126/science.1095455

Hald, Lea A., Esther G. Steenbeek-Planting, and Peter Hagoort. 2007. "The interaction of discourse context and world knowledge in online sentence comprehension. Evidence from the N400." *Brain Research* 1146 (May): 210–218. https://doi.org/10.1016/j.brainres.2007.02.054

Halle, Morris. 1995. "Feature geometry and feature spreading." *Linguistic Inquiry* 26, no. 1 (Winter): 1–46.

Halliday, M. A. K. 1967. *Intonation and Grammar in British English.* The Hague: Mouton.

Halliday, M. A. K. 1969. "Options and functions in the English clause." *Brno Studies in English* 8: 82–88. Reprinted in M. A. K. Halliday, and James R. Martin (eds.). 1981. *Readings in Systemic Linguistics*, London: Batsford.

Halliday, M. A. K. 1973. *Explorations in the Functions of Language*, London: Edward Arnold

Halliday, M. A. K. 1975. *Learning how to Mean: Explorations in the Development of Language.* London: Edward Arnold.

Halliday, M. A. K. 1978. *Language as Social Semiotic: The social interpretation of language and meaning.* Maryland: University Park Press.

Halliday, M. A. K. 1984. "On the ineffability of grammatical categories." In *The Tenth LACUS Forum*, edited by A. Manning, P. Martin and K. McCalla, 13–18. University Laval: Hornbeam Press.

Halliday, M. A. K. (1992/2005). "A systemic interpretation of Peking syllable finals." In *Studies in Systemic Phonology*, edited by Paul Tench, 19–34. London: Cassell. Reprinted in *Studies in Chinese Language; Vol 8 in the collected works of M.A.K. Halliday*, edited by Jonathan J. Webster 294–320. London: Continuum.

Halliday, M. A. K. 2014. "That 'certain cut': Towards a characterology of Mandarin Chinese." *Functional Linguistics* 1, no. 2 (April). https://doi.org/10.1186/2196-419x-1-2

Halliday, M. A. K. 2015. "The influence of Marxism." In *The Bloomsbury Companion to M.A.K. Halliday*, edited by J. J. Webster, 94–100. London and New York: Bloomsbury.

Halliday, M. A. K., and W. S. Greaves. 2008. *Intonation in the Grammar of English.* Sheffield: Equinox.

Halliday, M. A. K., and Ruqaiya Hasan. 1985. *Language, Context and Text: Aspects of Language in a Social-Semiotic Perspective.* Victoria, Australia: Deakin University Press.

Halliday, M. A. K., and James R. Martin. 1993. *Writing Science: Literacy and Discursive Power.* London: The Falmer Press.

Halliday, M. A. K. and Christian M. I. M. Matthiessen. 1999. *Construing Experience through Language.* London: Equinox.

Halliday, M. A. K. and Christian M. I. M. Matthiessen. 2014 (4th Edition). *Halliday's Introduction to Functional Grammar.* London and New York: Routledge.

Harbert, Wayne. 2007. *The Germanic Languages;* Cambridge: CUP.

Hare, Brian. 2013. *The Genius of Dogs; Discovering the Unique Intelligence of Man's Best Friend.* London: Oneworld.

Hare, Brian and Michael Tomasello. 2005. "Human-like social skills in dogs?" *Trends in Cognitive Sciences* 9, 9 (September): 439–444. https://doi.org/10.1016/j.tics.2005.07.003

Harré, Rom, and Luc van Langenhove, eds. 1999. *Positioning Theory*. Oxford and Malden, MA: Blackwell.

Harris, Roy. 1987. *Reading Saussure*. London: Duckworth.

Hart, Christopher. 2010. *Critical Discourse Analysis and Cognitive Science: New Perspectives on Immigration Discourse*. Basingstoke: Palgrave Macmillan.

Hasan, Ruqaiya. 1984. "What kind of resource is language?" *Australian Review of Applied Linguistics* 7, No. 1: 57–85. https://doi.org/10.1075/aral.7.1.03has

Hasan, Ruqaiya. 1987. "The grammarian's dream: Lexis as most delicate grammar." In *New Developments in Systemic Linguistics Volume 1*, edited by M. A. K. Halliday and R. P. Fawcett, 184–211. London and New York: Pinter.

Hasan, Ruqaiya. 1996. "Semantic networks: a tool for the analysis of meaning." In *Ways of Saying, Ways of Meaning: Selected papers of Ruqaiya Hasan*, edited by Carmel Cloran, David Butt and Geoff Williams, 104–132. London: Cassell.

Hasan, Ruqaiya. 2013. "Choice, system, realisation: Describing language as meaning potential." In *Systemic Functional Linguistics: Exploring Choice*, edited by L. Fontaine, T. Bartlett and G. O'Grady, 269–299. Cambridge: Cambridge University Press.

Hasan, Ruqaiya, and Peter Fries. 1995. *On Subject and Theme: A Discourse Functional Perspective*. Amsterdam. John Benjamins.

Hasan, Ruqaiya, C. M. I. M. Matthiessen and Jonathan J. Webster, eds. 2005a. *Continuing Discourse on Language: A Functional Perspective. Volume One*. Sheffield: Equinox.

Hasan, Ruqaiya, C. M. I. M. Matthiessen and Jonathan J. Webster, eds. 2005b. *Continuing Discourse on Language: A Functional Perspective. Volume Two*. Sheffield: Equinox.

Hauser, Mark D., Noam Chomsky and W. Tecumseh Fitch. 2002. "The Faculty of Language: What Is It, Who Has It, and How Did It Evolve?" *Science* 298, no. 5598 (November): 1569–1579. https://doi.org/10.1126/science.298.5598.1569

Hickok, Gregory. 2014. *The Myth of Mirror Neurons: The Real Neuroscience of Communication and Cognition*. New York. WW Norton.

Hjelmslev, Louis. 1961 [1943] (Revised English edition. Translated by F. J. Whitfield). *Prolegomena to a Theory of Language*. Madison: University of Wisconsin Press.

Hjelmslev, Louis. 1963. *A Prolegomena to a Theory of Language*. Translated by F. J. Whitfield. Madison Wisc. University of Wisconsin Press.

Hjelmslev, Louis. 1975. *Résumé of a Theory of Language*. Translated by F. J. Whitfield. Madison: University of Wisconsin Press.

Hockett, Charles F. 1960. "The Origin of Speech." *Scientific American* 203, 3 (September): 88–111. https://doi.org/10.1038/SCIENTIFICAMERICAN0960-88

Hodge, Bob. 2017. *Social Semiotics for a Complex World: Analysing Language and Social Meaning*. Cambridge: Polity Press.

Holquist, Michael. 2014. "What Would Bakhtin Do?" *Critical Multilingualism Studies* 2, No.1: 6–19.

Hood, Bruce. 2014. *The Domesticated Brain*. London: Pelican.

Hood, Susan. 2019. "Appraisal." In *The Cambridge Handbook of Systemic Functional Linguistics*, edited by Geoff Thompson, Wendy L. Bowcher, Lise Fontaine & David Schonthal, 382–409. Cambridge: Cambridge University Press.

Hopper, Paul, J, 1987. "Emergent Grammar." In *Proceedings of the 13th annual meeting of the Berkley Linguistics Society*, 139–157.

Huebner, Bryce, and Daniel Dennett. 2009. "Banishing 'I' and 'We' from accounts of metacognition." Response to Peter Carruthers 2008 "How we know our own minds." *Behavioral and Brain Sciences* 32, no. 2 (April): 148–149. https://doi.org/10.1017/S0140525X09000661

Hunston, Susan. 2010. *Corpus Approaches to Evaluation: Phraseology and Evaluative Language.* London: Routledge.

Hunston, Susan, and Geoff Thompson. 2000. *Evaluation in Text: Authorial Stance and the Construction of Discourse.* Oxford: Oxford University Press.

Hurford, James. R. 2012. *The Origins of Grammar: Language in the Light of Evolution.* Oxford: OUP.

Iosad, Pavel. 2018. "The study of phonology in the 21st century: overview and introduction to the Routledge Handbook of Phonological Theory." In *The Routledge Handbook of Phonological Theory*. Edited by S. J. Hannahs and Anna Bosch, 13–36. Abingdon, Oxon: Routledge.

Jakobson, Roman. 1942. *The Concept of the Phoneme.* Reprinted in *On Language.* Edited by Linda R. Waugh and Monica Moville-Burston, 218–241. Cambridge, Mass: Harvard University Press.

Jakobson, Roman, and Morris Halle. 1956. *Fundamentals of Language.* The Hague: Mouton.

Jakobson, Roman, and Linda Waugh. 1987. *The Sound Structure of Language.* Bloomington IN: Indiana University Press.

Jun, Sun A. 2005. *Prosodic Typology: The Phonology of Intonation and Phrasing.* Oxford: OUP.

Jun, Sun A., and H. Kubozono. 2020. "Prosodic Systems: Asian Pacific Rim in 2020." In *The Oxford Handbook of Language Prosody*, edited by Carlos Gussenhoven and Aoju Chen, 355–369. Oxford: OUP.

Kahneman, Daniel. 2012. *Thinking Fast and Slow.* London: Penguin.

Kanero, Junko, Mutsumi Imai, Jiro Okuda, Hiroyuki Okada, and Tetsuya Matsuda. 2014. "How Sound Symbolism Is Processed in the Brain: A Study on Japanese Mimetic Words." *PLoS ONE* 9, 5 (May): e97905. https://doi.org/10.1371/journal.pone.0097905

Kegl, Judy, A. 2002. "Language Emergence in a Language Ready Brain." In *Directions in Sign Language Emergence*, edited by G. Morgan and B. Woll, 207–254. Amsterdam: John Benjamins.

Kinzler, Katherine D., Kristin Shutts, Jasmine DeJesus, and Elizabeth S. Spelke. 2009. "Accent trumps race in guiding children's social preferences." *Social Cognition* 27, no. 4 (August): 623–634. https://doi.org/10.1521/soco.2009.27.4.623

Kirby, Simon. 1999. *Function, Selection and Innateness: The Emergence of Language Universals.* Oxford: Oxford University Press.

Kretzschmar, William A. 2009. *The Linguistics of Speech.* Cambridge: CUP.

Kretzschmar, William A. 2015. *Language and Complex Systems.* Cambridge: Cambridge University Press.

Kurth, Florian, Lutz, Jancke, and Eileen Luders. 2017. "The Sexual Dimorphism of Broca's Region: More Gray Matter in Female Brains in Brodmann Areas 44 and 45." *J Neurosci Res* 95, nos. 1–2 (January/February): 626–632. https://doi.org/10.1002/jnr.23898

Labov, William. 1972. "Rules for Ritual Insults." In *Studies in Social Interaction*, edited by D. Sudnow, 120–70. New York: The Free Press.

Laclau, Ernesto. 1988. "Metaphor and social antagonisms." In *Marxism and the Interpretation of Culture*, edited by C. Nelson and L. Grossberg. Urbana: University of Illinois.

Laclau, Ernesto, and Chantal Mouffe. 1985. *Hegemony and Socialist Strategy: Towards a Radical Democratic Politics.* London: Verso.

Ladefoged, Peter, and Ian Maddieson. 1996. *The Sounds of the World's Languages.* Oxford: Blackwell.

Ladd, D. Robert. 2008. *Intonational Phonology.* 2nd ed. Cambridge: CUP.

Ladd, D. Robert. 2014. *Simultaneous Structure in Phonology.* Oxford: OUP.

Lakoff, George. 1987. *Women, Fire, and Dangerous Things: What Categories Reveal about the Mind.* Chicago: Chicago University Press.

Lakoff, George, and Mark Johnson. 1999. *Philosophy in the Flesh: The Embodied Mind and its Challenge to Western Thought.* New York: Basic Books.

Lakoff, George, and Mark Turner, 1989. *More Than Cool Reason: A Field Guide to Poetic Metaphor.* Chicago: University of Chicago Press.

Laland, Kevin N. 2017. *Darwin's Unfinished Symphony: How culture made the human mind.* Princeton, NJ: Princeton University Press.

Lamb, Sydney 1999. *Pathways of the Brain.* Amsterdam: John Benjamins

Lee, Benny P. H. 2001. "Mutual knowledge, Background Knowledge and Shared Beliefs: their role in establishing common ground." *Journal of Pragmatics* 33, no. 1 (January): 21–44. https://doi.org/10.1016/s0378-2166(99)00128-9

Lein, Tatjane, Tanja Kupisch, and Joost van de Weijer. 2016. "Voice onset time and global foreign accent in German–French simultaneous bilinguals during adulthood." *International Journal Of Bilingualism* 20, no. 6 (July): 732–749. https://doi.org/10.1177/1367006915589424

Lemke, Jay L. 1984. "Semiotics and Education." In *Monographs, Working Papers and Prepublications of the Toronto Semiotic Circle, 2,* 23–62. Toronto: Victoria University.

Lemke, Jay L. 1992. "New challenges for Systemic-Functional Linguistics: Dialect Diversity and Language Change." *Network* 18: 61–68.

Lemke, Jay L. 1993. "Discourse, dynamics, and social change." *Cultural Dynamics* 6, no. 1: 243–275.

Lemke, Jay L. 1995. *Textual Politics: Discourse and Social Dynamics.* London and Bristol, PA: Taylor and Francis.

Lemke, Jay L. 2000. "Material Sign Processes and Ecosocial Organization." In , edited byP. B. Andersen, C. Emmeche and N. O. Finnemann-Nielsen, 181–213. Denmark: Aarhus University Press.

Lemke, Jay L. 2015. "Feeling and Meaning: A Unitary Bio-Semiotic Account." In *International Handbook of Semiotics*, edited by P. Trifonas, 589–616. Dordrecht: Springer.

Levelt, Willem, J. M. 1993. *Speaking from Intention to Articulation.* Cambridge MA: MIT Press.

Levelt, Willem., J. M. 1999. "Models of word production." *Trends in Cognitive Sciences* 3, no. 6 (June): 223–232. https://doi.org/10.1016/S1364-6613(99)01319-4

Levinson, Stephen. 2003. *Space in Language and Cognition: Explorations in Cognitive Diversity*. Cambridge: CUP.

Lloyd, Harriet, Tom Bartlett, Michelle Aldridge-Waddon, Tereza Spilioti, and Virpi Ylänne. 2021. "Opening up space for compassion in nurses' handover meetings." *Communication and Medicine* 16, no. 3 (January): 224–237. https://doi.org/10.1558/cam.38920

MacNeilage, Peter. F. 2008. *The Origin of Speech*. Oxford: OUP.

MacWhinney, Brian. 2005. "A unified model of language acquisition." In *Handbook of Bilingualism: Psycholinguistic Approaches*, edited by J. Kroll and A. De Groot, 49–67. Oxford and New York: Oxford University Press.

McGregor, William B. 1992. "Towards a systemic account of Gooniyandi segmental phonology." In *Studies in Systemic Phonology*, edited by Paul Tench, 19–34. London: Cassell.

McGregor, William B. 2019. "The evolutionary origins of interpersonal grammar." *Functions of Language* 26, no.1 (May): 112–135. https://doi.org/10.1075/fol.18018.mcg

McGurk, Harry, and John MacDonald. 1976. "Hearing lips and seeing voices." *Nature* 264: 746–748. https://doi.org/10.1038/264746a0

Maddieson, Ian. 2013. "Vowel Quality Inventories." In *The World Atlas of Language Structures Online*, edited by Matthew S. Dryer and Martin Haspelmath. Leipzig: Max Planck Institute for Evolutionary Anthropology. https://wals.info/chapter/2 (accessed 28 June, 2018).

Martin, James R. 2013. *Systemic Functional Grammar: A next step into the theory – Axial Relations*. Beijng: Higher Education Press.

Martin, James R., C. M. I. M. Matthiessen, and Clare Painter. 1997. *Working with Functional Grammar*. New York: Arnold.

Martin, James R., and David Rose. 2007. *Working with Discourse: Meaning beyond the clause*. London: Continuum.

Martin, James R., and Peter R. R. White. 2005. *The Language of Evaluation: Appraisal in English*. Basingstoke: Palgrave Macmillan.

Martinet, André. 1960. Éléments de Linguistique Générale. Paris: Armand Colin.

Martinez-Caro, Elena. 1993. Non SVO constructions in English: Some pragmatic and functional considerations. *Revisita Alicantina de Estudios Ingleses* 6, 115–130.

Mathesius, Vilém. 1964 [1928]. "On linguistic characterology with illustrations from Modern English." In *A Prague School Reader in Linguistics*, edited by Josef Vachek, 59–67. Bloomington: Indiana University Press.

Mathieus, Vilém. 1975. *A Functional Analysis of Present Day English on a General Linguistic Basis*, edited by Josef Vacek. The Hague: Mouton.

Matthiessen, Christian M. I. M. 1995. *Lexicogrammatical Cartography: English Systems*. Tokyo. International Science Publishers.

Matthiessen, Christian M. I. M. 2007. "The 'architecture' of language according to systemic functional theory." In *Continuing Discourse on Language, vol. 2*, edited by R. Hasan, C. M. I. M. Matthiessen and J. Webster, 505–561. London and Oakville: Equinox.

Matthiessen, Christian M. I. M. 2009. "Meaning in the making: Meaning potential emerging from acts of meaning." In *Language as a Complex Adaptive System*, edited by Nick C. Ellis and Diane Larsen-Freeman, 206–229. Malden MA and Oxford UK: Wiley-Blackwell.

Matthiessen, Christian M. I. M. 2015. "Halliday's conception of language as a probabilistic system." In *The Bloomsbury Companion to M.A.K. Halliday*, edited by Jonathan J. Webster. London, New Delhi, New York, Sydney: Bloomsbury.

Matthiessen, Christian M. I. M. 2021. "The architecture of phonology according to Systemic Functional Linguistics." In *The Collected works of Christian M.I.M. Matthiessen Volume 1*, edited by Kazuhiro Teruya, Canzhong Wu and Diana Slade. Sheffield: Equinox.

Matthiessen, Christian M. I. M. 2022. *System in Systemic Functional Linguistics: A System-based Theory of Language*. Sheffield: Equinox.

Maturana, Humberto R., and Francisco J. Varela. 1980. *Autopoiesis and Cognition: The Realization of the Living*. Dordecht, Boston and London: Springer Dordrecht.

Maturana, Humberto, Ximena Dávila Yáñez, and Simón Ramírez Muñoz. 2016. "Cultural-Biology: Systemic Consequences of Our Evolutionary Natural Drift as Molecular Autopoietic Systems." *Foundations of Science* 21: 631–678. https://doi.org/10.1007/s10699-015-9431-1

Mazoyer, Bernard, Laure Zago, Gaël Jobard, Fabrice Crivello, Marc Joliot, Guy Perchey, Emmanuel Mellet, Laurent Petit, Nathalie Tzourio-Mazoyer. 2014. "Gaussian Mixture Modeling of Hemispheric Lateralization for Language in a Large Sample of Healthy Individuals Balanced for Handedness." *PLOS ONE* 9, no. 6 (June): 1–14. https://doi.org/10.1371/journal.pone.0101165

Mielke, Jeff. 2008. *The Emergence of Distinctive Features*. Oxford: Oxford University Press.

Monaghan, Padraic, Karen Mattock, and Peter Walker. (2012). "The role of sound symbolism in language learning." *Journal of Experimental Psychology: Learning, Memory, and Cognition* 38, no. 5 (September): 1152–1164. https://doi.org/10.1037/a0027747

Morgan, Elaine, 2011. *The Aquatic Ape Hypothesis*. London: Souvenir Press.

Morton, Timothy. 2018. *Being Ecological*. London: Pelican

Mouffe, Chantal. 2000. *The Democratic Paradox*. London and New York: Verso.

Mulcahy, Nicholas, J. and Josep Call 2006. "Apes Save Tools for Future Use." *Science* 312: 1038–1040.

Muntigl, Peter. 2009. "Knowledge moves in conversational exchanges: Revisiting the concept of primary vs. secondary knowers." *Functions of Language* 16, no. 2, (January): 225–263. https://doi.org/10.1075/fol.16.2.03mun

Nathan, Geoffrey S. 2008. *Phonology: A Cognitive Grammar Introduction*. Amsterdam: John Benjamins.

O'Grady, Gerard. 2010. *A Grammar of Spoken English: The intonation of increments*. London: Continuum.

O'Grady, Gerard. 2013a. *Key Concepts in Phonetics and Phonology*. London: Palgrave Macmillan.

O'Grady, Gerard, 2013b. "Choices in Tony's talk: Phonological paragraphing, information nexuses and the presentation of tone units." In *Choice in Language: Applications in Text Analyses*, edited by G. O'Grady, T. Bartlett and L. Fontaine, 125–157. Sheffield: Equinox.

O'Grady, Gerard. 2014. "An investigation of how intonation helps to signal information structure in English." In *Systemic Phonology: Recent Studies in English*, edited by W. S. Bowcher and B. A. Smith, 27–52. London: Equinox.

O'Grady, Gerard, 2016. "Given/New: What do the terms refer to? A first (small) step." *English Text Construction* 9, no.1 (January): 9–32. https://doi.org/10.1075/etc.9.1.02ogr

O'Grady, Gerard. 2017. "Theme and Prosody: Redundancy or Meaning Making." *English Text Construction* 10, no.2 (January): 274–297. https://doi.org/10.1075/etc.10.2.05ogr

O'Grady, Gerard. 2020a. "Is there a role for prosody within register studies? And if so what and how?" *Language Context and Text* 2, No.1: 59–92. https://doi.org/10.1075/langct.00021.ogr

O'Grady, Gerard. 2020b. "Intonation and exchange: A dynamic and metafunctional view." *Lingua* 261, 102794: 1–14. https://doi.org/10.1016/j.lingua.2020.102794

O'Grady, Gerard. 2022. "A metafunctional analysis of two televised U.K. political interviews with Boris Johnson and Keir Starmer." In *Adversarial Political Interviewing: Worldwide Perspectives During Polarized Times*, edited by O. Feldman, 149–170. Springer, Singapore.

O'Grady, Gerard. Forthcoming. *Syllable and Syllable Onsets – Japanese and English: A systemic perspective.*

O'Grady, Gerard and Tom Bartlett. 2017. "Writing SFL." In *The Routledge Handbook of Systemic Functional Linguistics*, edited by Tom Bartlett & Gerard O'Grady, 634–646. London and New York: Routledge.

O'Grady, Gerard and Tom Bartlett. 2019. "Linearity and Tone in the Unfolding of Information." *Acta Linguistica Hafniensia* 51, No. 2, 192–221. https://doi.org/10.1080/03740463.2019.1668621

O'Grady, Gerard, Tom Bartlett and Lise Fontaine, eds. 2013. *Choice in Language: Applications in Text Analysis.* London and Oakville: Equinox.

Ohala, John, J. Leanne Hilton, and Johanna Nicholls. 1994. *Sound Symbolism.* Cambridge: Cambridge University Press.

Oteíza, Teresa, 2017. "The Appraisal framework and discourse analysis." In *The Routledge Handbook of Systemic Functional Linguistics*, edited by Tom Bartlett & Gerard O'Grady, 457–472. Abingdon, Oxon: Routledge.

Pagel, Mark. 2012. *Wired for Culture: The Natural History of Human Cooperation.* Harmondsworth: Penguin.

Pagel, Mark. 2014. "Creativity, like evolution, is merely a series of thefts." *Wired.* https://www.wired.co.uk/article/mark-pagel. Accessed 6/4/22

Painter, Clare. 2017. "Learning how to mean: Parent–child interaction." In *The Routledge Handbook of Systemic Functional Linguistics*, edited by Tom Bartlett and Gerard O'Grady, 619–633. London: Routledge.

Papagianni, Dimitra & Michael A Morse. 2015. *The Neanderthals Rediscovered: How Modern Science is Rewriting their Story.* Revised edition. London: Thames & Hudson,

Paradis, Johanne. 2001. "Do bilingual two-year-olds have separate phonological systems?" *International Journal Of Bilingualism* 5, no. 1 (March): 19–38. https://doi.org/10.1177/13670069010050010201

Patel, Aniruddh, D. 2007. *Music, Language and the Brain.* Oxford: OUP.

Peirce, C.S. 1883. Manuscript W4. (See Bergman 2009).

Peirce, C. S. 1907. Manuscript 318. (See Bergman 2009).

Peirce, C. S. 1909. Manuscript 364. (See Bergman 2009).

Peirce, Charles S. 1998 [2007]. *The Essential Peirce, Volume 2.* Peirce Edition Project (eds). Bloomington and Indianapolis: Indiana University Press.

Pennisi, Elizabeth. 2010. "Conquering by copying." *Science* 328, no. 5975 (April): 165–167. https://doi.org/10.1126/science.328.5975.165

Pennisi, Antonio and Alessandra Falzone. 2016. *Darwinian Biolinguistics: Theory and History of a Naturalistic Philosophy of Language and Pragmatics.* Cham, Switzerland: Springer

Phillippaki-Warburton, Irene. 1985. "Word Order in Modern Greek." *Transactions of the Philological Society* 83, no. 1 (November): 113–143. https://doi.org/10.1111/j.1467-968x.1985.tb01041.x

Pierrehumbert, Janet. 1980. "The phonology and phonetics of intonation in English." Unpublished PhD dissertation, *M.I.T.*3

Pierrehumbert, Janet. 2001. "Stochastic Phonology." *Glot International* 5, no. 6 (June): 195–207.

Pierrehumbert, Janet, and Julia Hirschberg. 1990. "The meaning of intonation contours in the interpretation of discourse." In *Intentions in Communication*, edited by Philip R. Cohen, Jerry Morgan and Martha E. Pollack, 271–311. Cambridge: MIT Press.

Pike, Kenneth, L. 1943. *Phonetics. A Critical Analysis of Phonetic Theory and a Technic for the Practical Description of Sounds.* Ann Arbor: University of Michigan Press.

Pinker, Steven. 1994. *The Language Instinct.* London: Penguin.

Prakasam, V. 2004. "Metafunctional profile of the grammar of Telugu." In *Language Typology: A Functional Perspective*, edited by Alice Cafferel, James, R. Martin and C. M. I. M. Matthiessen, 433–478. Amsterdam: John Benjamins.

Reboul, Anne. 2017. *Cognition and Communication in the Evolution of Language.* Oxford: Oxford University Press.

Rendell, Luke, R. Boyd, D. Cownden, M. Enquist, K. Eriksson, M. W. Feldman, L. Fogarty, S. Ghirlanda, T. Lillicrap, and Kevin N. Laland. 2010. "Why copy others? Insights from the Social Learning Strategies Tournament." *Science* 328, no. 5975 (April): 208–213. https://doi.org/10.1126/science.1184719

Rizzolatti, Giacomo, L. Fadiga, M. Matelli, V. Gallese and L. Fogassi. 1996. "Premotor cortex and the recognition of motor actions." *Cognitive Brain Research,* 3: 131–141. https://doi.org/10.1016/0926-6410(95)00038-0

Roca, Iggy, and Wyn Johnson. 1999. *A Course in Phonology.* Oxford: Blackwell.

Rogers, Alan R. 1989. "Does biology constrain culture?" *American Anthropology* 90, no. 4 (December): 819–831.

Rovelli, Carlo. 2016. *Reality is not what it seems: The journey to quantum gravity.* London: Allen Lane.

Sapir, Edward. 1921. *Language: An Introduction to the Study of Speech.* New York: Harcourt Brace.

de Saussure, Ferdinand. 1957. *A Course in General Linguistics.* Translated by Wade Baskin. New York: McGraw Hill.

de Saussure, Ferdinand. 1960. *Cours de Linguistique Générale.* Edited by Charles Bally & Albert Sechehaye, 3rd ed. Paris: Payot.

de Saussure, Ferdinand. 2006. *Writings in General Linguistics*, edited by S. Bouquet and R. Engler; translated by C. Sanders and M. Pires. Oxford: Oxford University Press.

Savage-Rumbaugh, Sue, J Murphy, R., Sevik, K. Brakke, S. Williams., and D. Rumbaugh. 1986. "Spontaneous symbol acquisition and communicative use by pygmy chimpanzees (*Pan paniscus*)." *Journal of Experimental Psychology*, 115: 211–235. https://doi.org/10.1037/0096-3445.115.3.211

Savage-Rumbaugh, Sue and Roger Lewin. 1994. *Kanzi: The Ape at the Brink of the Human Mind*. London: Doubleday.

Scollon, Ron. 2001. *Mediated Discourse: The Nexus of Practice*. London: Routledge.

Scollon, Ron, and Susie Wong Scollon. 2004. *Nexus Analysis: Discourse and the Emerging Internet*. London: Routledge.

Searle, John. 1969. *Speech Acts: An Essay in the Philosophy of Language*. Cambridge: CUP.

Silverman, K., Mary E. Beckman, J. Pitrelli, M. Ostendorf, C. Wightman, P. Price, Janet B. Pierrehumbert and Julia Hirschberg. 1992. "ToBI: A Standard for Labelling English Prosody." In *Proceedings of the International Congress on Speech and Language Processing*, 866–870. Banff: University of Alberta.

Silverstein, Michael. 2003. "Indexical order and the dialectics of sociolinguistic life." *Language and Communication* 23, Nos. 3–4: 193–229. https://doi.org/10.1016/s0271-5309(03)00013-2

Sinclair, John H., and Coulthard, Malcolm. (1975). *Towards an Analysis of Discourse*. Oxford: OUP.

Skopeteas, Stavros. 2016. "Information Structure in Modern Greek." In *The Oxford Handbook of Information Structure*, edited by C. Fery and S. Ishihara, 686–708. Oxford: OUP.

Sperber, Dan and Deirdre Wilson. 1995. *Relevance*, 2nd ed. Oxford: Blackwell.

Stalnaker, Robert C. 2002. "Common Ground." *Linguistics and Philosophy* 25, nos. 5–6 (December): 701–721. https://doi.org/10.1023/a:1020867916902

Steels, Luc. 1997. "The synthetic modelling of language origins." *Evolution of Communication Journal* 1, no. 1(October): 1– 34.

Steels, Luc. 2015. *The Talking Heads experiment: Origins of words and meanings*. Berlin: Language Science Publishers.

Stevens, Kenneth. 1972. "The quantal nature of speech: Evidence from articulatory-acoustic data." In *Human Communication: A Unified View*, edited by E. E. David Jr and P. B. Denes, 51–66. New York: McGraw Hill.

Stevens, Kenneth. 1989. "On the quantal nature of speech." *Journal of Phonetics* 17, nos. 1–2 (January–April): 3–45.

Tadros, Angela. (1985). *Prediction in Text: Discourse Analysis Monograph; no.10*. Birmingham: ELR, University of Birmingham.

Taverniers, Miriam. 2011. "The syntax–semantics interface in Systemic Functional Grammar: Halliday's interpretation of the Hjelmslevian model of stratification." *Journal of Pragmatics* 43, 4 (March): 1100–1126. https://doi.org/10.1016/j.pragma.2010.09.003

Taverniers, Miriam. 2018. *SFL Architecture: The Place and Role of Semantic Interfaces*. Talk given at the LinC SFL Summer School, Aachen, Germany.

Taverniers, Miriam. 2019. "Semantics." In *The Cambridge Handbook of Systemic Functional Linguistics*, edited by G. Thompson, W. Bowcher, L. Fontaine and D. Schönthal, 55–91. Cambridge: Cambridge University Press.

Taverniers, Miriam. 2021. "Modelling interfaces with context in SFL: Stratification, instantiation, metafunctions." *Functions of Language* 28, 3 (November): 291–314. https://doi.org/10.1075/fol.20015.tav

Taylor, Charles 2016. *The Language Animal: The full shape of the human linguistic capacity.* Cambridge MA: The Belknap Press of Harvard University Press.

Taylor, Kirsten, I. and Marianne Regard. 2003. "Language in the Right Cerebral Hemisphere: Contributions from Reading Studies." *News Physiol Sci* 18, no. 6 (December): 257–261. https://doi.org/10.1152/nips.01454.2003

Tench, Paul. 1990. *The Roles of Intonation in English Discourse.* Bern: Peter Lang.

Tench, Paul 1996. *The Intonation Systems of English.* London: Cassell.

Tench, Paul. 1997. "The Fall and Rise of the Level Tone in English." *Functions of Language* 4, no. 1 (January): 1–22. https://doi.org/10.1075/fol.4.1.02ten

Tench, Paul. 2003. "Process of Semogenesis in English Intonation." *Functions of Language* 10, no. 2 (January): 209–34. https://doi.org/10.1075/fol.10.2.04ten

Tench, Paul. 2017. "The phoneme and word phonology in systemic functional linguistics." In *The Routledge Handbook of Systemic Functional Linguistics*, edited by Tom Bartlett and Gerard O'Grady, 233–250. London: Routledge.

Teruya, Kazuhiro 2004. "Metafunctional profile of the grammar of Japanese." In *Language Typology: A functional Perspective*, edited by A. Caffarel, J. R. Martin and C. M. I. M. Matthiessen, 185–254. Amsterdam: John Benjamins.

Teruya, Kazuhiro. 2017. "Mood and Japanese." In *The Routledge Handbook of Systemic Functional Linguistics*, edited by Tom Bartlett and Gerard O'Grady, 213–230. London: Routledge.

Thibault, Paul J. 1997. *Re-reading Saussure: The Dynamics of Signs in Social Life.* London and New York: Routledge.

Thibault, Paul J. 2004b. *Agency and Consciousness in Discourse: Self-other dynamics as a Complex System.* London and New York: Continuum.

Thibault, Paul J. 2020. *Distributed Languaging, Affective Dynamics, and the Human Ecology Volume I: The Sense-making Body.* London: Routledge

Thibault, Paul J. 2021. "Selves, interactive representations and context: A systemic functional linguistic account of process in language and world." *Language, Context and Text* 3, no. 1 (February): 33–92. https://doi.org/10.1075/langct.00032.thi

Thierry, Guillaume, Panos Athanasopoulos, Alison Wiggett, Benjamin Dering and Jan-Rouke Kuipers. 2009. "Unconscious effects of language-specific terminology on preattentive color perception." *Proceedings of the National Academy of Science of the United States of America* 106, no. 11 (March): 4567–4570.

Thomas, Margaret. 2021. *Formalism and Functionalism in Linguistics: The Engineer and the Collector.* Abingdon, Oxon. and New York: Routledge.

Thompson, Geoff, Wendy Bowcher, Lise Fontaine and David Schönthal (Eds). 2019. *The Cambridge Handbook of Systemic Functional Linguistics.* Cambridge:Cambridge University Press.

Tomasello, Michael. 2003. *Constructing a Language: A Usage-Based Theory of Language Acquisition.* Cambridge, Mass. and London, UK: Harvard University Press.

Tomasello, Michael 2008. *The Origins of Human Communication.* Cambridge MA: MIT Press

Tomasello, Michael. 2014. *A Natural History of Human Thinking.* Cambridge MA: Harvard University Press.

Tomasello, Michael. 2019. *Becoming Human: A Theory of Ontogeny.* Cambridge MA: Harvard University Press.

Tomlin, Russell. S. 1986. *Basic Word Order. Functional Principles.* London: Croom-Helm.

Torfing, Jacob. 1999. *New Theories of Discourse: Laclau, Mouffe and Žižek.* Oxford: Blackwell.

Trubetzkoy, Nikolai. 1969. *Principles of Phonology.* Translated by C. A. M. Baltaxe. Los Angeles: University of California Press.

Trudgill, Peter. 2009. "Greek Dialect Vowel Systems, Vowel Dispersion Theory, and Sociolinguistic Typology." *Journal of Greek Linguistics* 9, no. 1 (January): 165–182. https://doi.org/10.1163/156658409x12500896406041

Turner, Mark. 2014. *The Origin of Ideas.* Oxford: OUP.Vallduví, Enric, 1992. *The Informational Component.* New York: Garland.

Vallduví, Enric, and Elisabeth Engdhal. 1996. "The linguistic realization of information packaging." *Linguistics* 34, no. 3 (January): 459–519. https://doi.org/10.1515/ling-2013-0041

Van Praet, Wout & Gerard O'Grady. 2018. "The prosody of specification: Discourse intonational cues to setting up a variable." *Journal of Pragmatics* 135 (October): 87–100. https://doi.org/10.1016/j.pragma.2018.07.013

Venditti, Jennifer, J. 2005. "The J_ToBI Model of Japanese Intonation." In *Prosodic Typology: The Phonology of Intonation and Phrasing*, edited by S Ah-Jun, 172–200. Oxford: OUP.

Venditti, Jennifer, J. Kikuo Maekawa, and Mary E. Beckman. 2008. "Prominence marking in the Japanese Intonation system." In *The Handbook of Japanese Linguistics*, edited by Shigeru Maekawa and Mamoru Saito, 456–512. Oxford: OUP.

Vygotsky, Lev S. 1978. *The Mind in Society: The Development of Higher Psychological Processes*, edited by M. Cole, V. John-Steiner, S. Scribner and E. Souberman. Cambridge, MA: Harvard University Press.

Wacewicz, Slawomir, and Przemyslaw Żywiczyński. 2015. "Language Evolution: Why Hockett's design features are a non-starter." *Biosemiotics* 8: 39–44. https://doi.org/10.1007/s12304-014-9203-2

Wang, Bo, and Yuanyi Ma. 2021. *Systemic Functional Translation Studies: Theoretical Insights and New Directions.* Sheffield: Equinox.

Warren, Richard M. 1970. "Perceptual restoration of missing speech sounds." *Science* 167, no. 3917 (January): 392–393. https://doi.org/10.1126/science.167.3917.392

Waugh, Linda, and Monique Monville-Burston. 1990. "Editor's note." In *Roman Jakobson On Language*, edited by L. Waugh and M. Monville-Burston, 259–260. Cambridge MA: Harvard University Press.

Wells. John C. 2000. *The Longman Pronunciation Dictionary of English.* London: Longman.

Wenger, Étienne. 1998. *Communities of Practice: Learning, Meaning, and Identity.* Cambridge: Cambridge University Press.

Wertsch, James. 1998. *Mind as Action.* New York: Oxford University Press.

West, Geoffrey. 2017. *Scale: The Universal Laws of Life and Death in Organisms, Cities and Companies*. London: Weidenfeld and Nicolson.

Westera, Matthijs, Daniel Goodhue, and Carlos Gussenhoven. 2020. "Meanings of Tones and Tunes," in *The Oxford Handbook of Language Prosody*, edited by Carlos Gussenhoven and Aoju Chen, 443–453. Oxford: OUP.

Whorf, Benjamin Lee. 1956. *Language Thought and Reality: Selected Writings*, edited by J. Carroll. Cambridge MA: MIT Press.

Wichmann, Ann. 2000. *Intonation in Text and Discourse: Beginnings, middles and ends*. London: Longman.

Wilkins, Wendy K., and Jennie Wakefield. 1995. "Brains, evolution and neurolinguistic preconditions." *Behavioral and Brain Sciences* 18, no. 1 (March): 161–182. https://doi.org/10.1017/s0140525x00037924

Willett, Michael (2015). "A Study of the Productivity of Twelve English Onset Phonaesthemes." Unpublished PhD dissertation, Cardiff University.

Wilson, Timothy. 2002. *Strangers to Ourselves: Discovering the Adaptive Unconscious*. Cambridge, Mass.: Harvard University Press.

Wittgenstein, Ludwig. 1922 [1921]. *Tractatus Logico-Philosophicus*. London: Kegan Paul.

Wrangham, Richard. 2019. *The Goodness Paradox*. London: Profile Books.

Wray, Alison. 2014. "Developing comprehensive criteria of adequacy: the challenge of hybridity." In *The Functional Perspective on Language and Discourse : Applications and Implications*, edited by Gómez-González, María de los Angeles, Francisco José Ruiz de Mendoza Ibáñez, Francisco Gonzálvez García and Angela Downing, 19–36. Amsterdam: John Benjamins.

Wray, Alison. 2017. "Formulaic sequences as a regulatory mechanism for cognitive perturbations during the achievement of social goals." *Topics in Cognitive Science* 9(3): 569–587.

Ylänne, Virpi, Michelle Aldridge-Waddon, Tereza Spilioti, and Tom Bartlett. 2021. "Managing information, interaction and team building in nurse shift-change handovers." *Journal of Applied Linguistics and Professional Practice* 16, no. 1 (November): 51–75. https://doi.org/10.1558/jalpp.19140

Ziles, Karl. 2018. "Brodmann: a pioneer of human brain mapping—his impact on concepts of cortical organization." *Brain* 141, 11 (November): 3262–3278. https://doi.org/10.1093/brain/awy273

Zuraw, Kie. 2006. "Language change, probabilistic models of." In *The Encyclopedia of Language and Linguistics*, edited by Keith Brown, 349–357. Oxford: Elsevier.

Index